Perspectives on Governance and Society

Perspectives on Governance and Society

Essays in Honour of Professor O.P. Dwivedi

Edited by

NEELAM TRIVEDI
TIM A. MAU
DHIRENDRA VAJPEYI
SHRINATH PRASAD DWIVEDI

RAWAT PUBLICATIONS

Jaipur • New Delhi • Bangalore • Hyderabad • Guwahati • Kolkata

ISBN 978-81-316-0537-0 (HB)
ISBN 978-81-316-0601-8 (PB)

Published by
Prem Rawat for **Rawat Publications**
Satyam Apts, Sector 3, Jawahar Nagar, Jaipur 302 004 (India)
Phone: 0141 265 1748 / 7006 Fax: 0141 265 1748
E-mail: info@rawatbooks.com
Website: www.rawatbooks.com

New Delhi Office
4858/24, Ansari Road, Daryaganj, New Delhi 110 002
Phone: 011 2326 3290

Also at *Bangalore, Hyderabad, Guwahati* and *Kolkata*

Typeset by Rawat Computers, Jaipur
Printed at Chaman Enterprises, New Delhi

Contents

Part II : Environment and Society

Preface

NEELAM TRIVEDI, TIM A. MAU, DHIRENDRA VAJPEYI AND SHRINATH PRASAD DWIVEDI

Greatness is not a destination; it is a continuous journey. This Festschrift commemorates the 75th year of the continuous journey of Professor O.P. Dwivedi, a man endowed with remarkable human qualities, who has imbibed in himself the unfathomable depths of knowledge. As one goes through this collection of essays it will be patently obvious that both the editors and all the contributors to this volume feel an inexpressible gratitude towards the person to whom this volume is dedicated. A brief glimpse on Professor Dwivedi's scholarly contributions and other accomplishments is presented towards the later part of this volume.

For quite a few years much discussion and debate has been going on among academics and policy makers about issues related to nation building and political development, and the role of governance in providing services to the general public in the most efficient manner. In short, there has been a quest to develop a functioning paradigm on the topic. What constitutes good governance, and how is it possible to implement those ideas where some consensus exists? It has been observed that 'good governance is, among other things, participatory, transparent and accountable ... effective and equitable' (Dwivedi, 2008). Another substantive issue that has been a major concern for Professor Dwivedi pertains to the value of environmental ethics; in this regard, his work, drawing from various religious and spiritual traditions, pleads for treating Mother Earth with respect and as though it were your family member. His belief is that those who see divinity in nature could not contemplate harming it in anyway.

Globalization has put further pressure on the need for good governance. While free trade and advancements in information and communication technologies are supposed to provide a 'flat field' for people to compete and be prosperous, it also requires a fair distribution of wealth to all people, not only to private corporations and a few countries. As the former Secretary-General of the UN argued, for globalization to succeed 'it must do so equally for the rich and the poor' (Annan, 2000: 126). What was 'lost' in the exuberance of material wealth was the value of politics—and not just any politics, but specifically the politics of good governance, liberty, equity and social justice (ibid.: 127). 'The development of a society based on the rule of law; the establishment of legitimate responsive uncorrupt government, respect for human rights and the rights of minorities, freedom of expression; the right to have fair trial—these essential universal pillars of democratic pluralism were in too many cases ignored ...' (ibid.).

The present anthology is a tribute to Professor O.P. Dwivedi's life-long dedication to multidimensional scholarship and concern about good governance and political development. The rich diversity of topics in this collection reflects Professor Dwivedi's broad scholarship in areas as diverse as public ethics, religion/spirituality and global environment.

II

The book is divided into two parts comprising essays on ethics of governance and environment and society, respectively, written specifically to celebrate Professor Dwivedi's contribution to scholarship and intellectual discourse spanning more than four decades. Besides a short biographical sketch of Professor Dwivedi, reflecting in part his journey through life, has been presented.

Part I, which consists of eight essays, begins with the paper by Melchior D. Powell entitled, 'The Convergence of Citizen Distrust in Governments and Financial Institutions, and the Global Decline of Citizen Optimism and Confidence'. It discusses the relationship between citizen participation and confidence in shaping the civic/political culture of a society. The author points out that 'trusting societies create strong legal systems that maintain trust and confidence of citizens ... Societies that trust their governments ... will have less corruption'. R.B. Jain follows in the next essay discussing the topic of reinventing good governance. He specifically focuses on India's administrative development, identifying the challenges and strategies to achieve good governance. Chapter 3 by M.V. Naidu is a case study and examines the broad framework on democratic theory and practice in India.

In Chapter 4, Tim A. Mau examines the limited contributions of Canadian political scientists and public administration scholars to the study of leadership and argues that 'if our cumulative knowledge about leadership is to expand in any meaningful way, more researchers must strive to recognize the artificiality of their disciplinary boundaries and begin to theorize based on empirical studies from across the full spectrum of research'. His call to action, while directed at Canadian scholars, is germane to all those who aspire to contribute to the advancement of knowledge in leadership studies.

Chapter 5, 'My Land, My Niche and a Lost Home', by Amita Singh highlights humans' love for land as a much misunderstood phenomenon in policies for urbanization or industrialization. Discussing land acquisition in the context of special economic zones proposed by the Government of India's legislation Land Acquisition, Rehabilitation and Resettlement Bill, 2011, she points out that land does not just provide a habitation and a home, but also an eco-system, which carries with it the unwritten history of many past generations of human and non-human inhabitants who shared that space in perpetuity. Any disruption of this heritage and honour is most likely to create inseeurities, loss of confidence and weakening of self-esteem amongst communities. That is why, one must understand the nature of 'land'.

In the next chapter, entitled 'The Diasporic Identity and Globalization: New Cultural Politics in Hindi Cinema', Reeta Chowdhari Tremblay suggests that 'cinema acts as a symbolic construct in structuring social relations and represents the pan-Indian homogeneous nationalist project, constructed and constantly reinforced in light of the majoritarian community and religions politics in India'. She also thinks that the invasive transnational consumer industry is being assisted by a conscious and concrete effort on the part of the political elite in developing economies that wish to establish political control over their nations' cultural politics.

Chapter 7 by R.K. Mishra analyses the pivotal role of public enterprises in economic development in many developing countries by examining the role played by technology in uplifting and maintaining growth, the R&D investment scenario, and trends in growing innovativeness in selected Central Public Sector Enterprises (CPSEs) in India. For example, over the past two to three decades, India's CPSEs have played a key role in contributing to the rapid economic growth of the nation. Moving on from the topic of public enterprises, the next chapter by Deeptima Shukla discusses the Mahatma Gandhi National Rural Employment Act (MGNREGA) passed by the Indian

Parliament in 2005 to provide full-fledged rights and employment guarantee for one hundred days to all households in rural India. It also empowers women to achieve economic independence. The author feels that by altering the socio-economic conditions of the affected areas, women, the disadvantaged and the poor shall greatly benefit.

Part II of the book consists of nine essays related to such issues as environmental policy and management, global sustainability, use of medicinal plants and the role of religion in defending the environment. The first essay by Bruce Mitchell analyses the close link between governance and water management by highlighting the Chinese approach to these issues. The author concludes by making policy suggestions related to the issue. He believes that the concept of Integrated Water Resource Management (IWRM), while it may not be a panacea to resolve water management problems, is nonetheless a worthwhile strategy to be tried by many countries around the globe. Chapter 10 by Kirit Patel and Kathryn Dey provides the trajectory of environmental justice in India and its prospects and challenges for turning the nation green. The authors discuss the efforts made by the Government of India to empower the judiciary to provide effective and expeditious disposal of cases related to the environment, to enforce any legal right related to the environment, provide relief and compensation for damages caused to person and property and for dealing in matters connected therewith or incidental thereto. This essay is followed by the chapter 'Environment and Climate Change-Induced Natural Disasters in India' by Vinod K. Sharma and A.D. Kaushik. These authors discuss the greenhouse effect on climate change in general and on India in particular. They maintain that climate-induced natural disasters, such as droughts, floods and cyclones, have an adverse impact on India's economy. The chapter also reports on the measures taken in India to meet these challenges.

Production of green products is the theme of Chapter 12 by R.K. Trivedi. Based on his experience with Shastri Indo-Canadian Institute funded research (sponsored by the Canadian International Development Agency (CIDA), Harcourt Butler Technological Institute (HBTI), Kanpur, and the University of Guelph, Canada), the essay is a case study of developing green products by using environment-friendly industrial production processes.

The next three essays switch the discussion towards the role of sacred plants and religions in protecting the environment. In Chapter 13, Christopher Key Chapple analyses global sustainability in the context of broader Indian traditions with a specific focus on Hinduism, Sikhism and Mahatma Gandhi's values of non-violence (*ahimsa*) and power of truth (*satyagraha*). He points out that 'the *dharma* traditions of India suggest that we can and must learn to live within limits, that we must seek inner peace, not outward acquisition'. Chapter 14 by B.N. Tiwari and Neelam Trivedi discusses the spiritual/religious aspects of the Hindu religion, which provides the basic foundation and exhortations to work towards environmental protection and the preservation of nature. Drawing on Hindu scriptures and philosophical beliefs that the main objective of human and environmental sustainability is the well-being of all, the authors assert that our spiritual heritage (of any faith and religion) can provide new ways of valuing, thinking and acting towards nature and its sustainability. Next, Mukund R. Shukla and Praveen K. Saxena analyse the role of the Tulsi (Holy Basil) plant not only in Hindu religious and cultural traditions but also because of its medicinal qualities in fostering health promotion, disease prevention and longevity of life. They assert that Tulsi-based natural health products can serve as a model for the introduction of many other Ayurvedic medicinal preparations in other countries, as these are commonly used by South Asian ethnic communities all over the world.

The penultimate chapter by Anil K. Gupta examines how traditional knowledge along with an environmental quality approach, if encouraged, can provide grassroots innovations for poverty alleviation. His case study of Honey Bees (an environmental NGO that he founded) is a shining example of how such traditional knowledge and its network of people can mitigate the negative side effects of agro-industrial farming by acquiring, processing and disseminating stories of innovations in different languages. Finally, in Chapter 17, 'A Thousand Small Windows: Pondering the Role of Global IT Communication Towards Adult Education for Sustainability', Jane Dougan analyses the crucial role of information technology in adult education for sustainability. Based on her teaching experience, she points out that in the context of environmental education, the disparate location of learners within different bioregional and social ecologies is not incidental but pedagogically powerful, and active reference to this can become a critical and complex part of the learning process.

No work is ever a product of a solitary scholar. While working for this project, we came across many people who helped us to make this possible. We wish to express our deep sense of gratitude to the contributors, who sent their essays in time, which enabled us to produce this volume in a timely fashion. Without their cooperation this endeavour would not have been possible.

We worked closely with each other to produce this volume, but we were fortunate to have had the kind guidance and support of Professor Dwivedi throughout this project. In addition, we offer our special thanks to Dr Deeptima Shukla of Jaipur, who acted as our emissary with the publishers and co-ordinated various aspects of production and distribution of this volume. Lastly, we are grateful to Acharya Shrinath Dwivedi (of Surrey, BC, Canada) for reviewing the contributions in the Hindi language.

Personally, Dhirendra Vajpeyi would like to thank his very hardworking Graduate Assistant Yuna Rusinova for her considerable effort in putting the manuscript together in a pre-publishable form.

Neelam Trivedi would like to acknowledge her gratitude to Professor Dwivedi, without whose consent and blessings this project would not have been realized. In addition, she expresses her indebtedness to him for his encouragement and enthusiastic guidance during the initial phases of her research activities as well as her ongoing association with him, which has been an enlightening experience. She would also like to offer her heartfelt thanks to Dr Nagendra Swaroop, Secretary, Dayanand Shiksha Sansthan, Kanpur, for being a constant source of inspiration. Finally, a special note of thanks is due to Abhinav Trivedi for his valuable technical assistance.

Professor Mau fondly acknowledges the contribution of his family, who have always been supportive of his academic and other pursuits, and to Professor O.P. Dwivedi, a friend, colleague and mentor to whom he owes a great debt of gratitude.

Finally, we would like to offer our sincere thanks to Rawat Publications, Jaipur for undertaking the task of publishing this felicitation volume within the stipulated time frame.

References

Annan, Kofi (2000). "The Politics of Globalization", in Patrick O'Meara et al. (eds.), *Globalization and the Challenges of a New Century*, Bloomington, Indiana: Indiana University Press.

Dwivedi, O.P. (2008). "The Well-being of Nations: Reflections on Integrating the Human and Ecosystem Well-being", in Dhirendra Vajpeyi and Renu Khator (eds.), *Globalization, Governance and Technology*, New Delhi: Deep & Deep Publications, pp. 60–75.

Preface Addendum

In the first printing of this felicitation volume there was a third part to the book that included selected photographs of my father, Professor Dwivedi, followed by several messages and tributes sent by his friends, family and well-wishers, such as Dr Karan Singh, John Meisel, T.N. Chaturvedi, Professor Allan Rosenbaum, Meera Mishra, D.S. Mishra, Gerald E. Caiden, Ram Naresh Tripathi, Sarla Dwivedi, Kanti Dwivedi, Shrinath Prasad Dwivedi, Shailendra Kumar Awasthi, Suresh Awasthi, Inakshi Chaturvedi, Bhagwat Saran Srivastava, Bhartendu Srivastava and Dhirendra Vajpeyi.

This book has provided a cherished memento for all of the recipients, who included friends, colleagues and family. I would like to thank the authors for their contributions.

My father was a tireless academic, who fussed over the list of contributors, the edited manuscripts and was worried about its completion – even though he was neither an editor nor a contributor! I remember early on in its inception, he asked me if I would like to write a message, but then quickly cautioned me about the stress of writing a tribute to a living parent. Sadly, I took his caution to heart and did not write about him. If I did, it would have been a lengthy chapter on the moral fibre he instilled in me, something that I have spoken about many times, and which is the foundation of the actions I take every day.

I was able to show my father the first print of this book in the hospital. He took great interest and pride in the volume, and was happy to know it was published. It sat by his bedside for all visitors to see.

He passed away on January 29, 2013 at the age of 76 from complications due to cancer. He wanted more time on earth to continue to seed projects that he knew would surpass him. He wanted to leave his mark on this world, and he did: he left it a better place than how he found it.

I, like many family members, friends and colleagues, miss him dearly.

Prateek Dwivedi

PART I

Ethics of Governance

1

The Convergence of Citizen Distrust in Governments and Financial Institutions, and the Global Decline of Citizen Optimism and Confidence

MELCHIOR D. POWELL

The decline of citizen trust in governmental institutions in societies across all social and economic characteristics has been highlighted in the past several years by an awareness of corruption in the workings of both public and private institutions, with responses ranging from demands by citizens for greater accountability and transparency, to demands for regime changes that have resulted in violent overthrow of

---

I am pleased to contribute to this felicitation book honouring the life and work of Professor O.P. Dwivedi as a scholar and teacher of immense impact on the understanding of ethics in governance, and for his efforts in influencing governmental leaders in fostering accountability and trust on an international level. I have known Professor Dwivedi for almost 30 years, and have worked with him closely in the direction and guidance of a Working Group for the International Association of Schools and Institutes of Administration that has produced several hundreds of research papers from international scholars on accountability, culture and trust, further expanding our understanding of ethics in government. Professor Dwivedi's scholarship and publications on ethics in government has made enormous contributions to democratic governance and has expanded peaceful co-existence between and among all cultures.

several governments in North Africa as well as changes in governmental leadership in several European nations.

Concurrently, suppressed public disdain and distrust of authoritarian governments has been translated into worldwide mass civilian protests directed against international financial institutions, with demands for increased transparency and accountability, and demands for societal transformations designed to reduce special economic and business privileges for elites and their families.

The Arab Spring that transformed Tunisia, Egypt and Libya, with uncertain outcomes for Syria and Yemen, is now transforming into constitution writing and the solidification of 'rights' considered vital to moderates and protestors in those countries. Of significance is the inclusion of rights for minorities and women. Other elements of constitutional governments will also need to be included if the emerging democratic governments are to be restrained from returning to autocracies.

Independent courts and checks and balances will also need to be institutionalized to prevent the continuation of controls by elites over economic development, capturing contracts with international companies seeking to invest and create jobs, and the continuation of infrastructure projects that are inferior in quality, or dangerous for citizens. Moreover, legal systems will need to be secured that resist the restraining of transparent contractual relations that are necessary for the growth of private sector institutions that produce jobs for citizens and opportunities for citizen satisfaction with progress toward individual economic growth and personal advancement.

The Loss of Optimism for a Better Future

It is a principle of democratic societies that citizen optimism for a 'better' future is the driver that sustains trust and confidence in government institutions, in private institutions, in legal systems, and in all institutions that alter or affect one's future well-being (Banfield, 1958; Seligmen, 1997; Putnam, 2000; Uslaner, 2002; Johnston, 2005).

Optimism and trust may be most apparent, however, when economic survival is threatened, or at an extreme, non-existent. The persistent economic condition and lack of optimism in developing countries, characterized by the persistence of corruption in all or most areas of contact with public officials and institutions and in perceptions of contractual favouritism with private sector activities and elites cements the belief in the minds of citizens that economic opportunity is not available for those who work hard to achieve a higher standard of living, and reinforces a persistent and persuasive belief that elites will thwart one's personal freedom. Further, corruption strengthens a perception that one's ability to enter into enforceable contracts, or to achieve social advancement, educational opportunity, or a better life for one's children, is not feasible (Johnston, 1997).

The acceleration of distrust in advanced democracies is perhaps a response to failures of private sector financial institutions in the 2008 financial crisis accompanied by a reduction in jobs, and a general loss of confidence in governmental institutions to effectively manage, regulate, or coerce financial institutions, that has given new energy to a loss of optimism and distrust (Spitzer, 2011). It may be argued that the loss of optimism is the factor that is creating the greater sense of distrust currently apparent in the full range of societies.

Legalisms, Constitutions and Legal Systems that Inspire Trust

Many Western scholars look at the relations of citizens and their governments in terms of 'a turning over' to their governments' powers that will benefit citizens, maintaining that government is the 'servant' to its citizens. The English philosopher John Locke may have convinced the founders of the American Republic that the creation of a new government following the American Revolution, the voluntary act by citizens in the newly independent colonies 'turning' power over to a 'national' government, was a contractual agreement because the public agreed that their condition in the state of nature is unsatisfactory, and therefore the public agreed to transfer some of their natural rights to a new (and central) government (Bailyn, 1967). While accepting this view of the role of government, issues of trust are characterized as general 'distrust' by citizens of all decisions made by governments, with a continuing need to create and maintain institutional arrangements that keep governments in check, with transparency as a necessary characteristic of all government activities and actions.

This is to say that the question of trust of government may realistically be viewed as a forceful and energetic distrust of government, and that such distrust is a healthy state of mind for a modern society that reflects a maturity of a developed and open culture with established and accepted concepts of freedom of speech and thoughts and other institutional balances that maintain a government that is 'in check'.

With a society that inherently distrusts government, complaints by citizens, groups or private institutions against any government action may be viewed as a positive statement about the rights of citizens to complain, demand accountability and transparency, slur public officials if that is necessary to bring attention to a contention, and call for their defeat in future elections.

But distrust and disagreement are actions that are possible only when a society comprises citizens who have trust in each other and in their legal systems. Having an adopted constitution that guarantees citizens in all of their natural concerns about the powers of government may be desirable, but it also may be a waste of paper if distrust prevails (Johnston, 2005; Hardin, 2004).

While democracies may be established relatively quickly (as in formally communist nations of central and eastern Europe), history tells us that economic equality changes slowly over a long period of time. Legal systems must be trusted to be effective. A culture filled with acts of favouritism, bribes, and a lack of optimism on the part of citizens, cannot foster and support a culture of trust. Citizens must believe that equality is gaining in the race against corruption for a culture of trust to be nourished and flourish as a necessary element in creating an effective legal system (Uslaner, 2002; Montinola, 2004).

Emerging societies resulting from The Arab Spring may justifiably demand a 'Bill of Rights' amended to their new constitution that protects them from reprisals, such as imprisonment without trial, discrimination in employment, or freedom from discrimination against women and minorities. But it is doubtful that civil rights for women and minorities can be institutionalized if the emerging governments are not civil, particularly if favouritism in those societies is institutionalized by religious leaders or a strong military.

Governments can write as many guarantees as possible, but written constitutions neither be substitutes for nor will they create trust between citizens and governments. In the long run, only honest citizens write constitutions that work. And a society that is distrustful, with divisions and corrupt intentions, will not produce guarantees through the devise of constitution writing. Idealist may assume that relations between government and citizens are like relations between corporations, where contracts for doing business, consideration for gain, money for service, or whatever the bargain, is the same as a constitution. Thus, a constitution is viewed as a contract. But, the public is not a customer, corporation, or a business. As anyone in business learns, a handshake with trust and the existing condition, is better than a contract. Law professors tell their students that lawyers that trust each other can do business with a handshake.

As Uslaner (2002: 46) argues in *The Moral Foundations of Trust*:

> There is a linkage between confidence in the legal system and trust in people; the direction of causality goes from trust to confidence in the legal system. Trusting societies have strong legal systems, able to punish the small number of scofflaws.

The best example of the above is illustrated in the belief that the citizens in some formerly communist societies have little trust in their legal systems, principally because they do not trust each other. Of course that culture was born during the years when those societies were police states and citizens were encouraged to spy on each other. Thus, attempting to create a trusting society by orders from the top of government to the lower levels of citizen participation is unlikely to work (Levi, 1996; Johnston, 2005).

Influence of a Strong Military

The question may well be asked whether a strong and unified military would be a necessary advantage and condition in a society to avoid the rule by religious leaders. In emerging societies recovering from secular autocratic rule, secular societies, protected from religious law during the long reign of autocratic rulers, may have reason for concern. It may indeed be argued that the Egyptian revolution was moderated by a strong military establishment that supported an overthrow of the Mubarak regime, but that it is unwilling to relinquish the influence of the military to an uncertain and possibly uncontrollable and corrupt Islamic regime.

But constitutional protections, including the right of free speech and the right to state publicly negative views of sitting government, may also be triggers for the claims that such guarantees are the 'seeds' of Western ideas imported from, or imposed by, the West, either through the writing and speeches of Western educated native scholars and business leaders, or surreptitiously introduced by intelligence or other institutions of the West working to influence or capture the future of a society.

It may be reasonable to expect that even in modern and seemingly civil democracies, hatred of and discrimination toward a political group or group of citizens may be the real agenda in demonstrations of disdain of government and its leaders. It may be thus argued that such ruses and conspiracies are the price that is paid by reasonable citizens in a free society. The unknown is the question of reasonableness of citizens that have become unaccustomed to actions that are not designed to control lives and economic conditions.

A frequent device in attacks on the viability and rationality of government action may also have as its goal a partisan view utilizing freedom of speech mechanisms to attack public policies by wrapping such arguments in negative terms emphasizing anti-government slogans, and negative stereotypical statements of 'big government' or 'inefficient government' or 'central government' or 'authoritative government' or 'Western controlled government', or a wide variety of slurs and complaints couched in negative terms.

In the United States, partisan rancour has evolved to form a new conservative political movement that has challenged the premise that government should be engaged in regulating business. It has successfully elected a sufficient number of members to the House of Representatives to create a Republican majority, challenging not only the Administration of President Barack Obama but many of the reforms initiated by the United State Congress to correct the shortcomings of practices and policies of regulatory agencies captured by the finance industry and the oil industry (Pew Research Center, 2010; Spitzer, 2011).

In developed democratic societies, it may be reasonable to anticipate that a more contemporary view of trust in government exists, one that looks at strategies that may be legitimately employed by governments to learn from the public those attributes, policies, and desires that citizens wish to express, or may fear have been suppressed. A complex set of tools providing information by government to the public, such as variations of citizen participation, performance measurements and successes, strategic planning, and other devices may be employed as strategies that 'develop trust'.

The Role of Business in Combating Corruption

A somewhat different agenda becomes apparent when we analyse the causes and goals of distrust of private sector organizations. The distrust of private institutions may not have the same basis as the trading of natural rights for a government that provides order but which is checked by institutional instruments balancing power. Private institutions provide goods and 'ends' that cannot be provided by governments, but instead are delivered by private or quasi-private institutions, and they offer economic benefits and other economic interactions with the public that may well extend beyond government's ability or capacity to provide. It is apparent that in many developing societies, including those transformed by The Arab Spring, a large percentage of jobs are in government, reportedly as great as 50 per cent in Egypt. Opportunities in the private sector are limited in developing cultures, to a large extent because of the pervasiveness of corruption. Perhaps the more precise approach is to understand the pervasiveness of cultural conventions. In many developing nations, what constitutes corruption is read as the 'way to do business', while Western laws may define corruption more simply as the payment of a bribe to a government official (Heiman, 1997).

Perhaps the interpretation of corruption at its extreme may be that action defined by the American government as the bribing of employees of a 'state-owned' company. American company officials are fined by the United States government for such actions. On the other hand, employees of state-owned companies in developing nations generally see the right to bribe as part of their compensation and an accepted practice without legal penalty. The costs associated with bribes, and the uncertainties associated with continuing bribery, generally leads to reluctance by private investors to enter a market where the only recourse is to deliver less than would be delivered in a more open and legally protected contractual arrangement. Thus, the result may be the use of inexpensive or defective materials or equipment in the construction of roads, dams or bridges, and the greater cost to the nation's citizens for a defective project.

When the services that private institutions provide are deficient, or threaten the economic viability of citizens, or there are apparent failures on the part of governments to provide adequate oversight or regulatory actions to protect the safety and well-being of citizens, citizen reaction can be negative, and even the cause of a revolution. Citizen reactions may be as extreme as the occupation of a government square, or the overthrow of a government, or, as may be the case in the recent occupations of government spaces by 'Occupying Wall Street' protestors of banking and other financial firms, the emergence of distrust of governments, and a lack of trust in these private institutions.

More Trust by the Young in Social Media than in Establishment Media

Disillusionment and a loss of optimism are now prevalent among the youth of many developed societies. The apparent lack of opportunity for jobs and for advancement is a major cause of this loss. The debt-ridden nations of southern Europe have also created a crisis in confidence, a loss of optimism about the future, about the need for jobs, and the realization that level of unemployment for several southern European nations is as high as 44.1 per cent for Spain for 18 to 24-year-olds, and

38.5 per cent for youths in Greece. They now have a lowering of expectations that were enjoyed by earlier generations of youth.

In some ways, the proliferation of social media networks and the openness of the Internet has its greatest impact on young people. Newscasts produced by the established governments and media outlets have less trust for the young underemployed youth. They may not have come to a belief that 'idealism' is dead, but they are making their own decisions, and less willing than in the past 50 years to trust the established media, or government programmes that promise much, but deliver more to senior citizens with government largess than to younger generations.

Impact of Failing Private Sector Industries on Accelerating Citizen Distrust

Private financial institutions are generally blamed for creating the recent global financial crisis, impairing the basic requirements of a society for economic security. The 'Wall Street' protesters take the view that failed private financial institutions no longer protect all citizens in their economic viability. This view may also be extended to the personal safety and health of citizens, to a loss of personal safety created by the BP oil crisis in the Gulf of Mexico in 2010 and the many recalls of medications deemed unsafe and also responsible for deaths—with an accompanying perception of the part of the public that government institutions, in their failure to adequately regulate those industries, were part of a programme of corruption, possibly including bribes, or at best, suggesting ineptness and incompetence (Powell, 2010).

Pervasiveness of Bribes and Enhanced Citizen Distrust

There is a tendency to focus on corruption from the perspective of government employees accepting or demanding bribes from corporations attempting to enter into contracts for the delivery of products or services. Less focus is placed on the executives and sales representatives of western companies that are both willing and anxious to obtain business and willing to pay bribes. Both the United States Foreign Corruption Act and the OECD Convention on Combating Bribery of Foreign Public Officials in International Business Transactions have had an influence on the reduction of bribery in developing nations (Foreign Corruption Act of 1977; OECD, 2011).

It may be appropriate to surmise that the willingness of Western businesses to pay bribes may be a more appropriate path for further analysis and study to an understanding of the pervasiveness of corrupt practices in developing countries than simply focusing on the education and training requirements frequently presented by public administration scholars as the solution to the persistent practice of corruption in developing countries (Johnston, 2005; Horne, 2004). The willingness to pay bribes by Western businesses may be illustrated by current lobbying efforts by the United States Chamber of Commerce to have the inclusion of employees of government-owned foreign corporations excluded from the administration of the Foreign Corruption Act, thus freeing American companies from the penalties currently being levied by the American government.

The global economic crisis, with a growing lack of trust by citizens in powerful private institutions, has weakened the global financial system. It can be suggested that a large percentage of the world's population believes that it is vulnerable to forces outside of their control, even by their governments, and believes that a large part of its 'vulnerability' is the result of a sizable power imbalance that enables corporate executives and corporations as entities to assume far less risk than the average citizen.

The Role of Banking in Enhancing Citizen Distrust

This belief of helplessness by citizens has been exacerbated by governments using citizens' tax dollars to shore up private financial institutions, banks, and other industries, whose chancy behaviour has placed the global financial system, and the personal investments of citizens, at risk.

In September 1998, AIG, the largest insurance company in the world, was taken over by government; The Bank of America was forced by government to take over a failed Merrill Lynch. But when the US government refused to rescue Lehman Brothers, the value of personal investments and public pension plans that had invested in stocks and securities, all fell by 25 to 50 per cent in value. Banks that were saved by government purchases began hoarding their cash; corporations could issue commercial paper only for short terms and high interest, and London interbank lending collapsed. The International Monetary Fund estimated that 10 trillion in mortgaged backed securities would be written. And, the public's trust in the relatively secret world of finance fell dramatically (Spitzer, 2011).

The cause of the current financial crisis is unlike past crises, where financial institutions experienced bank runs by depositors and central bank cut-backs. The problem this time was a loss of trust in the safety of investments, of financial firms and their actions (Paulson,

2010). Central banks can and did provide liquidity, presidents and prime ministers have assured their citizens and businesses that their economies are resilient, captains of industry have assured future profits for their companies, and governments have reduced spending and lowered taxes. But whether any of these actions have revived citizen trust once distrust has taken hold is the question.

The global economic crisis, with a growing lack of trust by citizens in powerful private institutions, has weakened the global financial system. It is suggested by this author that a large percentage of the world's population believes that it is vulnerable to forces outside of their control, even control by their governments, and thus citizens believe that a large part of their 'vulnerability' is the result of a sizable power imbalance that enables corporate executives and corporations as entities to obtain financial relief and to exist with far less risk than the average citizen.

Further exasperating citizen displeasure with bailouts, banks that were saved by United States government bailouts began hoarding their new bailout cash rather than making loans to citizens and corporations needing credit to rebuild their inventory, rehire 'let go' employees, hire new employees, and further the expansion of the economy. It was almost as though an utter disconnect existed between the federal United States government and banks (Spitzer, 2011).

Economic Disparities between the Wealthy and the Majority

As stated above, the cause of the current financial crisis is unlike past crises, where financial institutions experienced bank runs by depositors and central banks failed to cover losses of local failing banks. The problem this time has been a loss of trust in the safety of investments, of financial firms that had been viewed by the public as the backbone of capitalism, and by the actions of investment firms in trading in very risky investments not backed by substantial equity *(The Financial Crisis Inquiry Report, 2011)*.

A recent accumulation of extreme wealth in the hands of a very small population in the United States during the years of President George W. Bush's administration created economic disparities that likely influenced and accelerated the declining level of citizen trust in the US, and placed into jeopardy the faith of banks and other investment industries in the value of sovereign funds of several nations, as evidenced in the recent crisis in Greece, the threat of national bankruptcy in Spain and Portugal, and in the financial crisis following rapid rises in the cost in interest of Italian bonds resulting in a resignation of the prime minister of Europe's fourth wealthiest nation, and the world's eighth largest economy.

The relative increased wealth and extremely high salaries of executives and employees in the world's leading investment firms and banks, as well as manufacturing firms, uncovered during the financial crisis, also contributed to a loss of citizen trust in corporations and business executives. The arrogance of these firms following through with their practice of millions in bonuses for individual executives was more that the public could comprehend as a justified practice for smart and clever business icons, especially given that it was the public's tax dollars that had just bailed them from certain bankruptcies.

Concurrently, a perspective that national politicians were not 'managing' the fiscal crisis, and that the newly elected President Barack Obama was not managing the fiscal crisis, also contributed to a growing perception that there were severe economic disparities in the United States culture. To a degree, similar reactions to extremely high executive salaries in investment firms were cause for national actions in the United Kingdom.

Distrust by the public in its largest financial institutions has extended to all businesses, in all fields of enterprise. And distrust has also extended to governments at all levels. Many corporations have avoided perilous financial conditions during the current financial crisis; however, business in general is seen by the public as part of a large 'alliance of corporate greed' and risky financial behaviour that has caused much of the discomfort experienced by citizens.

Citizen Protests in Reaction to Failing Investment Entities

The Occupy Wall Street movement is, to a large extent, the realization that no one has been held accountable for the 2008 financial crisis and the altered and negative economic climate in nations around the globe (Spitzer, 2011). Persistent high unemployment numbers in developed nations, particularly for the young graduates of universities, are now reaching the level of unemployment in underdeveloped nations. Although banks were at the heart of the economic crisis, they have grown wealthier and more powerful. Moreover, there is evidence of malfeasance and illegal actions, with little success by regulatory agencies to bring individuals causing economic chaos to trial, much less to prison (ibid.). The 'feeling' of economic stagnation, high unemployment, distrust of government officials who are viewed as elites and unresponsive, and the loss of economic opportunities with a stagnant economy. Citizens are now asking for more voice in economic affairs, and a fairer distribution of wealth. The perception that the wealthy are growing wealthier while the rest of society is stagnant is driving many citizens to protest. While their message is not coordinated, and not a comprehensive call for a reduction in corruption, together the hundreds of 'Global Change' groups are exhibiting their distrust of their governments, and also their large corporate enterprises (Samuelson, 2011; *Final Report of the National Commission on the Causes of the Financial and Economic Crisis in the United States*, 2011).

There has traditionally been an expectation that private organizations are competent in doing what they are meant to do in serving the public's interests. For most of their rise in the last century and into the first decade of the current century, they have successfully promoted social engagement, the funding of neighbourhood baseball teams, horse racing the square of Sienna, and proclaimed their ethical standards and their contract with citizens for the public welfare. Environmental damage, death through pharmaceuticals, and undercapitalized derivatives trading, have collectively created a sense of distrust.

The onset of distrust was not sudden; the realization of the health damaging effects of tobacco was played out over a decade, and the dangers of automobiles with steering posts designed to spear drivers in a collision took several decades to overcome with federal regulations. A citizen's inability to control large private institutions, and the lack of information about the workings of such institutions, has created public distrust in the intent or ability of large corporations to operate efficiently, safely and in the public interest.

The founding and growth of the Tea Party movement in the United States following the election of President Barack Obama was undoubtedly a defensive reaction to the remedies under development by the United States Congress and additional federal regulations being created to harness the larger and more powerful banks. The counter revolution was effective in electing a majority in the Congress opposed to the new President's programme for reform of the powers of financial firms and the return of economic stability programmes that failed. The resulting stagnation in the economy has in turn led to the 'Occupy Wall Street' movement. Ironically, the Occupy movement is now an international movement with thousands marching in developed, developing and underdeveloped nations.

When private institutions no longer warrant the trust of citizens, such as in the current world economic crisis initiated by banks and other financial institutions, the public perceives that its trust has been abused, and a degree of growing distrust in those large and anonymous institutions will be, and most likely has been, transferred to all large institutions, both private and public, leading to a corresponding growing lack of trust in government (Powell, 2010).

We live in a time of incredible access to information of all kinds. We are plainly drowning in facts and statistics. There is a large amount of information that the Internet and the latest technology is making available to us about the loss of trust in government and particularly about government institutions and also about major private institutions that are under duress or failing. We can begin to make sense about what implications we can draw from this information.

Most societies have experienced urbanization and have recognized that a modern industrial society is replacing homogeneous social relations associated with village life from a recent past. This gravitation has been a century long in progress for developed nations, and more recently, accelerated by globalization, very rapid for most developing nations. Citizens are, to a greater degree, living in cities that are part of an interdependent world, rather than in homogeneous villages with strong family bonds, and perhaps tribal bonds that tend to make trust of strangers more difficult to accept. And further, trust of far-off government institutions is almost an impossibility. Certainly newly urbanized citizens are having difficulty learning to accommodate our human differences and to survive interdependently of village and family loyalties (Fukuyama, 1995).

Toward a Theoretical Basis for Citizen Trust in Government

The breath of scholarship in the area of trust is very broad, ranging from concepts of social contracts justifying the need for checks and balances in government institutions to avoid the re-emergence of monarchies, to public reactions to catastrophes, both natural and economic, and concern about the impact such crisis might have on daily life and survival in the new global economy (Hardin, 2002, 2004; Uslaner, 2002; Johnston, 2005). For some developed societies, the question of distrust of government has a long tradition. Certainly that is valid for the United States. In effect, to the American view, any power given to government is necessarily subtracted from the liberties of the governed (Wills, 1999).

But critical to the study of trust in government is the realization that a 'certain' level of distrust is healthy and constructive given that it serves as motivation for accountability by government for its actions. The American concept of balance of power and the emergence internationally of transparency and the need for audits and accountability are institutionalized expressions of citizen distrust (Hardin, 2004; Kenney, 2009).

What is clearly understood is that when a society is corrupt in all of its government institutions, and criminalized as far as allowing dissent or criticism of ruling authorities, discussions of trust have little meaning. At this extreme, individuals are merely trying to survive and are viewing their environment only in terms of immediate survival. Without the rule of law, without the security of contracts, a viable justice system, and without efficient governmental administration, distrust is not a viable issue.

If democratic societies are more trusting, with a high level of security in citizens' safety, with the rule of law secure, then, why the decline in citizen trust in democratic and developed nations? One may argue that it is not democracy that creates citizen trust, but instead, a 'trusting society' that creates a democracy, and a society that invests its government with the authority to be more responsive to the needs of its citizens, and to 'redistribute wealth' in an egalitarian fashion (Hardin, 2002).

The answer may be in an examination of the causes and consequences of trust. But causes and effect may be difficult to identify, and will vary from culture to culture. Certainly democracy tends to assure a supportive political culture and consequently an increase in citizen trust in government, but economic equality may be a more substantive cause of trust in government. The two are essential causes of trust in government, democracy and economic equality.

Meddling with constitutions as a means of causing a more trusting citizenry may not work, in that the creation of new legal systems presented in the form of new constitutions will not by themselves 'create' a more trusting society—and one might add that strong legal systems do not assure citizen trust in government.

Developing stable governmental institutions requires transparency and accountability to the public over a long period of time. The length of time, of course, is difficult to predict for any society, and depends on hundreds of variables relating to jobs, security, peace and prosperity, and open and transparent government, and a sense of participation in the selection of elected officials beyond the selection of individuals by autocratic institutions.

Nation-building is a process that takes time, with the intervention of leaders that are in turn trusted. Ironically, today's political leaders, both executive leaders and parliaments, have the lowest level of trust in modern times, while government institutions are experiencing a higher, and in some instances, such as in South Korea, a very high level of trust and confidence.

It may be argued that trusting societies create strong legal systems that maintain the trust and confidence of citizens. And strong legal systems are accompanied by courts that enforce contracts, protect basic freedoms, protect against governmental abuse, and assure the viability of contracts and commercial activity. Societies that trust their governments, it is thus suggested, will have less corruption.

References

Bailyn, Bernard (1967). *The Ideological Origins of the American Revolution*. Cambridge, Mass: Harvard University Press.

Banfield, Edward (1958). *The Moral Basis of a Backward Society*. New York: Free Press.

"Capitalism at Bay", in *The Economist*, October 16, 2008, p. 15.

Fukuyama, Francis (1995). *Trust: The Social Virtues and the Creation of Prosperity*. New York: Free Press.

Hardin, Russell (2002). *Trust and Trustworthiness*. New York: Russell Sage Foundation, Inc.

——. (Ed.) (2004). *Distrust*. New York: Russell Sage Foundation, Inc.

Heinman, Fritz F. (1997). 'Combating International Corruption: The Role of the Business Community'. In Elliot, Kimberly Ann (Ed.), *Corruption and the Global Economy*. Washington, DC: Institute for International Economics, pp. 147–61.

Horne, Cynthia M. (2004). 'Distrust as a Trade Impediment: European Trade Policy Toward Nonmarket Economies'. In Hardin, Russell (Ed.), *Distrust*. New York: Russell Sage Foundation.

Johnston, Michael (1997). 'Public Officials, Private Interests, and Sustainable Democracy: When Politics and Corruption Meet'. In Elliot, Kimberly Ann (Ed.), *Corruption and the Global Economy. Institute for International Economics*. Washington, DC, pp. 61–82.

——. (2005). *Syndromes of Corruption: Wealth, Power, and Democracy*. Cambridge, UK: Cambridge University Press.

Kenney, Sheila Suess (2009). *Distrust American Style: Diversity and Crisis of Public Confidence*. New York: Prometheus Books.

Montinola, Gabriella R. (2004). "Corruption, Distrust, and the Deterioration of the Rule of Law". In Hardin, Russell (Ed.), *Distrust*. New York: Russell Sage Foundation.

OECD Convention on Combating Bribery of Foreign Public Officials in International Business Transactions (2011).

Paulson, Henry (2010). *On the Brink: Inside the Race to Stop the Collapse of the Global Financial System*. New York: Business Plus.

Pew Research Center (2010). *Distrust, Discontent, Anger and Partisan Rancor: The People and Their Government*. Washington DC: Pew Research Center for the People and the Press.

Porte, T.R. and D.S. Metley (1996). "Hazards and Institutional Trustworthiness: Facing a Deficit of Trust". *Public Administration Review,* 56 (4): 341–47.

Powell, Melchior D. (2010). "Conceptions and Management of Trust in Government and Business in a Globalized World" (paper presented at the 2010 Annual Conference of the International Association of Schools and Institutes of Administration, Bali, Indonesia, July).

Putnam, Robert (2000). *Bowling Alone*. New York: Simon and Schuster.

Rose-Ackerman, Susan (1999). *Corruption and Government: Causes, Consequences and Reform*. Cambridge, UK: Cambridge University Press.

Seligman, Adam B. (1997). *The Problem of Trust*. Princeton: Princeton University Press.

Samuelson Robert, J. (2011). "Rethinking the Great Recession". *Wilson Quarterly,* Winter.

Spitzer, Eliot (2011). *Government's Place in the Market*. Cambridge, Mass: The MIT Press.

The Financial Crisis Inquiry Report: Final Report of the National Commission on the Causes of the Financial and Economic Crisis in the United States. 2011. Washington DC: Superintendent of Documents, US Government Printing Office.

The Foreign Corrupt Practices Act of 1977. Pub. L. 95–213.

Ullmann-Margalit (2004). "Trust, Distrust, and Inbetween". In Hardin, Russell (Ed.), *Distrust.* New York: Russell Sage Foundation.

Uslaner, Eric M. (2002). *The Moral Foundations of Trust*. Cambridge, UK: Cambridge University Press.

Wills, Garry (1999). *A Necessary Evil: A History of American Distrust of Government*. New York: Simon and Shuster.

Wolak, Jennifer and Christine K. Palus (2010). "The Dynamics of Public Confidence in US State and Local Government". *State Politics & Policy Quarterly,* 10: 421–45.

2

Reinventing Good Governance

Challenges and Strategies in India

R.B. JAIN

The advent of the 21st century has been characterized with the rising of poor quality governance and unsustainable development that has gripped the so-called Third World countries into a new form of maladministration found rampant everywhere. Many of the characteristics of the colonial governments have permeated the successor states. In addition, because of the growing intervention of the state in most human collective activities and resultant public enterprises, the states of the Third World have found themselves deficient in skilled, technically competent and specialist manpower necessary for their development purposes resulting in low administrative capacities (Jain, 1989, 362–74). After experimenting with different systems and models of public administration to achieve developmental goals, most developing countries (including India) are now in the process of formulating strategies to meet the challenges of 'governance' rather 'good governance'—the concepts that have become quite popular, as a result of the impact of globalization, liberalization and the impact of New Public Management (NPM) movement of the early 1990s, coupled with the sustained efforts of the World Bank to pressurize the governments to undertake constructive reforms in their administrative system to fully achieve the benefits of the World Bank initiatives for development.

Concept of Good Governance

The term 'governance' in its earlier interpretation was used to describe the 'activity of decision-making and the process by which decisions are implemented (or not implemented)'. However, it has now become a very fashionable and a broad concept, which is defined as the exercise of authority through formal and informal traditions and institutions for the common good. Governance encompasses the process of selecting, monitoring, and replacing governments. It includes the capacity to formulate and implement sound policies, and it assumes a respect for citizens. From this framework governance can be construed as consisting of six different elements. These are: (i) voice and accountability, which includes civil liberties and freedom of the press, (ii) political stability, (iii) government effectiveness, which includes the quality of policy-making and public service delivery, (iv) quality of regulations, (v) rule of law, which includes protection of property rights and an independent judiciary, and (vi) control of corruption.

Improving the quality of governance requires a system of checks and balances in society that restrains arbitrary action and harassment by politicians and bureaucrats, promotes voices and participation by the population, reduces incentives for the corporate elite to engage in state capture, and fosters the rule of law. A meritocratic and service-oriented public administration is a salient feature of such a strategy. However, synthesizing the strategy of key reforms for improving governance and combating corruption is a particularly daunting challenge, as is the task of detailing and adapting a strategy to each country-specific reality. Governance is more than fighting corruption. Improving governance should be seen as a process integrating three vital components: (a) knowledge, with rigorous data and empirical analysis, including in-country diagnostics and dissemination, utilizing the latest information technology tools, (b) leadership in the political, civil society and international arena, and (c) collective action via systematic participatory and consensus-building approaches with key stakeholders in society (for which technology revolution is also assisting). No two countries arrive at the same strategy, but to maximize the prospects of success, any country serious about improving governance for sustainable development must involve all key stakeholders, guarantee a flow of information to them, and lock in the commitment of the leadership (ibid.: 6).

The World Bank has incorporated these features of quality governance in the concept of 'good governance' as 'the one epitomized by predictable, open, an enlightened policy-making, a bureaucracy imbued with a professional ethos acting in furtherance of the public good, the rule of law, transparent processes, and a strong civil society participating in public affairs. Poor governance, on the other hand, is characterized by arbitrary policy-making, unaccountable bureaucracies, enforced or unjust legal systems, the abuse of executive power, a civil society engaged in public life, and widespread corruption'.

India's Experiences in Governance and Administrative Development

The threshold of the new millennium has furnished us with a good occasion to reflect upon and evaluate India's experiences in administrative development towards its pursuit of good governance and ponder over the likely emerging trends and the lessons learnt for the future. Reflecting upon the realities of public administration system in India over the last half a century is not a simple exercise, for India is a complex society comprising a diversity of languages, social systems, ethnic, tribal and caste groups, various religions, regional disparities, different cultural patterns, and unlimited environmental factors that shape the behavioural pattern of the masses and public functionaries at all levels, which affect the idea of rationalism in administrative behaviour. It is indeed very difficult to objectively evaluate the impact of all these factors on governance. The Government of India has since independence in 1947 taken a number of steps to revamp the system of administration at different stages of its evolution with a view to secure objectivity, transparency, efficiency and responsiveness. In the administrative process, the basic ingredients of good governance in a democratic system are based on the concepts of rule of law and public welfare.

As it appears, the search for the elusive goal of good governance in India has been simultaneous with the evolution of a constitutional democratic government—a government which is limited, stable and truly representative of the majority of the people, maintains its territorial integrity and national sovereignty, accelerates economic growth and development, upholds the rule of law and renders justice without fear or favour and without delay, and ensures welfare of all sections of the people. These objectives were sought to be achieved through the adoption of the Republican Constitution in 1950. However, despite the lofty ideals and the values of good governance enshrined in the Constitution, we find ourselves today in a state where the system has not been able to provide either a stable government or stable policies. What has gone wrong in our constitutional and administrative system during the last fifty years has been a subject of endless debate and discussions, and a number of prognosis have been made by constitutional and administrative experts, political leaders and policy-makers, various commissions and committees to reform and restructure the system to be able to achieve the objectives of good governance. 'Has the system of government failed in India or the people have failed the system' is an oft repeated question being raised again and again without any satisfactory answer. As was so emphatically suggested by the author elsewhere (Jain, 2001), it is wrong to always blame the structural aspects of governmental system for our failures. Given the normal wear and tear in the edifice of the governmental and administrative system over a period of over fifty years, the system as a whole has not only survived, but also admirably borne the brunt of time, in comparison to the scores of examples of other countries in the developing world where such structures have crumbled completely.

However, at the same time, a number of serious distortions have crept in the system during all these years, giving validity to the dictum of Woodrow Wilson that it is easier 'to make a constitution than to run it'. The foremost and fundamental reason for all these aberrations has firstly, been the existence of a dual system of values on the part of political and administrative elites in India, who have the basic responsibility of implementing the system. In their public pronouncements and external behaviour, they are highly idealistic and show deep concern for integrity, equity and justice—the prime values of good governance, but in practice, when it comes to actual decision-making and its implementation, the same political and administrative elites are vulnerable to all kinds of narrow prejudices, biases and pressures of caste, community or religion, or political compromises in order to continue to remain in power by all possible means—fair or dubious. This has been a marked trend in India's political and administrative development especially since the 1960s. The public postures of political and administrative leaders hardly match their actual behaviour on the positions they hold and the values they espouse.

Secondly, there has been a growing sense of zealousness amongst the people from all walks of life in India about the constitutional rights and administrative privileges without paying due attention to the corresponding duties that go with them. The level of tolerance among the people in India, which was the hallmark of their social, cultural and political behaviour in the first two decades of the Republic, seems to have been lost somewhere in the labyrinthine struggle for power. People will go to any length of aggressive, unfair, immoral and unjudicial conduct to achieve their selfish goals. This general decline in standards of behaviour and conduct of mutual relations have been more prominent in the floors of legislatures—once considered the temples of democracy. The honourable members of these august bodies increasingly seem to settle their individual and political scores by blocking the proceedings, creating pandemonium, showing fists, hurling shoes, chairs and microphones, and breaking the heads and teeth of political opponents. All these happenings have some disastrous consequences for the social and political system as a whole. People in all fields of professions and occupations will go to any extent and resort to any form of agitations demanding their rights, but would not care for the obligation that such rights carry. Whether it is the student bodies, academics, the labour organizations, business or industrial groups, there are agitations galore for all kinds of demands from the state and against any move of the government to bring about any reform or semblance of discipline in the system, holding the citizens at large to ransom and throwing the lives of the people out of gear and at the same time put strains and pressures on the performance of the system.

Thirdly, at the same time, the total lack of a notion of accountability and responsiveness on the part of both legislators and administrators has eroded the very essence of a responsible government. There are political rhetoric and polemics, but no substantial accomplishment in respect of the citizens' needs and aspirations. There are innumerable grandiose policies, plans, programmes and projects, which we are very apt to formulate, but there are no plans or will to implement these four p's. The result is either stagnation or a very slow growth in the realm of progress and development. On top of it, the bureaucracy in India is cold, slow and somewhat inhuman in dealing with the complaints of the citizens. Worst of all it carries an image of being the most corrupt amongst the world bureaucracies. Instances of administrative excesses, police brutality and the nexus between politicians, bureaucrats and criminals for securing political and personal ends appear endlessly in the media practically every day. Billions of rupees are being spent every day on the security, privileges and 'welfare' of the politicians, legislators, ministers and other political and administrative functionaries, but without any proportionate returns on the welfare of the masses. There is an open exploitation and the use of money power, muscle power and mafia power all around for securing personal and material gains without the slightest qualms on one's conscience or on one's moral sense of responsibility for efficient and effective governance.

Fourthly, in India, the poor are still poor and have even increased in absolute numbers. Economic gains have been wiped out by population growth. Though India has an economically powerful middle class, a vibrant software industry, and nuclear capability, a huge number of India's citizens continue to eke out a living under conditions of extreme poverty and deprivation. The government's capacity to perform is still weak, resources available for public investment and development are still scarce and local jurisdictions are particularly starved. The critical basic needs in education, health, welfare, infrastructure and the very basic need of clean drinking water for the masses still go unmet. Many of the poor are in fact worse-off now than they were a decade ago. No wonder that India ranks very low in the Human Development Report prepared each year by the UNDP. Human development is the strand which holds together concerns on political institutions and governance, social institutions and culture, and science and technology. Ultimately, what really matters is how the interaction between globalization and these different institutions redounds to higher levels of human development.

As one of the observers of the Indian political scene has rightly put it, 'poverty is the biggest political constituency in India. Not only do our politicians feed-off it like vultures but supposedly pro-poor activists and NGOs also rush around condemning economic reforms on the grounds that the poor will not benefit .... A favourite whipping boy of the "pro-poor" activists is globalisation. This they tell us is definitely anti-poor but again they do not ask if globalisation is an option anymore or a reality we have to face. There are not many countries left in the world so over regulated as we are ... there is much we can gain by learning from other kinds of systems of governance where we went wrong' (Singh, 2000: 26). What particular social and economic model can be devised at this juncture of the evolution of the Indian polity, with vociferous disruptive tendencies without any coherent ideological stance remains the biggest challenge for the policy-makers in India at the beginning of the millennium.

Strategies Needed for Good Governance and Sustainable Development

In the perspective of these developments worldwide and in India, the fundamental question that arises is to devise the strategies that would be conducive for the developing nations, particularly India, to strive towards sustainable development. Besides the institutional and structural innovations that make for a system of good governance, a corruption-free sustainable development requires a 'moral determination' (Dwivedi, 1987: 607–9 and 2001). Recognition of that moral determination in governance marks the direction in which those who govern must channel their efforts toward the common good if they are to justly serve the society. That direction calls for individual 'moral responsibility and accountability, sacrifice, compassion, justice and an honest effort to achieve the common good'. Ultimately, it is the moral determination which provides the foundation for governance towards a corruption-free sustainable development.

(i) *Adopting a normative model of good governance*: Thus, the need at present seems to be to adopt a normative model of good management incorporating both the politico-administrative as well as the moral dimensions of good governance. This should include: (a) a more strategic or result-oriented (efficiency, effectiveness and service quality) orientation to decision-making; (b) replacement of highly centralized organizational structures with decentralized management environment integrating with the new rural, urban and municipal institutions, where decisions on resource allocation and service delivery are taken close to the point of delivery; (c) flexibility to explore alternatives to direct public provision, which might provide more cost-effective policy outcomes; (d) focusing attention on the matching of authority and responsibility as a key to improving performance, including a mechanism of explicit performance contracting; (e) creating competitive environments within and between public service organizations; (f) strengthening of strategic capacities at the centre to steer government to respond to external changes and diverse interests quickly, flexibly and at the least cost; (g) greater accountability and transparency through requirements to report on results and their full costs; (h) service-wide budgeting and management systems to support and encourage these changes; (i) the most important task is to break the growing nexus of bureaucrats, politicians and criminals leading not only to a breakdown of the total system but also to a sense of cynicism amongst the citizenry; (j) adapting of innovations and evolving suitable mechanism to eliminate corruption at both political and administrative levels and strengthen citizens' grievance redressal system; (k) improving the system of delivery at the cutting edge of administration by replacing the existing archaic bureaucratic procedures by absorbing some appropriate precepts inherent in the philosophy of New Public Management; and (l) making improvements in the working atmosphere of the government institutions and offices to reflect a new work culture and a changed administrative behaviour incorporating the principles of transparency, responsiveness, accountability, participative and citizen-friendly management.

(ii) *The public-private sector synergy*: There is no doubt that the process of globalization and the simultaneous rapid economic and technological changes have greatly affected the pattern of governance in modern times. Scholars have argued that the actual pattern of governance in internationalized environments can be related to the respective governance capacity of public and private actors, which hinges in turn on the strategic constellations underlying the provision of public goods. The specific strategic constellations vary along three dimensions, namely, the congruence between the scope of the underlying problem and the organizational structures of the related actors; the type of goods problem; and the institutional context. For their part, each of these combines a number of factors (Knill and Lehmkuhl, 2002: 41–63). On the basis of this concept four ideal types of governance, enabled by their differing configurations of public and private capacities to formally or factually influence in various ways the social, economic and political processes employed in the provision of certain goods, have been identified. Assessing the implications of economic and political internationalization on the governance capacities of public and private actors, internationalization has been described as a process in which the patterns of governance are transformed along three paths: from interventionist regulation to regulated self-regulation; from interventionist regulation to private self-regulation; and from interventionist regulation to interfering regulation. The analysis of the consequences of internationalization for the patterns of governance further suggests that the expectation of the weakening of the state, or a mutual driving out of governance activities of public and private actors can hardly be confirmed. The relationship between public and private actors is neither free from conflict, nor is it paralysed by conflict; in essence, there is a dynamic, synergetic relationship, with public and private contributions reinforcing each other over time. However, such mutual dependencies between public and private actors and their concept to cope with specific problems are apparent only in the implementation of certain regulatory arrangements and do not take into account the problems related to accountability and the democratic legitimacy of regulatory structures. Thus, a crucial question becomes important: how is it possible to ensure that private governance activities are kept responsive to wider societal interests (ibid.: 57–58)? The question of accountability, therefore, becomes a key factor along with the issue of good government. Nowadays, a new model is also being discussed, called the Public-Private Community Partnership (PPCP) model, wherein both the government and private players work together for social welfare, eliminating the prime focus of private players on profit. This model is being applied more in developing nations as in India. Success is being achieved through this model too. It mainly helps to ramp up the development process as the focus is shifted towards target achievement rather than profit achievement. These not-for-profit organizations bridge public and private sector interests, with a view toward resolving the specific incentive and financial barriers to increased industry involvement in the development of safe and effective pharmaceutical and other types of products (Wikipedia, culled from Google, 20 September 2010).

(iii) *Accountability as a basic requisite for good governance*: If the concept of accountability refers to the degree to which public servants and others in non-governmental sectors providing public programmes are responsive to those they serve, then there is a need for multidimensional methods to measure how different institutional arrangements advantage different forms of responsiveness. The traditional measures of accountability that rely upon line or top-down measures do not necessarily provide a good guide to the accountability culture as a whole. As service delivery systems move to more complex forms of agency, accountability at other levels must be expected to undergo a dynamic process of evolution and adaptation. It is clearly not enough to bemoan the decline of a parliament or the weakness of the consumer. Institutional development must fit each case. Vertical strength can be improved with stronger roles for parliamentary committees, ombudsmen, and so on. Tools for greater horizontal accountability will need to be different for competitive systems and for those using more collaborative methods. In both cases, a focus upon the role of reflexive feedback or improvization offers a means to reopen the organizational process box without the perils of re-regulation. This new domain of accountability will take sometime to develop its own regime of measures, standards and rules. Perhaps the most important step needed is the recognition that multidimensionality of accountability means both multiple measure and new mandates (Considine, 2002: 21–40).

(iv) *Adoption of IT and the concept of e-governance*: The revolution in information technology has brought into focus its adoption for good governance. There is a talk of e-governance all over the world. E-governance implies a smoother interface between government and citizen. While it cannot entirely replace manual governance, even its limited applications are good enough to affect day-to-day living. It can fulfil roughly speaking, the four purposes for which citizens generally interact with the government: (i) paying bills, taxes, user fees and so on, (ii) registration formalities, whether of a child's birth or a house purchase or a driving license (in Tamil Nadu, for instance, one can download 72 application forms), (iii) seeking information, and (iv) lodging complaints. E-governance can reduce distances to nothing, linking remote villages to government offices in the cities, can reduce staff, cut costs, check leaks in the governing system, and can make the citizen-government interaction smooth, without queues and the tyranny of clerks. But it must be remembered that e-governance is only a tool for good governance. It cannot succeed independent of responsive officers, and it has to be owned by the political leadership. Otherwise it will only be a bureaucrat's game

(*India Today*, 11 December 2000: 70–76; also see Jain, 2007: 1418–23). How to rebuild the system of governance on these new premises without the majority of population even being literate is a real challenge for all concerned with new innovations in the performance of the Government in India. E-governance initiatives are common in most countries as they promise a more citizen-centric government and reduce operational cost. Unfortunately, most of these initiatives have not been able to achieve the benefits claimed. Often the reason for this failure is a techno-centric focus rather than a governance-centric focus. Therefore, the aim is to explore the necessary attributes of a governance-centric initiative under the banner 'excellent e-governance', and describe a methodology for ensuring such excellence in e-governance implementations. There should be a case study approach for developing the concept of excellent e-governance. Thus, a methodology, which may be called e-governance engineering, should be developed, which when applied to an e-governance initiative, will ensure excellence.

(v) *The citizen-oriented paradigm of good governance*: The corporate millennium has brought into focus a new concept of governance based on the interests of the shareholders, i.e., the citizens, which has signalled the role of transparency, accountability and merit-based management and a sense of morality and ethics that rests on the principle of 'concern for others'. An ethical organization, more so a government not only stands for people with a set of values, but a positive attitude which generates a culture within the organization in which every member feels a sense of loyalty and belonging and the leaders are responsible for initiating dialogues across a wide range of levels and functions so as to operationalize values in practical policies.

Modernization of government and public administration involves a redefinition of government responsibilities. The state system of the 21st century will have to see a redistribution of duties and responsibilities between government, business and society. The guiding principle is the idea of the 'empowering state', which leaves more space for society and individual commitment. The internal structures of government administration should also become part of this developmental process. This would require the introduction of modern management techniques with quality control, budgeting and cost-benefit analyses. In future, public authorities are meant to be results-oriented in providing public services. Modern management and e-government are two central means of achieving fundamental changes in public administration. The goal is an administration that does more and costs less. E-governance projects are not only modernizing public agencies and authorities, but also making administrative procedures more transparent for ordinary citizens, which in turn also makes new demands on personnel to be more accountable.

Managers must respond flexibly to the changing demands and expectations of the public and the ever-changing nature of public problems, yet they must do so in a manner that provides accountability to the public and political overseers. A dichotomous approach to the study of leadership as management action and the governance structures within which managers operate has inhibited the search for a public management theory that reconciles the dilemma. Managers must attend to demands for both flexible leadership action and structures that promise accountability. The capacity to perceive this relationship offers managers a means to keep flexibility and accountability in a dynamic tension. It has been suggested that public management scholars can elevate this understanding from an implicit 'theory in use' to an explicit 'espoused theory'. This approach could be a productive one for public management scholarship and ultimately for its practice (Feldman and Khademian, 2001: 339–61).

(vi) *Combating corruption for good governance*: From the foregoing discussion, it is more than evident that the concept of quality governance is premised on a corruption-free administrative system. Combating corruption for sustainable development calls for: (a) reducing opportunities and incentives for corrupt behaviour and increasing the sense of accountability on the part of public officials; and (b) effective implementation of anti-corruption measures, which would imply that measures should be logically consistent with regard to the phasing of a time table for speedy investigation and conviction; a strong political commitment to implement the strategies and enforcing anti-corruption measures; and people's active participation from below in the enforcement of administrative, legal and judicial measures, thus mobilizing the public against corruption in public life.

Apart from the above fundamental conditions it must be emphasized that fighting corruption requires: (a) formation of a national coordinating body that should be responsible for devising and following up on a strategy against corruption, along with a citizen's oversight board; (b) the existence of a high-powered independent prosecuting body to investigate and prosecute all such known cases of corruption; (c) and the setting up of special courts for trying such cases at a stretch so that the cases come to their legitimate conclusion without any delay; (d) thoroughly overhauling and reforming the system of electoral laws and economic regulations minimizing the temptation to indulge in corruption practice; (e) enactment of appropriate legislation to limit the number of ministries and departments both at the centre and in the states so that the temptation of expanding ministries only for political gains could be minimized; and (f) by providing specialized technical assistance to anti-corruption agencies organizing high-level anti-corruption workshops or strategic consulting or hiring international investigations to track down ill-gotten deposits overseas. At the same time, it is also important that international institutions should take steps to encourage participatory approaches in developing countries in order to build consensus for anti-corruption drives and associated reforms. Civil society is likely to be a major ally in resisting corruption. More and more it is this ally that seeks concrete support from more developed Western countries and international agencies in actively combating corruption (Kaufman, 1997: 130). International cooperation can help national leaders develop political resolve, and international action can convey the useful truth that we are all involved in the problem of corruption and that we must find solutions together.

Concluding Observations

In conclusion, however, it should be remembered that for achieving good governance, no amount of planning and thinking in all these areas would be useful unless the governments at all levels of the polity are capable enough to take hard and unpleasant decisions and have the will and capacity to implement and continuously monitor and evaluate their impact. At the same time, the political leadership has to demonstrate its strong determination to undertake reforms by first cleaning its own stable from corrupt and criminal influences, and setting ethical standards of quality governance both at the political and administrative levels. For changes to come, it is necessary to change the mindset and attitudes of both the public administrators and the politicians in power (Mathur, 2005: 343).

In the perspectives of the worldwide developments at the threshold of the 21st century, we have attempted to discuss some of the emerging challenges to quality and 'good governance', on which the strategies for growth and sustainable development in India and in other transitional societies can be built and operationalized. It is heartening that people in almost all developing countries have recognized their importance, and it is likely that the growing concerns towards sustainable development, fighting corruption and devising innovations for 'quality governance' may turn out to be a concerted international movement, not confined merely to the realm of academic discussions or writings in specific contexts like India, but of taking constructive actions for positive results transcending the jurisdictions of national boundaries. This is the only hope for achieving a universally good, and corruption-free good governance, for the very survival of humanity, towards which we must all strive.

References

Brinkerhoff, Derick W. and Jennifer M. Coston (1999). "International Development Management in a Globalized World" in *Public Administration Review*, July–August, Vol. 59, No.4, pp. 346–61.

Considine, Mark (2002). "The End of the Line? Accountable Governance in the Age of Networks, Partnerships, and Joined-up Services" in *Governance: An International Journal of Policy, Administration and Institutions*, Vol. 15, No.1 January 2, pp. 21–40.

Dwivedi, O.P. (1987). "Moral Dimensions of Statecraft", *Canadian Journal of Political Science*, Vol. 20, No.4, pp. 609–709 and "The Challenge of Cultural Diversity for Good Governance", a paper prepared for presentation at the UN meeting on Managing Diversity in the Civil Service, organized by the UN Division of Public Economics and Public Administration (DPEPA), UN Department of Economic and Social Affairs, New York, NY, USA, 3–4 May 2001.

Feldman, Martha S. and Anne M. Khademian (2001). "Principles for Public Management Practice: From Dichotomies to Interdependence" in *Governance: An International Journal of Policy and Administration*, Vol. 14, No.3, July, pp. 339–61.

Fuhr, Harald (2003). "Constructive Pressures and Incentives to Reform: Globalization and its Impact on Public Sector Performance and Governance in Developing Countries", a paper presented in Panel RC 4.2 at the 19th Congress of the International Political Science Association, held at Durban (South Africa), June–July.

India (2000). *Economic Survey*, 1999–2000, New Delhi, Government of India, Ministry of Finance, p. 164.

——. (2001). *Approach Paper to the Tenth Five Year Plan* (2002–07) (New Delhi, Planning Commission), para 1.9, p. 2, and 49.

——. (2007). *Towards Faster and More Inclusive Growth: An Approach to the XI Five Year Plan* (2007–12), Government of India, Planning Commission, New Delhi, December.

India Today, 11 December 2000, pp. 70–76.

Jain, R.B. (1989). *Bureaucratic Politics in the Third World*. New Delhi, Gitanjali Publishing House, pp. 362–74.

Jain, R.B. (2001). *Public Administration in India: 21st Century Challenges to Good Governance*, New Delhi, Deep & Deep.

——. (2006). "Opening Government for Public Scrutiny: An Analysis of Recent Efforts in India to Make Governance More Transparent and Accountable" in *Indian Journal of Public Administration*, Vol. 52, No. 3, July–September). See pp. 555–60 for a detailed discussion and analysis of the enactment and implementation of the Right to Information Act, 2005.

——. (2007). "Revamping the Administrative Structure and Processes in India for Online Democracy" in Ari-Veikko Anttiroiko and Mtti Malkia (eds.,) *Encyclopedia of Digital Government*, Finland, Vol. III (I-Z), pp. 1418–23.

Kaufman, Daniel (1997). "Corruption: The Facts", *Foreign Policy*, Summer, p. 130.

——. (2001). "New Empirical Frontiers in Fighting Corruption and Improving Governance-Selected Issues", a paper presented at the OSCE Economic Forum, Brussels, January 30–31, p. 6.

Knill, Christoph and Dirk Lehmkuhl (2002). "Private Actors and the State: Internationalization and Changing Patterns of Governance" *in Governance: An International Journal of Policy, Administration and Institutions* (Oxford), Vol. 15, No.1, January), pp. 41–63.

Mathur, B.P. (2005). *Governance Reform for Vision India*. New Delhi, Macmillan, 2005, p. 343.

Parr, Saikko Fuuda (1997). *Sustainable Human Development in a Globalizing World*, New York, Human Development Report Office, pp. 1–2.

Singh, Tavleen (2000). "Poverty Politics" in *India Today*, 11 December, p. 26.

Stuijvenberg, Peter A. Van (1996). "Structural Adjustment in India: What About Poverty Alleviation?", in Hanumantha Rao, C.H. and Hans Linnemann (eds.), *Economic Reforms and Poverty Alleviation in India* (New Delhi: Sage Publications), pp. 31–89.

3

Indian Democracy

Ideology and Reality

M.V. NAIDU

The world's biggest democracy—India—held, in 1996, its eleventh national elections, with 443 political parties wooing 600 million voters to win 543 seats in Lok Sabha, the lower house of Indian parliament, which selects the government (Basu, 1996: 6–9). Since attaining independence in 1947, India has remained a democracy. Democracy is the polity that is most conducive to peaceful conflict resolution, development and peace building.

In spite of initiating many unprecedented political and economic experiments, Indian democracy has lasted for the last sixty years without violent disruptions, while all its neighbouring sister states—Pakistan, Bangladesh, Myanmar, Nepal and Sri Lanka—have suffered military *coups d'état*, civil wars, dictatorships, territorial disintegration or political instabilities. For that matter, all other countries of Asia and Africa, the Middle East and Latin America that were decolonized in the pre-war and post-war eras have also succumbed to authoritarianism of one form or another. In countries such as Greece, Italy and Turkey, democracy was often suspended during the last sixty years. European countries such as Spain and Portugal and former Communist satellites have become democratic only during the last decade or two. Authoritarian states of Germany, Italy and Japan were forced into democratization under the allied occupation; so far they have remained democratic.

The six factors that seem to destroy, distort or inhibit democracy may be identified as the following: (1) military coups; (2) civil wars; (3) neighbourhood wars; (4) autocratization of the regime; (5)

national disintegration; and (6) massive deportation or displacement of the people.

Why has Indian democracy survived and flourished while 70–80 per cent of countries in the world today are being run by anti-democratic autocracies (Kousoulas, 1982: 24)?

In assessing India's record we must realize that until recently most Western sources of information on India have been cynical and sensational.

Democratic Theory and Practice

Ideal democracy is a political system that is committed to human equality, individual liberty and humanism (Naidu, 1992: 8–9), and is built on the foundations of non-violence and rationalism that give rise to pluralism, secularism, toleration and empathy. In constitutional terms, democracy is a government of the people (i.e., popular sovereignty), for the people (i.e., government responsible to the people) and by the people (i.e., public participation in legislative, executive and judiciary). In operational terms, democracy is a system in which people choose their government leaders through universal adult franchise and free and fair elections held at regular and reasonable intervals, without undue influence of money and mass media, and without coercive or violent interventions of the police, the secret service and the military, but with the availability of the free press and an independent judiciary. In political-administrative terms, the constitutional structure of democracy is supported by two pillars—the pillar of fundamental freedoms and the pillar of rule of law (due process of law).

If violence is seen as physical, structural and psychological, then the ideal democracy, in essence, is a non-violent system. Gandhi defines democracy as 'the rule of unadulterated non-violence' (*Harijan*, 1940). Increasing coercion, militarization and authoritarianization in a democracy can undercut existing democratic structures and processes, and can eventually lead to an atrophy of democracy.

On the basis of the above ingredients, at least three types of democracy can be identified—nominal or minimal, considerable or substantive, and advanced or maximal democracy. However, to be considered as a democracy, a political system should have maintained, continuously not intermittently, a democratic constitution, structures, policies and functions for at least five decades, not just five months or five years or on five occasions.

As commonly understood, dictatorship is the opposite of democracy. An ideal typology of dictatorship is based upon violence and irrationalism, monism, theocratism, intolerance, hatred and the non-acceptance of equality, denial of liberty and the absence of humanism. A dictator usurps powers and sets up an arbitrary regime through the suspension of rights, and elimination of the elected legislature, avoiding an independent judiciary, the rule of law and freedom of the press; it is accomplished with the help of guns, soldiers, religious or ideological fanaticism and jingoistic chauvinism. Dictatorship is the embodiment of violence.

A political system represents not only a system of government but also a way of life. In other words, constitutional philosophy, political institutions and political activities are built upon the foundations of the social values, the psychological behaviours and the cultural patterns of the society. Thus, culture and politics are intertwined and interdependent.

If politics and culture are attuned to non-violence and democracy at home, they could not induce aggressive or militaristic foreign policy and support for authoritarianism abroad, unless domestic democracy is superficial or immature, or unless the nation develops a split personality. When foreign policy is consistently and persistently contradictory to domestic democracy, and when the chickens come home to roost, they can bring home the foreign disease of anti-democratism that is sure to undermine the health of domestic democracy.

Of course, democracies could be dragged into military conflicts. But a mature democracy will have two strategies in meeting such challenges. First, it will choose to fight, if unavoidable, a defensive war, and will be willing to terminate or suspend the war as soon as possible, bilaterally or multilaterally or through the United Nations. Second, a thoughtful democracy will carefully disallow any such military enterprise to have a long-lasting impact on domestic affairs and its national values and goals. The introduction of conscription, joining military alliances, increased militarization and militarism (Naidu, 1985: 2–10), an enhanced role for the industrial-military complex and lasting hate campaigns are bound to weaken democratic politics and democratic culture. A mature democracy should not allow the foreign aggressor to intervene and reshape and dehumanize its domestic democracy.

Through all its structures and functions, democracy relies heavily upon non-violent conflict resolution that invariably results in peace building.

Contemporary Challenges to Democracy

Many of the newly independent states and some of the old established states have suffered during the last sixty years many internal crises that have led to violent conflicts, territorial disintegration, political instabilities and authoritarian regimes. What factors caused these tragedies? Did not Indian democracy also face similar challenges?

The seven evils that have plagued many democratic countries could be identified as the following: (1) racial/ethnic hatreds; (2) religious bigotry; (3) linguistic rivalries; (4) separatist violence; (5) communist terrorism; (6) crises of industrialization; and (7) participation in the Cold War and proxy wars.

While racial hatreds have damaged the political systems in South Africa and the United States, ethnic antagonisms have led to inhuman atrocities and national disintegration in Afghanistan, Burundi, Cyprus, East Pakistan, East Timor, Iraq, Lebanon, Myanmar, Nigeria, Palestine, Rwanda, Somalia, the former Soviet Union, Sri Lanka, Tibet, Turkey and the former Yugoslavia.

Religious bigotry and fundamentalism have led to hate-filled violence and political instabilities in Afghanistan, Algeria, Lebanon, Iran, Israel, Ireland, Pakistan, Sri Lanka and so on.

Linguistic chauvinism in some countries has not only created hatreds and bitter political disputes, but has also generated demands for separatism. The Bengali-speaking in East Pakistan, the French-speaking in Canada, the Tamil-speaking in Sri Lanka and the Flemish-speaking in Belgium have fought linguistic battles. Almost every country in Africa is multilingual and has language conflicts. Unilingual bigots in the United States have already started an agitation to discourage any concession to minority languages, like the Spanish, even though the Spanish-speaking Hispanic population is close to 30 per cent of the American population.

Separatist violence has caused gruesome atrocities or political disintegration in Bosnia-Herzegovina, the Congo (Zaire), Cyprus, Ethiopia, Nigeria, Pakistan and Sri Lanka. So far the French-speaking Quebec Separatist movement in Canada has remained mostly peaceful.

Communist terrorism or guerrilla movements have created civil wars, peasant revolts, political breakdowns and economic disruptions in many countries including Afghanistan, Angola, Bolivia, Cambodia, China, Cuba, Ethiopia, Indonesia, Laos, Malaysia, Mozambique, Peru, Somalia, Vietnam and South Yemen. Communist terrorism flares up occasionally in India.

Industrial development in the West was attained and is being sustained through colonialism—domestic, foreign and neo-colonialist—militarization, bureaucratization, authoritarianization and wars. Since 1945, there have been 250 wars in the Third

World that killed 40 million people. Western development took 100–150 years of uninterrupted industrialization. Under Nazi, Fascist and communist totalitarianism, development occurred within 50 years, but at an enormous cost of human life and liberty. Initial industrialization everywhere arose on the foundations of authoritarian politics (Naidu, 1994: 1–17). Many Third World countries, wanting to imitate Western industrialization, but without all the necessary factors and advantages possessed by the West, have been facing serious crises. In their blind enthusiasm and hurry for Westernization, they have all abandoned their original goals of democratization and humanism and have resorted to militarization and dictatorship.

In the name of defending democracy and capitalism, the Western powers launched the Cold War in the post-war period. In this power struggle the American bloc befriended and bolstered dictators all over the world by providing them military aid and by inducting their countries into the anti-Communist alliances of NATO, CENTO, SEATO and the OAS (Naidu, 1975). Among such patronized dictators were Franco of Spain, Salazar of Portugal, Menderes of Turkey, and the military juntas of Italy, Greece and South Vietnam, King Faisal of Iraq, the Shah of Iran, General Ayub Khan of Pakistan, Marcos of the Philippines, Chiang Kai-shek of Taiwan, Sygman Rhee of South Korea, Diem of Vietnam and so on. Besides, the American bloc also attempted to undermine a democracy like India and non-aligned countries like Yugoslavia, Egypt, Indonesia, Ghana and others.

In the name of proletarian democratism and communist solidarity, the Soviet Union launched the Warsaw Treaty Organization to fight capitalism and imperialism. All East European communist countries, calling themselves 'people's democracies', set up dictatorships that became satellites of the Soviet Union called 'proletarian democracy'. In the early phase the Communist bloc condemned Indian non-alignment, as a pro-West and anti-progress movement.

Both the Communist bloc and the Western bloc proclaimed that their respective Cold War preparations and strategies had established peace by avoiding a Third World War. Yet there were 250 wars in which more than 40 million people were killed; of course all outside Europe (Ball, 1994: 216–17). These wars were helped through weapons, finances and propaganda supplied by the major Cold War protagonists.

War, by definition, is anti-democratic and anti-peace. Countries deeply involved in war and in the Cold War have undermined their domestic democracy, more or less, directly or indirectly. Warring states are, therefore, opposed to peaceful settlement of disputes and to measures towards peace building.

The Case of Indian Democracy: Background Factors

India had to face, like most other nations on earth, all the above-mentioned seven challenges. One cannot, therefore, argue that the Indian polity is a system of perfect democracy or of total non-violence. Far from such perfection, India has been facing innumerable crises and has developed numerous defects. The Western media have been propagating day-in and day-out, how poor India is, how caste-ridden it is, how problematic is its democracy, and how anti-West has been its non-aligned policy. Indeed in the political field, India suffers from general corruption, periodic religious riots, forces of regional separatism, terrorist uprisings, police excesses, bureaucratic red tape and judicial slowness. Socially, the nation is still handling informal and politicized caste and class barriers, incidents of nepotism and bribery, thirty per cent illiteracy and so on. Economically, industrial productivity is low, job creation is slow, unemployment stands high, standards of living for the lower classes are still very low and the distribution of wealth is far from being equitable.

All the above faults and failures of Indian democracy must be placed in the proper context and be viewed within the framework of the following factors: (1) India has a population of 1.2 billion spread over a subcontinent of 3.3 million square kilometres. In the light of the enormous dimensions of population and territory, one must be extremely careful, against all natural propensities, to generalize based on a few cases of any act or event. (2) The incomparable dimensions of India's multiracial, multilinguistic and multicultural realities must be remembered when comparing India's problems with those of any small or monolithic society with a unicultural or bicultural population. (3) It must not be forgotten that India attained freedom after having suffered British imperialism for 150 years. Imperialism is not just a system of military occupation, economic exploitation and political oppression, but also a powerful force that causes the degeneration of culture and the dehumanization of its victim peoples. Besides, the ghosts of colonialism linger on long after decolonization. (4) Britain dragged colonized India into the world wars, and the Cold War bullied and battered independent India. (5) Many contradictory facets co-exist in contemporary India, e.g., hunting-fishing; agriculture; high industrialization and nuclear and space technology; abject poverty, rising middle class and the rich elite; illiteracy and intellectual sophistication. (6) Development under Indian democracy is sixty-year-old, compared to the 200-year-old development and experience of the Western countries. (7) The main sources of our information on India are the writings of the former British colonial officers, bigoted Christian missionaries, prejudiced Zionists, American and Soviet ideologues, spokesmen of the industrial-military complex and Western authors and journalists who become 'instant experts' after a six-week or six-month tour of India.

While not ignoring the above-mentioned background factors, one can provide broad and in-depth analyses on how India has been able to confront the seven evils that have been threatening the peace and stability of most nations in the world.

Non-violent Absorption of Ethnic and Religious Refugees

The first challenge that Indian democracy had to deal with was the influx of millions of Hindu, Sikh, Christian, Buddhist and Zoroastrian refugees escaping Pakistan. After the 1947 partition, 4.5 million Hindus, Sikhs and others left West Pakistan for India; another one million left East Pakistan for India. Six million Muslims went to Pakistan from India. Half a million people were killed in the partition conflicts (Hardgrave, 1986: 51–52). But within a decade these refugees were absorbed into the Indian society without conflicts, ethnic rivalries or religious intolerance. The same process was used in accepting refugees from Bangladesh, Tibet, Nepal, Sri Lanka, Uganda, Fiji, etc.

This fact can be appreciated when one compares the tragic situation of the refugees (called 'Muhajir') who moved to Pakistan from India. Though all of them were Muslims, they were ethnically different from the indigenous Sindhis, Punjabis, Baluchis and Bengalis who constituted the new state of Pakistan. Even after sixty years, the refugees have remained so-called Muhajir; to this day and they are still being excluded from Pakistan's society, economy and politics. In the absence of democracy and peaceful channelization, the continuing ethnic conflicts have been using the methods of sabotage, terrorism, murder, rape, looting and arson, while Pakistani dictators continue to use these ethnic conflicts to rationalize their hold on political power by declaring that the people of Pakistan are unfit for democracy.

Non-violent Political Integration of the Princely States

Independent India ended up with more than 562 so-called princely states of Maharajas (Menon, 1956) whose legal status was left ambiguous by the Raj. The British law on Indian independence made the provision that the autocratic princes had the authority to decide if they chose to let their territories become part of free India or Pakistan by signing the 'instrument of accession'. By implication the princes could also decide to declare their sovereignty. This political mischief was Britain's last act of divide-and-rule; it was meant to be a British concession to its erstwhile loyal servants, the princes, who had supported the British Raj by opposing Indian independence and democratization. If the princes had chosen to declare their own independence, India could have ended up as political Swiss cheese with 562 holes in its territorial solidarity. Such a catastrophe was avoided when through peaceful persuasion and political concessions all the princely states except two were integrated into the Indian republic. The people of Hyderabad fought the last significant battle of Indian independence. Token Indian force was necessitated by the demand of the citizens of Hyderabad state, whose ruler, the Nizam, was oppressing the people for agitating to remain a part of free India. In the case of the state of Jammu & Kashmir, the Maharaja at first was opposed to the popular demand to 'accede' to India. But when Kashmir was attacked by Pakistan, the Maharaja signed the instrument of accession to India and appealed for India's help against Pakistan's aggression.

Peaceful Settlement of Linguistic Conflicts

A land of more than 1,600 languages and dialects (Hardgrave, 1986: 131), India could not avoid linguistic conflicts. In many parts of the world linguistic parochialism has caused untold prejudice, hate and violence. However, in India such conflicts were avoided or dissolved and settled through democratic solutions and peaceful adjustments.

First of all, the Indian Constitution acknowledges the equality and importance of 15 languages. Under Article 343, Hindi in Devanagari script is the 'official language'. English will continue to be the official language for the first 15 years, and later on for any extension provided by the Parliament. Article 345 acknowledges that states may adopt one or more languages. English could continue.

Second was a dramatic and far-reaching solution—the map of India was redrawn on linguistic lines. No other democratic country in the world tried such radical and peaceful reorganization of its political units (ibid.: 123–28). Thirdly, a bilingual language formula was devised for official purposes—Hindi is to remain the national language and English is accepted as the official and administrative language (ibid.; Constitution of India, 1981). Fourthly, for educational purposes, a trilingual formula was devised. Education could be in the national language or in English or in the regional language. However, educational institutions are expected to encourage students to learn at least one language of another region (ibid.: 131–32). The peaceful coexistence of the constitutionally reorganized 15 languages of India is nothing short of a modern miracle performed through non-violence and democracy.

Overcoming Separatist Violence

As the most multiracial, multireligious and multilingual nation in the world, India has faced the violent challenges of multiculturalism. While bicultural Canada is facing a potential break-up, tricultural Bosnia-Herzegovina has suffered the cruelties of ethnic cleansing and the multicultural Soviet empire has already broken up into 22 new states and their ethnic conflicts, India has maintained, since independence, its territorial integrity, its political sovereignty, and its democratic existence. In the earlier phase, when the Tamils and the Telugus in South India developed some separatist tendencies, they were quickly won over through democratic compromises and peaceful reorganization of the state on linguistic-cultural lines. Next, the tribal conflicts in the northeast region of India raised the slogans of separatism, inspired and encouraged by neighbouring East Pakistan (which later became Bangladesh), China, Burma (which later was named Myanmar), and some Western Christian missionaries. After its initial military response, New Delhi sought a peaceful and democratic solution. The region was reorganized into the six new states of the federal union.

In recent years separatism raised its ugly head in the northern states of India. The Sikh separatism in the Punjab and the Islamic terrorism in Kashmir have produced considerable death and destruction. With its strategy of flexible response of carrot and stick, and its ever-ready willingness to seek peaceful settlement, New Delhi has been able to curtail separatist terrorism and to channel it into electoral participation, thereby providing the separatists a role in democracy and a stake in the country. As a result, in the 1991 elections the Congress party captured 12 of the 13 parliamentary seats in the Punjab (*India Today*, 1996: 42). Even some of the Sikh separatists' factions of the Akali Dal entered the 1996 election. Similarly, some of the Kashmiri terrorists have decided to abandon the guns and to pick up the ballots. Javed Ahmed Shah, the 'Supreme Commander' of Al-Fateh, a terrorist group, became a candidate for the May 1996 election. He told reporters, 'I regret having picked the gun. Now I realize this was a mistake'. His colleague, Gulam Nabi Mir, also a candidate, said: 'Guns have brought disaster to Kashmiris. I am trying to forget the past. It is a new beginning'. Gulam Nabi Azad, leader of Muslim Mujahideen, a pro-Pakistan terrorist group, became a candidate in South Kashmir and said: 'Elections are the only way out of the current turmoil in Kashmir'.

For an objective appreciation, the achievement of Indian democracy should be compared with what happened in other multicultural nations. East Pakistan broke away to become Bangladesh, Eritrea separated from Ethiopia, and Singapore was thrown out of Malaysia. Yugoslavia broke up into six new states and Czechoslovakia into two new states. The separatism of Katanga in Congo, of Biafra in Nigeria, of Eastern Cyprus, of Northern Ireland, and of Tamils in Sri Lanka has caused mass massacres and vast devastations.

Racially and religiously homogeneous Canada is now facing the serious challenge of Quebec separatism. Earlier, when a dozen FLQ (Naidu, 1995: 105–14) terrorists indulged in a few letter bombs, a barn burning, two kidnappings and one murder, the Trudeau government invoked the War Measures Act, let loose the Canadian army on the Quebecers and set up a dictatorial regime all over Canada. Proclaiming to suppress an 'apprehended insurrection' by French separatists, Trudeau ended up charging four persons under the criminal code and providing them gold and a plane to fly to Cuba. It can be argued that by resorting to a cannon to kill a fly, Trudeau even bolstered Quebec separatism. If Trudeau were the Indian prime minister, how would he have handled hundreds of bombings, kidnappings and murders carried out by the Sikh separatists in the Punjab and by the Muslim fundamentalists in Kashmir, who were being helped by Pakistan, by many Islamic states and by the pro-Pakistan US lobbies?

Transforming Communist Terrorism into Democratic Politics

A serious challenge to Indian democracy came from the terrorism of peasant guerrillas, organized in 1948 by the Indian Communist Party along the lines of Maoist guerrillas in China, in the Telangana district of the southern state of Andhra Pradesh. The Telangana terrorism was later re-enacted by the Indian Maoists in Naxalbari in West Bengal and some other regions during the 1960s. This challenge of peasant violence against feudalism was met in India through two approaches: one, Bhoodan, the non-violent 'land gift' movement; the other, democratic legislation to end landlordism. Bhoodan, organized by Vinoba Bhave, a disciple of Gandhi, appealed to the conscience of landlords and collected and distributed among the landless peasants more than five million acres of land. This non-violent process was furthered and supplemented by democratic decision-making in state legislatures that acquired from the feudal and absentee landlords millions of acres of 'surplus lands' for free distribution among the landless peasants and the rural poor. The non-violent abolition of Indian feudalism was one of the most significant economic revolutions of history.

Thus, the poor farmers of India were endowed with two new powers—land and the vote. The land gave them hope to live for; the vote gave them power to influence political policies. Thus empowered, the peasant had no need for violence or guerrilla war. In this way the peasant resentment was channelled into the non-violent processes of elections, legislation and judicial adjudication. All these activities enhanced participatory democracy. Losing their guerrilla wars, the communist movements were driven to seek a role in democratic politics. India was the first country where a communist revolutionary movement felt compelled to abandon terrorism and violence in favour of electoral politics. Two of the 25 states in the Indian Union—Kerala and West Bengal—have been on occasions under communist administrations, which were indistinguishable from any pragmatic left-leaning governments that welcome private enterprise and foreign investment.

Thus, Indian democracy proved its unique capability of transforming communist terrorism and peasant revolution into peaceful electoral politics for conflict resolution and peace building. The Maoist uprisings, that appear periodically, will have to be eliminated.

Combining Democracy and Industrialization

The initiation of industrialization and full democracy, as defined earlier, has never been combined anywhere in the world. Looking at the history of industrialization, one can detect various combinations of democracy and industrialization since the Industrial Revolution of the 18th century. The Soviet Union never showed any concern for democracy, and became within sixty years the second most industrialized state. Democracy was very limited in Britain and the US when they initiated industrial development and it took them 100–200 years to reach mature industrialization and full-fledged democracy. Gorbachev in the Soviet Union tried to develop political democracy without economic liberalization and he faced problems. Deng's attempt in China to industrialize without political liberties is boosting the economy and suppressing democracy. India was bold and wise in attempting to combine right from start democracy and industrialization. Thus, early industrialization in the West rose on the foundations of domestic colonialism characterized by militarism, authoritarianism and violence. Substantial democracy in Britain, France, Germany and Japan appeared only after the advantages of foreign colonialism/ neo-colonialism were firmly established and industrialization had reached the take off stage some 100–150 years after the initiation of the industrial revolution in those countries (Naidu, 1994: 2).

During the initial stage in the developing countries, democracy was very limited, while violence (physical, structural and psychological) was extensive. In fact, the more authoritarian and violent a state was, the faster was the growth of its industrialization. Examples of this trend include the Soviet Union, Communist China, Nazi Germany and Fascist Japan.

In defiance of the traditional Western approach to industrialization, India started its industrialization with full-fledged democracy, a combination that had no precedent. The seemingly insurmountable challenges of industrialization have been met so far with a maximum of democracy and minimum of violence. Besides, there is no precedent in the West of industrialization being attained or sustained without colonies and colonialism. Again, there is no example of a country, with a population of 900 million people emerging out of 150 years of colonial exploitation that has attained within fifty years such high levels of industrialization within the framework of full democracy right from the initial stage.

Before independence, under the British rule, the industrial base was very small contributing only 5 per cent of the Gross National Product (GNP). By 1980 industries were contributing 29 per cent of the GNP. By then India had become, in terms of industrialization, one of the 20 most industrialized nations. In 1947–50 Indian food production was only 50 million tonnes. The figure rose to 100 million tonnes in 1971 and to 150 million tonnes in 1983. By 1984 India became a net exporter of food. During 1900–1946 Indian national income rose by just 0.8 per cent per annum. Between 1950–1990, India achieved an annual growth rate of 3.9 per cent. In the 1980s the growth rate was 5.2 per cent per year. In 1994–95 the Gross Domestic Product (GDP) growth rate was 6.3 per cent (Almond, 1996: 715–18). In spite of all possible criticisms and defects, thoughtful and objective commentators must admit the unique and the overall achievements of Indian democracy through peaceful policies and democratic processes.

Facing the Challenges of the Cold War and the Proxy Wars

If Indian democracy has remained mostly non-violent and effective and if domestic democracy should induce foreign policies that are non-militaristic and supportive of foreign democratic forces, how then can one explain the facts that India was involved in wars with Pakistan and China?

First of all, even though a democracy may formulate and pursue non-militarist and non-aggressive foreign policies, it cannot inhibit, ban or prevent the pursuit of militarist foreign policies by other countries that are inimical towards that democracy. Secondly, when it is the object of aggression, a democracy may not surrender or accept the terms of the aggressor, and may decide to defend itself. Thus, a democracy may be dragged into a war against its own intentions.

On the other hand, dictatorship, by definition, is a system that greatly depends upon or results from militarization that becomes essential for the dictator's retention of power against his/her own countrymen. A dictator depends upon tanks not elections, upon guns and not votes, upon soldiers not peaceful protesters, upon propaganda not education, and upon religionism not rationalism (Naidu, 1993: 1–10). Very often, when a dictator has troubles or failures in domestic affairs, he/she turns to foreign affairs to divert the attention of the dissatisfied citizens. The foreign dangers are identified and presented in the irrational and emotional terms of racism, religionism and chauvinism, the three most effective ideologies for mass mobilization. Besides, there is built-in antipathy in dictatorship towards democracy. Dictators detest, in particular, neighbourhood democracies that could become dangerously appealing to the citizens under the dictatorship.

Independent India entered the world arena with its unique, innovative and bold foreign policy of non-alignment, which was aimed at avoiding a world conflagration, at reducing global militarization, and at ending dogmatic ideological rivalries. The central goal of non-alignment is to seek peaceful coexistence of all ideologies, political systems and national hopes. But the non-alignment policy displeased both the Soviet communist bloc and the American capitalist bloc that were engaged in the Cold War. In 1949, Mao Tse-tung wrote: 'Not only in China, but also in the world without exception, one either leans to the side of imperialism or to the side of socialism. Neutrality is mere camouflage and a third road does not exist' (Tse-tung, 1952: 111–12). On 12 March 1947 President Harry Truman said: 'At the present moment in world history nearly every nation must choose between alternative ways of life ... one way of life is based upon the will of the majority ... freedom of speech and religion, and from political oppression. The second way of life is based upon terror and oppression ... and the suppression of personal freedom.' Both blocs were feverishly preparing for a world war they both considered inevitable and even necessary (Lenin, 1941: 122; Stalin, 1946; Grant, 1944).

Failing to persuade the Maharaja of Kashmir to join Pakistan, Pakistan took the major step of attacking Kashmir in 1949. When the

Maharaja signed the instrument of accession to India making Kashmir a part of India, the Nehru government felt the legal and political obligation to rescue Kashmir and to protect Indian territory. Indian forces had to be dispatched to Kashmir. The Pakistani forces were pushed back. But before completely vacating the Pakistani aggression, India held back its seemingly successful military action and took the complaint of Pakistani aggression to the United Nations to seek a peaceful withdrawal of Pakistan. In spite of its military advantages India even agreed to a military truce.

At the United Nations, Western powers, especially the United States, that were critical of India's non-alignment decided to support Pakistan, hoping to draw Pakistan into the anti-communist alliance. Under the influence of the Cold War, the Security Council avoided naming Pakistan the aggressor, even after Pakistan confessed to the participation in the military attack on Kashmir (Naidu, 1995; Jain, 1972). Instead, Pakistani supporters transformed the issue of Pakistani aggression into a Hindu-Muslim religious conflict and an India-Pakistan dispute. India's original complaint of Pakistani aggression remains frozen and forgotten, and Pakistan continues to occupy a part of Kashmir and continues to foment trouble in the Indian part of Kashmir by raising the slogan that 'Islam is in danger in Kashmir', and that Pakistan has the moral obligation to conduct a *jihad* against 'Kafir' India.

Pakistan quickly realized the advantages of pleasing the United States, of alienating India from the West and of increasing Pakistan's military power. Pakistan readily agreed to join the American-sponsored anti-communist alliances—the Central Treaty Organization (CENTO) and the Southeast Asia Treaty Organization (SEATO) while seeking military alliance with Communist China. Ever since Pakistan has remained a pet protégé of the United States.

Encouraged by the military help received from the United States and China, then the bitter foe of the USA, Pakistan's dictator launched a second jihad on India in 1965 by invading the Rann of Kutch in Gujarat. India responded militarily, but was quick to agree, once again, to a negotiated truce reached through Soviet mediation.

The third Pakistani aggression on India came in 1972. When General Yahya Khan, the military dictator of Pakistan at the time, began to lose his grip on controlling the rebellion of the Bengalis in East Pakistan, he tried to transform Pakistan's civil war into an international war and to shift India's attention away from East Pakistan; he launched a blitzkrieg attack on India in several places along the

Western borders of India. In this plot, capitalist United States and Communist China expressed support to the Islamic dictatorship of Pakistan against the liberation struggle of East Pakistan and democratic India. Indian troops responded by marching quickly and effectively against Pakistani forces in East Pakistan. Within days India defeated Pakistan, captured thousands of Pakistani soldiers, and occupied East Pakistan. But when Pakistan sued for peace, India acted generously and readily. It released the Pakistani soldiers, vacated East Pakistan, handed over the power to the new independent state of Bangladesh and signed the Simla Peace Agreement with Pakistan.

In recent years the Pakistani government has resorted to indirect aggression on India by arming, training and financing not only the Muslim fundamentalists in Kashmir, but also the Sikh separatists in the Punjab. In these attempts Pakistan's success has been limited.

Through most of its existence since its creation in 1947, Pakistan has remained a dictatorship. There were five military coups, averaging one every decade. Besides, Pakistan has been shaped into an Islamic theocracy in which the political leadership invokes religious bigotry whenever convenient or necessary. Thus, Pakistan's conflict with India has three facets: (a) Pakistan's theocratic state is a sworn enemy of Indian secularism; (b) Pakistan's pro-Western militarism contributed to the Cold War, while India's non-alignment was opposed to the Western camp and the pursuit of Cold War strategies; and (c) Pakistan's military dictatorship has been the bitter foe of India's democracy that upholds civilian supremacy.

And, there are no signs that these formulations are about to change in the near future. Any day India could be dragged into another military conflict with Pakistan. However, when drawn into a military conflict, India, as an effective democracy committed to peaceful settlement of disputes, should pursue three possible strategies: (a) India should never raise the stakes and prolong war beyond certain reasonable limits; (b) India should never hesitate to stop or end such a war through mutual agreements to establish a truce or to withdraw forces or to sign a peace treaty; and (c) India should never allow Pakistan to indirectly or subtly undermine India's domestic democracy by inducing long-lasting militarization or initiating a hate Pakistan campaign.

India-China relations are built upon two fundamental conflicts: one, Chinese dictatorship has always considered Indian democracy a rival that cannot be tolerated or allowed to supersede China; the other, Chinese communist philosophy, however diluted it may seem presently, rests upon a monolithic ideology, militarism and state authoritarianism, while Indian social democracy is nurtured by the ideology of pluralism and toleration, the policy of peaceful settlement of disputes, the strategy of non-politicization of the armed forces and de-emphasis of militarization, the politics of responsible government and the rule of law.

In 1950 when Communist China was condemned by the West and isolated by the rest, India was the only major non-communist country that befriended China, recognized the communist government, continuously pleaded for its seating in the United Nations, introduced China to the Afro-Asian world community by sponsoring China to the Banding Conference, even handed over to China its own diplomatic supervisory role over Tibet inherited from the Raj, and signed the Panchasheel Agreement embodying five principles of peaceful coexistence.

But by the 1950s the Soviet Union began snubbing China and befriending India, while India emerged as the de facto leader of the Third World. Frustrated, China took the desperate step of attacking India in 1962 without any provocation. This was utterly shocking to the Nehru government of India that was totally unprepared for a major war and was against India's militarization. China thought it was killing two birds with one stone (Naidu, 1996). By attacking India, China had placed the Soviet Union on the spot—would Communist Russia support sister Communist China, or the non-aligned India? Secondly, by demonstrating Chinese military superiority over India, China was hoping to prove to the Afro-Asian countries that the communist military dictatorship was a better model to emulate than the peace-loving non-aligned Indian democracy.

China failed to achieve both of its goals. The Soviet Union came out expressing its sympathy for India; China became more alienated in the communist bloc; secondly, most of the world condemned Chinese aggression against India, while few Afro-Asian countries adopted the Chinese communist model of polity (Mitra, 1996: 715–18).

Without yielding to Chinese bullying or blackmail, India agreed to a truce with China and the India-China border conflicts remain frozen to this day. However, Indian democracy suffered to some extent by having to increase India's militarization after 1962. Between 1950–61, Indian defence expenditures declined. After the 1962 Chinese invasion, defence budgets averaged 3–4 per cent of the GNP, or 20 per cent of the national budget. This was, at that time, still far below the world average of 7 per cent (Mitra, 1996). In 1987, the defence expenditure was 3.9 per cent of the GNP while the world average was 5.1 per cent (cf. Sward, 1991).

Still India has limited its militarization to reasonable proportions, and has maintained its forces on defensive rather than adopting aggressive strategies.

Fundamental Forces Shaping Indian Democracy

In spite of confronting the serious challenges of the seven evils, the agents of violence and disintegration, Indian democracy has survived and flourished. Why? What are those fundamental forces that have shaped and sustained Indian democracy's capacities to solve conflicts peacefully and to develop its civil society, while many other political systems have succumbed, in one form or another, to the seven evils? Some explanations of those fundamental forces are outlined below.

Only a Non-violent Revolution can Establish a Non-violent Democracy

The nature of a revolution predetermines the nature of the political system that the revolution establishes. A violent revolution cannot establish a non-violent polity. In other words, the values, the tools and the techniques of the pre-revolutionary phase continue to colour and characterize the post-revolution concepts, structures and functions. History provides ample evidence that the dogmatism, hatred and violence that shape a violent revolution continue and undermine all attempts to build an effective and peaceful democracy at the end of the revolution.

The bloody French Revolution of 1789 led to a chain of violent repercussions, including 'the reign of terror', and ended up in the Napoleonic dictatorship and imperialist wars. The Chinese civil wars and the Maoist guerrilla wars paved the path for the bloody Cultural Revolution of 1966–76, the Tiananmen Square massacre of 1991 and the continuing persecution of the latest dissidents in China. The violence of the American War of Independence of 1776 continued in the Civil War (1861–65), in the American involvements in the two world wars, the Korean War (1950), the Vietnam War (1954–74), the Iraqi War (1991), the invasion of Afghanistan and continues in the recent rise of anarchist militia organizations, the killing of hundreds of individuals by the society and the state. The American prejudice, hate and violence that inspired the aboriginal Indian massacres and the Negro lynching, lingered on in the McCarthyism of 1950s, and the Oklahoma bombing. The Bolshevik *coup d'état* (1917) and the long-drawn-out Russian civil war, led to the massacre of millions of anti-communist citizens, the organization of slave labour camps, and the establishment of totalitarianism. The present gangsterism and murders by the new Russian Mafia are the latest reflections of the hatred and violence that were entrenched in the Communist system. Almost every country in Latin America has embodied in its political culture revolutionary violence that has led to dozens of *coups d'état* and to long periods of dictatorship. Most countries of Africa that struggled for independence through violence are today suffering from civil wars, political instabilities and authoritarian regimes that are, indeed, replicas of the regimes they experienced under European colonialism.

The contrary examples are countries like Canada, Australia, New Zealand and India. The first three did not have to wage a revolution for freedom and they have remained non-violent democracies. After the violent uprising of 1857 against the British occupation of India, the Indian freedom struggle rarely resorted to violence. Until the 1920s, the Indian struggle used the techniques of petitions, appeals and court actions; later came the use of the agitational methods of marches, demonstrations and protest meetings. In the 1920s, the Gandhian leadership transformed the freedom struggle into a genuine mass movement that used the methodologies of *satyagraha* (non-violent struggle) in the forms of non-violent non-cooperation and civil disobedience. *Satyagraha* used peaceful strikes, marches, demonstrations, sit-ins, hunger strikes and courting imprisonment.

The Dynamics of Satyagraha

The principles and the practices of *satyagraha* produced multifarious effects. Firstly, by avoiding violence and military means, *satyagraha* develops rational debate and emphasizes political process. Secondly, by undermining the power of the police and by avoiding the politicization of the military, *satyagraha* prepares the grounds for the acceptance of 'civilian supremacy', a basic condition of democracy (Plano, 1990: 518–19). Thirdly, *satyagraha* builds among the masses the habits and behavioural patterns of peaceful discussion, compromises and non-violent settlement of disputes. These methods of conflict resolution are indeed the methods of democracy. Fourthly, *satyagraha* demands the avoidance of psychological violence, i.e., prejudice, hatred, disrespect towards those who disagree or who oppose (Naidu, 1989: 53–55). *Satyagraha* believes that because human beings are not evil by nature, *satyagrahis* should not hate individuals while fighting evil social institutions (ibid.: 50–52); they should win their opponents through love, service and sacrifice; they should build bridges between all human beings. Thus, *satyagraha* stands firm on the principles of equality of all, freedom for all and fraternity among all human beings. Because democracy demands respect for differences and cooperation of all citizens, *satyagraha* prepared the Indian masses for accepting the rules and regulations of democracy. Finally, while violent struggle needs a small and clandestine group of young and physically fit people (mostly men) who are equipped with weapons, *satyagraha* depends upon open and active participation of the masses consisting of all types of men and women, who possess self-confidence, courage and goodwill to carry on non-violent campaigns in non-cooperation and civil disobedience. The national Congress movement under Gandhi involved millions working at all levels—village, district, province and nation—and organized through democratic structures and functions.

Women's Liberation

Gandhi was the greatest 'liberator' of women in the 20th century. His *satyagraha* drew millions of women who were ready to disregard the traditional taboos and religious orthodoxies against women's activism and politicization. They marched, faced police beatings and bullets and went to jails. The training of women in active non-violence prepared the grounds for sustained democratic functioning of the nationalist movement and of the country after independence.

Peasant Liberation

Ending feudalism (landlordism) and distributing land among the landless peasantry have produced blood baths, civil wars and military coups in every country. India is only one exception where feudalism was eliminated and peasants were liberated from slavery and exploitation through peaceful Gandhian methods. Equipped with a piece of land and the democratic vote, the Indian peasantry shunned guerrilla wars and civil wars and became highly politicized and involved in the democratic process.

Gandhian 'Constructive Programme'

The Gandhian impact was holistic. The Gandhian movement was not only agitational, but also 'constructive', laying the foundation for future democracy. Gandhi designed the so-called 'Constructive Programme' that included campaigns for literacy, health and hygiene, cottage industries, *khaki* production, animal husbandry, ending untouchability and religious bigotry and inculcating the spirit of self-reliance, community service and peaceful settlement of disputes. These programmes prepared the way for democratization and peace building.

Of course, all the followers of Gandhi and all the *satyagrahis* did not all the time follow the way of non-violence that Gandhi had prescribed. In other words, all the 500 million people of India were not strict adherents of non-violence; many did not agree with Gandhi's ideas of political unity, religious harmony, caste elimination, women's liberation, limited industrialization and so on. Against all his preachings and pleadings, the country was partitioned in the end. Yet the facts remain that millions followed Gandhi and participated in non-violent struggles; many more, though politically inactive, admired and appreciated, and accepted Gandhian ideas and methods of non-violence. Thus, the Gandhian non-violent revolution paved the way for a post-revolution non-violent democracy. This was a unique achievement. Will the Gandhian influence continue to shape the democratic way of life in India for a long time to come? No one can predict. Indian democracy has lasted for half a century and there are no signs of its collapsing entirely or soon!

Universal Adult Franchise

Until the successful Indian experiment with universal adult franchise, the Western democratic theory insisted that democracy can function only in a highly educated society. This thesis had been challenged by Communist and Fascist states. Communist Russia, Nazi Germany and Fascist Japan were the most literate nations, but they did not produce democracy. Though illiterate, Indian masses were trained in democratic values, attitudes and behaviours through their participation in Gandhian non-violent movements. Indian democracy has thrived for the last 70 years. Today, India has an electorate of 600 million voters. In the recent national elections, 14,000 candidates and 443 political parties contested for the seats in the national parliament. So far 11 general elections, 250 by-elections and 300 state elections have been held, averaging one election every six months. Normally, 50–60 per cent of the voters cast their ballots.

Dictatorship cannot Lead to Democracy

Karl Marx said, 'the dictatorship itself only constitutes the transition to the abolition of all classes to a classless society'. The Marxist doctrine states that a proletarian dictatorship can lead to a classless and ultimately to a stateless society is a fundamental fallacy. In terms of logic and in terms of praxis, the proletarian dictatorship did not and cannot lead to the 'withering away of the state' (Marx, 1934: 450). In Russia, Lenin's so-called proletarian revolution was really the

Communist Party's *coup d'état*. This proletarian revolution established an authoritarian government. This led to dictatorship of the state, which in fact became the dictatorship of the Communist Party. This in practise meant the dictatorship of the top leaders (politburo), which became the carrier of state dictatorship. The politburo was then taken over by the supreme leader. Lenin rationalized these developments as 'democratic centralism'. After the death of Lenin, Stalin succeeded and established the personality cult, thus establishing the totalitarian state under a dictator, a far cry from a classless and stateless society.

Even many of the non-Marxist leaders in the world who hoped to build democracy, felt the necessity of using limited violence and temporary authoritarianism, ended up becoming dictators establishing authoritarian regimes. Napoleon Bonaparte, Kamal Pasha of Turkey, Chiang Kai-shek of China (and of Taiwan later), Sygman Rhee of South Korea, Sukarno of Indonesia, Nkrumah of Ghana, General Ayub Khan of Pakistan, and so on, professed democracy, but established dictatorships.

India was fortunate in its leadership that conscientiously created democratic structures and functions for the very revolutionary movement of the Congress organization. Congress organization rose from village, district and provincial committees to the highest level of national committee and national leadership. Elections, debates and discussions, accountability of the leaders, regular meetings, democratic decision-making, etc., were the features of every village and district Congress committee. Special facilities were provided in these committees for the representation of minorities, women and the so-called untouchables. All these elements were essential for the non-violent mass movement. Unlike terrorist or guerrilla or army movements, non-violent revolution depends upon mass participation and support, personal commitment of the *satyagrahis* to the values and goals of the movement, democratic leadership that depends upon the consent of the followers, and open and public activities. Thus, the non-violent freedom struggle led by the Congress was a long and trying preparation for arriving at the post-independence democracy.

After the attainment of independence, the Indian leadership had no difficulty or hesitation in making the historic decision that a free India would start as a full democracy, with republicanism, secularism, a charter of fundamental rights, an independent judiciary, rule of law, a free press and universal adult franchise—all this in spite of high illiteracy, widespread poverty, and little national experience in full-fledged democracy. Western observers were very negative and cynical on the creation of the world's biggest electorate (Hanson, 1972: 54); Western trained Indians were also sceptical of the immediate introduction of full-fledged democracy. Ideologically committed to democracy and willing to place their faith in the Indian masses, the Indian leaders took the courageous step to create democracy by practising democracy (Pylee, 1977: 26), unlike those leaders in other countries who believed the masses were unfit for democracy or those who felt that paternalistic authoritarian government is the necessary first step to lead the public to the ultimate goal of full democracy. Article 326 of the Indian Constitution provides adult franchise. In a speech before the Constituent Assembly, A. Krishna Swami Aiyer argued that the adult franchise would 'bring enlightenment and promote the well-being, the standard of life, the comfort and decent living of the common man .... If democracy is to be broad-based, and the government is to have the ultimate sanction of the people as a whole, in a country where the large mass of people are illiterate, and the people owning property are so few, the introduction of any property or educational qualifications for the exercise of franchise would be a negation of the principles of democracy' (Pylee, 1977: 26).

By empowering the masses with the power of the ballot, Indian democracy weaned the Indian public away from the temptation of the power of the bullet. Over the last fifty years and through the last eleven national elections, the masses of India have become sophisticated voters by exercising their ballot power to punish or to empower their leaders. The voter turnout in national elections is around 60 per cent. In some states it was up to 75 per cent (Basu, 1969: 6).

An interesting contrast is presented by the sister nation of Pakistan, where dictators right from the beginning felt that the citizens of Pakistan were unfit for democracy and needed the tutelage of military generals for learning democracy. The fact remains that even today there are Muslim families that have members in both India and Pakistan. How could one part of the family suddenly become unfit for democracy? The leaders of Pakistan, not its masses, have indeed been unfit for democracy.

Conclusions

As a test case in conflict resolution and peace building, Indian democracy leads us to the following conclusions:

First, non-violence can be psychological, structural and physical. The practice of non-violence can shape intellectual, social, economic, environmental and political aspects of human existence.

In its ideal form, democracy is a system that rests on non-violence. As such, non-violent democracy is the best guarantee for conflict resolution and peace building.

As the opposite of democracy, dictatorship is least conducive for peaceful resolution of disputes and is more prone to militarism, war, political instabilities and disintegration.

Second, violent revolution cannot lead to or sustain meaningful democracy in the post-revolution phase. The values, tools and techniques of revolutionary violence linger on for a long time after the revolution; the ghost of dictator cannot easily be exorcised.

Third, dictatorship, however benevolent and well-intentioned, cannot develop democracy or nurture non-violence.

Fourth, Indian democracy in real terms has been largely successful in practising non-violent conflict resolution and in building peaceful civil society, as practically vindicated by India's unique experiments and unprecedented policies—non-violent revolution, peaceful ending of feudalism, combining democracy and industrialization, adoption of universal adult franchise in a highly illiterate society, conducting the world's largest elections regularly every five years, defusing the Cold War through non-alignment and sustaining, without military coups, civil wars or political disintegration for 70 years, the world's largest democracy with the most multiracial, multireligious, and multicultural population on the planet Earth.

Winston Churchill, a diehard imperialist opposed to India's freedom, described Indian leaders such as Gandhi and Nehru as 'men of straw' (Brecher, 1969). Other Westerners who could not forgive India for having caused the downfall of the British empire, and for not joining the Western bloc, prognosticated that India would fall to pieces without British 'guardianship' or would be taken over by militaristic Pakistan, or revolutionary communists, or disgruntled armed forces, or it would be broken up through civil wars into more than 20 states. Falsifying such cynicism, India has survived and progressed. Indian democracy has been tested and tried during the last half a century. With all its imperfections, Indian democracy has adhered, broadly speaking, to the ideals of peaceful management of domestic affairs and the pursuit of non-alignment and peaceful coexistence in foreign relations. As a genuine, thoughtful and effective democracy among some 25 meaningful democracies in the world, India is worthy of study. India's maximal democracy deserves sincere understanding, honest analysis and objective appreciation.

References

Almond, G.A., Powell, G.B. and Mundt, R.J. (1993). *Comparative Politics Today: A Theoretical Framework,* 3rd edn. NY: Harper Collins.

Ball, N. (1994). "Demilitarizing the Third World," in M. Klare and D. Thomas (eds.), *World Security: Challenges for a New Century*. NY: St. Martin's Press.

Basu, T. (1996). "Frequent Elections a Boon to Democracies," *India Abroad* (Weekly) Canadian Edition, 6 April: 6; 12 April: 9. *India Today* (Fortnightly) (New Delhi), 30 April 1996: 14–15 and 42.

Brecher, M. (1962). *Nehru: A Political Biography.* Boston: Beacon Press.

Constituent Assembly Debates, Vol. X: 834. New Delhi.

Documentary History of Chinese Communism (1952). Cambridge: Harvard University Press, 453–54.

Grant, D.D. (1944). *Canada and the Building of Peace*. Toronto: Canadian Institute of International Affairs.

Hanson, A.H. and Douglas, J. (1972). *India's Democracy.* NY: Weidenfeld and Nicolson.

Hardgrave Jr., R.L. and Kochanek, S.A. (1986). *India: Government and Politics in a Developing Nation.* San Diego: Harcourt Brace Jovanovich, 51–52.

House of Commons Debates (1946).

India Abroad (1996). weekly Canadian edition. Toronto.

India Today (1996). New Delhi.

International Conciliation (September 1948). U.N. Document, 443.

Jain, A.P. (1972). *Kashmir: What Really Happened* (Jaico Publishing House), 30.

Joshi, B. (1996). "Ex-Militarists in Kashmir will contest Elections," in *India Abroad*, 12 April, 10.

Kousoulas, D.G. (1982). *On Government and Politics: An Introduction to Political Science*. Brooks/Cole Publishing Company, 24.

Lenin (1941). *Works*. Moscow: State Publishing House, Vol. 24.

Marx, Karl (1846). *Selected Correspondence of Marx and Engels 1846–1895*. London, U.K.

Mayo, H.B. (1960). *Introduction to Marxist Theory*. NY: Oxford University Press.

Menon, V.P. (1956). *The Story of the Integration of the Indian States,* Bombay: Orient Longmans.

Mitra, S.K. (1996). 'Politics in India' in G.A. Almond and B. Powell (eds.), *Comparative Politics Today*, N.Y.: Harper Collins.

Naidu, M.V. (1975). *Alliances and Balance of Power: A Search for Conceptual Clarity*. London and Delhi: Macmillan.

——. (1985). "Military Power, Militarism and Militarization: An Attempt at Clarification and Classification," *Peace Research*, 17(1): 2–10.

——. (1989). "Gandhian Humanism and Contemporary Crises," *Peace Research*, 21(4): 53–55.

——. (1992). "Human Rights: Concepts and Prospects," *Peace Research*, 24(1): 8–9.

——. (1993). "Religionism, Rationalism and Peace Education: An Attempt at Model Building," *Peace Education Miniprints No.45* (April 1993) (Malmo, Sweden: School of Education, Lurid University), 1–10.

——. (1994). "Initial Development: An Attempt at Conceptualization for Comparative Analysis of Models of Development," *Peace Research*, 26(1): 1–17.

——. (1995). *Quebec Separatism, Canadian Unity*. Oakville, Ontario: MITA Press, 105–14.

——. (1995). "The Origins of UN Peace-Enforcement and Peacekeeping: Re-examination," *Peace Research*, 27 (1): February.

——. (1996). *War, Security, Peace*. Oakville, Ontario: MITA Press, 156–59.

Peace Research: The Canadian Journal of Peace Studies (1985–96). Canada Brandon University.

Plano, J.C. (1990). *The American Political Dictionary*. NY: Holt, Rinehart and Winston.

Pylee, M.V. (1977). *Constitutional Government in India*. Bombay: Asia Publishing House.

Sivard, R.L. (1991). *World Military and Social Expenditures 1991*. Washington, D.C.: World Resources Institute.

Stalin, J. (1946). *Works*. Moscow: State Publishing House, Vol. 5.

Truman, H. (1956). *Years of Trial and Hope: 1946–1953*. London: Hodder and Stoughton.

Tse-tung, Mao (1952). *A Documentary History of Chinese Communism*. Cambridge: Harvard University Press.

4

A Wellspring of Opportunity

Political Science Research on Public Sector Leadership

TIM A. MAU

Introduction

Echoing the earlier lament of Burns (1978), Bennis and Nanus (1985: 20) argued in their classic work on leadership that it 'is the most studied and least understood topic of any in the social sciences'. Despite some significant advances, this claim is as valid today as when they wrote their book almost three decades ago. Of the numerous studies of the leadership phenomenon that are produced each year, many of them lack the empirical evidence and academic rigour to truly enhance our collective understanding of leadership. Moreover,

---

Whether through deed or action, leaders motivate and inspire their followers. Moreover, one of their critical responsibilities is to mentor others so as to foster the leadership cadre of the future. When measured against this standard, O.P. Dwivedi is an unmistakable leader in not only the public administration community but indeed academia more broadly. In an association that goes back nearly 25 years, from the day I first arrived at the University of Guelph as an undergraduate student studying political science to our more recent relationship as departmental colleagues, I am proud to call myself one of OP's followers. He is, to borrow a term he used to describe the late Ted Hodgetts, the father of Canadian public administration, my guru. Although small in stature, OP leaves an indelible impression on those who have had the good fortune of knowing him. For me, his impact has been profound. From the moment I decided that I wanted to pursue a full-time career in academia, OP has been an unabashed champion of mine. I am deeply indebted to him for his support and encouragement over the years, but more importantly for

the field is riddled with conceptual confusion and a true understanding of the phenomenon of leadership defies the often simplistic explanations that are offered. Washbush (2005: 1084) even goes as far as suggesting that the concept of leadership is meaningless. He wrote: 'Having built the "tower of leadership babble", we might be better served if it were to crumble'.

Fortunately, that is not a widely shared view. Many scholars from a variety of perspectives, including anthropology, social psychology, political science, history, military/strategic studies, human resources, sociology and, above all, business, are of the mindset that leadership does matter and are producing some sound academic research demonstrating the link between effective leadership and organizational performance. These developments notwithstanding, the challenge for leadership studies is two-fold: firstly, it is to enhance the overall quality of the research that is being produced, ensuring that the trivial does not cloud the important; and secondly, it needs to address one a commonly cited shortcoming of the state of research on leadership, which is that these various disciplines have conducted their studies in isolation with relatively few attempts to incorporate advancements from each one into a more holistic theory or approach.

Political scientists and public administration scholars are not immune to these criticisms, but for them the challenge is more fundamental: despite the obvious shared interests that they have with students of leadership—with respect to power, authority, decision making and

---

the opportunities to collaborate with him on a number of research initiatives. These endeavours have been both interesting and enjoyable; however, I am particularly grateful for his 'gentle prodding' because in doing so he has forced me to grow as a scholar, broadening my interests and understanding of important aspects of public administration that, regrettably, had been hitherto neglected.

OP is notable for many achievements, all of which merit recognition, but I will focus on one in particular: his prodigious scholarly output. OP's record of publication, which continues to grow unabated well into his retirement years, serves as a constant reminder of the responsibility I bear as an academic to engage in research that will both contribute to and push the frontiers of knowledge. The challenge is a formidable one, but like any good leader OP has modelled the way for me—indeed the global public administration community—to follow. While I cannot begin to imagine replicating the influence that OP has had in his career, I will nonetheless walk quite proudly in his shadow as I research, write and talk about public administration issues that ultimately promote good governance.

the mobilization of support, for example—their contributions to the advancement of knowledge in this area have been rather limited (Peele, 2005). As Trottier, Van Wart and Wang (2008: 329) noted: 'Despite an enormous amount of discussion about leadership in public agencies, there has been relatively little broad-scale empirical analysis'.

As will be argued in this chapter, if our cumulative knowledge about leadership is to expand in any meaningful way, more researchers must strive to recognize the artificiality of their disciplinary boundaries and begin to theorize based on empirical studies from across the full spectrum of research. This is particularly true for public administration scholars and political scientists who, until about the last two decades, either ignored the subject matter altogether or, in the latter instance, examined it from very narrow perspectives. It should be noted that while this has also been problematic in the US and the UK, the deficiency has been particularly glaring in the Canadian context. Public sector leadership, however, is simply too important an issue to suffer from this ongoing neglect. In short, while the subject matter has been 'gaining the attention of a growing number of scholars dedicated to the notion that the words public and leadership are not mutually exclusive' (Kellerman and Webster, 2001: 487), much remains to be done to bolster our knowledge and understanding of leadership in the context of the public sector.

The chapter begins by examining how Canadian political scientists have traditionally broached the subject of leadership. It will focus specifically on the limited Canadian scholarship in this area, but it will be placed in the context of contributions that emerged in the US since American academicians tend to dominate the field of leadership studies. Consideration will then be given to the public administration literature, demonstrating how initial disinterest in the subject matter has started to undergo a transformation in recent years. Virtually all of the journal articles and books dedicated to the study of public sector leadership that have emerged, however, have been produced by American and European scholars. Canadian contributions to the public sector leadership literature continue to be negligible. In the final section of the chapter, a case will be made that future research on public sector leadership—both political and administrative—must more overtly embrace leadership theories and concepts developed in other disciplines and, in doing so, strive to develop and test integrative models.

A Neglected and Narrowly Construed Concept: Political Science Treatments of Leadership

For the most part political scientists have not been overly concerned with the concept of leadership. This is as true in the US as it has been in Canada. An examination of the more than 2,500 articles published in the *American Political Science Review* between 1906 and 1963, for example, revealed that only seventeen titles made reference to the words 'leader' or 'leadership' (Paige, 1977: 11). A decade later, Blondel (1987) still lamented that there were relatively few studies of leadership in political science, except with respect to the institutional study of political executives. Examining the relationship between leadership and public policy, Pal (1988: 16) concluded:

> ... the study of public policy has taken almost no serious account of leadership. It has had something to say about specific leaders and administrative processes at the executive level, but with only a few exceptions has preferred to explain the policy process in macro-political terms such as class, bureaucracy, federalism or ideology.

The reality is that political scientists generally have not devoted their attention to understanding what constitutes a leader in the political realm, let alone an effective one, by explicitly situating their analyses in any of the four key approaches—behaviour, power-influence, trait and situational (Yukl, 1998)—that characterize the leadership field.

Rather, when the issue of leadership has been examined, the focus has been on prime ministers and the political executive more generally or, in some instances, those who head up the various political parties. Studies in Canada have typically focused on how party leaders are selected (Michelmann et al., 2007; Leduc, 2001; Cross, 1996; Smiley, 1968), the position and power of the prime minister (Aucoin, 1994), cabinet as the 'single most important instrument of governance' (Bakvis and MacDonald, 1993: 47; Bernier, Brownsey and Howlett, 2005) and how the institutions of our parliamentary democracy serve to place restrictions on the power and authority of those who have ostensibly been chosen to 'lead' (Whittington, 2004; Mancuso et al., 1994; Pal and Taras, 1988; Hockin, 1971).

An obvious limitation of these studies is that these political scientists have fallen into the trap of ascribing leadership to the occupant on the basis of his or her status, position or power-base in the political organization. A similar problem has emerged in the US with much of the work on individual leaders in that country focusing on the presidency, which 'is considered an office so important and powerful that those who fill it ... are, by definition, grist for the leadership mill' (Kellerman and Webster, 2001: 489). But, as Burns (1978: 18) noted, 'all leaders are actual or potential power holders, but not all power holders are leaders'. While it may be true that '... no matter the circumstances, the prime minister remains "the boss"' (Savoie, 1999: 71), this is not akin to being a leader. Being 'the boss' is more analogous to being a manager or what Burns (1978) called transactional leadership, whereby rewards or punishments are conferred in order to influence behaviour, and management, as several contributors to the study of leadership have noted (Kent, 2005; Kotter, 1998; Bennis and Nanus, 1985), should not be confused with leadership. Joseph Rost (1991: 10), in his impressive critique of the state of leadership studies, has perhaps gone the furthest in that regard by issuing a passionate plea for a new school of leadership to replace what he termed the outmoded existing 'industrial paradigm' of 'leadership as good management'.

But perhaps this critique of the political science literature on leadership is misplaced. After all, politicians, by virtue of being elected into their roles either by the members of their parties and their constituents or, in the case of the US president, the electorate more broadly, do have some modicum of followership and will invariably possess some of the traits and exhibit some of the behaviours associated with leadership. For that reason, a convincing case can be made that all elected politicians are *de facto* leaders. The reason why it is so easy to question or forget that fact is that we are inundated with politicians who provide what Kellerman (2004) referred to as 'bad leadership', that is to say leadership that is either unethical or ineffective, and the reality is that there has been a widespread tendency in the literature since Burns (1978) first articulated the concept of the transformational leader that leadership is inherently good—that those who are leaders ultimately are competent individuals of high moral character. This bias of assuming that leaders only use their power and ability to influence others to successfully pursue positive ends goes a long way towards explaining why there is such a widespread perception that the public, private and non-profit sectors all suffer from a paucity of leadership. But the problem is not that we have too few leaders in our social, political and economic institutions, but rather that so few of them can be classified as good.

As Kellerman (2004: 33) states: 'Ineffective leadership fails to produce the desired change. For reasons that include missing traits, weak skills, strategies badly conceived, and tactics badly employed, ineffective leadership falls short of its intention'. In the cases of Canada and the US, bad leadership in the political realm has rarely meant unethical, but political leaders quite frequently prove to be ineffective—whether it was because of incompetence, rigidity or intemperance. To suggest that these individuals are not leaders then, is confusing, misleading and seriously impedes our ability to truly understand the leadership phenomenon. Therefore, the real failure of political scientists has not been the tendency to automatically equate leadership with the political executive but rather to focus almost exclusively at that level and to undertake investigations of political leadership without embracing the mainstream concepts and knowledge that have been generated by other disciplines.

One notable exception in that regard was the study conducted by Léon Dion (1968). Drawing on the nascent and limited mainstream leadership literature of the day, he explicitly recognized that political leadership was a dynamic process of interaction, that is to say a group process involving both the leader and one or more followers submitting to the influence attempts of the former, and explored whether there were qualities and traits endemic to political leaders. At the conclusion of his article, Dion (1968: 17) actually apologized for having relied on a corpus of research outside of political science:

> The impossibility of treating political leadership as a distinct concept, separate from the generic concept of leadership, may have obscured some parts of the analysis. This kind of approach was necessitated by the present state of social science research. I am convinced however that, given tools of analysis for the study of leadership, it will be possible eventually to present an analysis of the concept of political leadership.

He then went on to say, '... a close study of those who have stood or now stand at the apex of political organizations would undoubtedly help towards a deepening of our understanding of the whole political process' (ibid.). It is not without irony, therefore, that nearly 45 years later the discipline of political science is being indicted, firstly, for having focused too much on the upper echelons of our political institutions and organizations; and secondly, for having neglected to bridge the disciplinary divide by utilizing the theories and concepts from the mainstream of leadership studies into the study of political leadership.

Public Sector Leadership: An Oxymoron No More

Turning our attention to the realm of public administration, the historic neglect of leadership has been even more pronounced. Larry Terry (1995), in offering his compelling public sector leadership theory of the bureaucratic administrator as conservator, highlighted this deficiency. Ultimately, he identified a number of reasons why public administration researchers have given such short shrift to leadership: first, there was a view that bureaucratic leadership was an affront to democratic theory since the duly elected politicians were the ones who had the legitimacy to provide leadership, while bureaucrats were merely responsible for the technical implementation of those policy decisions; second, given the complex forces at play in the public sector, the impact of public servants to influence bureaucratic outcomes was thought to be rather limited; and third, public administration scholars were preoccupied with other issues of greater interest. Nearly a decade later, Van Wart (2003: 215) surveyed the public sector literature on leadership theory and research and discovered that 'administrative leadership literature ... has experienced neither the volume nor the integration of the mainstream'.

To what extent does that still characterize the public administration literature both in the US and Canada? The results are decidedly mixed. Integration—or the lack thereof—remains a glaring weakness of the literature, both in the US and Canada. On the issue of outputs, there has been an explosion of interest by US-based academics in the subject of public sector leadership in the past two decades. While there is no disputing that the public administration literature on leadership remains underdeveloped when compared to the mainstream, in recent years we have witnessed the publication of a number of studies and books dedicated to understanding the role and importance of leadership in the public sector. Significantly, there are few voices suggesting that the exercise of leadership is incongruent with the public sector, although some scholars continue to recognize that the ability to innovate and be entrepreneurial, hallmarks of an effective leader, are more difficult to materialize in bureaucratic organizations. Instead, there is widespread agreement with the view of Robert Behn (1998: 209), who eloquently and forcefully made the case that 'leadership is not just a right of public managers. It is an obligation'.

It is beyond the scope of this chapter to offer more than a cursory overview of the American public administration literature dedicated to the theory and practice of leadership. It is worth noting, however, that is was only a decade ago that Rusaw (2001) published what is considered to be the first full-scale textbook treatment of public sector leadership, which provided an overarching survey of the mainstream literature and applied it to the public sector. Shortly thereafter, Van Wart (2008; 2005) offered his own comprehensive treatment of the subject matter; in addition to reviewing the main theories of leadership, his work presented the competencies associated with his model of the Leadership Action Cycle. Building on the contribution of Van Wart's work to integrate leadership and public administration is the edited volume by Raffel, Leisink and Middlebrooks (2009a), which thematically examines public sector leadership issues in more than a dozen countries. It is notable for its attempt to go beyond the American experience, a blatant limitation of much of the existing scholarship, and provide an understanding of public sector leadership on a global level. In addition to these book-length treatments of public sector leadership, a number of relevant studies has emerged. Suffice it to say that there have been many public sector studies dedicated to the various aspects of the leadership phenomenon: it includes, among others, the importance of vision (Elden and Sanders, 1996), culture (Schraeder, Tears and Jordan, 2005) and strategic planning (Bryson, 2004); the empowerment of employees (Pitts, 2005); the use of leadership competencies for recruiting, selecting, assessing, developing and compensating public sector employees (Ingraham and Getha-Taylor, 2005); and training and development programmes for nurturing effective leadership (Ingraham and Getha-Taylor, 2004; Blunt, 2003).

Important gaps in the American public sector leadership literature remain to be sure (Raffel, Leisink and Middlebrooks, 2009b), but with a flurry of research activity since the early-to-mid 1990s tangible progress is unquestionably being made. The same cannot be said, however, for Canadian contributions to this body of scholarship. But the lack of public sector leadership research is not the only area where Canadian public administration scholars have been inattentive. Plumptre (1991[1988]) even lamented the deplorable state of the literature on management in the Canadian public sector, although, in addition to his own *tour de force*, there has been some treatment of that subject matter (Bourgault, 2002; Mintzberg and Bourgault, 2000; Doerr, 1981: Ch. 4).

What, then, is the nature and scope of the literature on public sector leadership in Canada? The first observation to be made is that unlike the US, where most of the standard generic public administration textbooks contained a chapter that provided a broad treatment of leadership (Van Wart, 2003: 157), most Canadian public administration textbooks have largely been silent on the matter (for example, Barker,

2008; Inwood, 2009[1999]; Adie and Thomas, 1987; Wilson, 1981). The absence of any meaningful discussion of leadership in the Barker and Inwood textbooks is particularly striking given that successive Clerks of the Privy Council have prioritized leadership development and the recruitment of the best and the brightest to the ranks of the public service for the better part of the past 15 years. How these themes did not emerge in their respective chapters devoted to human resources management in the public sector at the very least is astounding.

But even with respect to the textbooks that do overtly address the topic of leadership, the results are less than satisfactory. Johnson (2011[2006]), for example, has a chapter entitled, 'The Challenges of Leadership', but his primary focus is to make the argument that the exercise of leadership is the most important means of addressing the key challenges of public administration, namely, to be responsive to the needs of society, ensure that there is accountability in government and to deliver government programmes and services with economy, efficiency and effectiveness, rather than to provide an overarching examination of the most seminal contributions to leadership studies and how this knowledge applies to the Canadian public service. Even Kernaghan and Siegel (1999[1987]), who produced four editions of the textbook that became the Canadian standard for more than a decade, only dedicated part of a chapter (along with the topics of communication and motivation) to the role and importance of leadership in the public sector. This represented a mere five pages in a book in excess of 700 pages, which, to state the patently obvious, is hardly sufficient for presenting an adequate understanding of the complex phenomenon of leadership.

Considering the Canadian public administration literature more broadly only serves to confirm that the study of public sector leadership to date has been wholly inadequate. The only book-length treatment of the subject has been a recent edited volume that examines the role of highest ranking public servant in Ottawa and the provincial and territorial governments, namely, the clerk or secretary to cabinet (Dutil, 2008). As welcome as this book has been for starting the dialogue about the leadership potential for the incumbents of this critically important position in the public bureaucracy, it nonetheless suffers from a number of limitations. First, like the studies of political leadership referred to earlier in the chapter, many of the contributions to this collection start with the faulty premise that those who are secretaries to cabinet are *ipso facto* leaders. Second, the book relies too heavily on case studies for providing rich description of the position of the secretary to cabinet. There is no overarching model or theoretical framework presented from which to generate insights into the nature of leadership exhibited by individuals occupying this senior position in the public bureaucracy. This leads to a third shortcoming, which is that by focusing narrowly on the secretary to cabinet position, there is neither an appreciation of the potential for leadership to emerge at various levels throughout the public service nor how it is manifested in those instances.

Other studies can be identified but they are rather disparate and relatively few and far between. Attempts have also been made to examine the 'leadership paradigms' of prime ministers to determine the impact they had on the design of the machinery of government (Aucoin, 1986) and the public service (Zussman, 1986). Ingstrup and Crookall (1998), in their study of well-performing public organizations, identified nine key elements (grouped according to three pillars) that appeared to be essential to good performance, one of which was leadership, although the chapter dedicated to that specific element made no effort to critically engage with the mainstream leadership literature. Borins (2002) established a link between leadership and innovation, discovering that much of it materializes as a result of middle managers and frontline employees rather than from the top, which is the conventional wisdom. Some scholarship has been produced on leadership training and development in the federal public service (Mau, 2007; Wilson, Stanford and Dwivedi, 2004; Boase, 1994) as well as the use of leadership competency models (Mau, 2009). The intention of these studies was to analyse how the federal government has attempted to ensure that it will possess the leadership cadre necessary to contend with the societal forces, increasingly global in nature, that will stress our public organizations. More recently, Siegel (2010) has written about the leadership of the municipal CAO, arguing that these individuals need to lead down, lead up and lead out to effectively fulfil their organizational roles.

There are a few additional studies on public sector leadership in Canada, some of which have been written by researchers either based at think-tanks, like the Public Policy Forum or the Conference Board of Canada, or outside of the discipline of public administration, but this very brief synopsis outlined above essentially captures the state of existing scholarship in this area. The paucity of Canadian scholarship dedicated to public sector leadership is as disheartening as it is problematic. However, perceived more positively, for those public administration scholars interested in exploring the concept of leadership in the Canadian public sector, there is a veritable wellspring of opportunity to make a contribution. The next section of the chapter sets out a call to action for political scientists and public administration scholars who are interested in understanding the nature of political and administrative leadership, both of which are essential to ensuring good governance.

Breaking Down the Silos: Towards an Enhanced Understanding of Leadership

It should be evident from the preceding discussion that, aside from the esteemed political scientist, James MacGregor Burns, whose conceptualization of transactional and transformational leadership has radically transformed the field of leadership studies, the contributions of political scientists and public administration scholars has been rather limited. This is especially true if consideration is given only to those Canadian academics who have conducted research in this area. Canadian political scientists have typically examined political leadership from an institutional perspective by focusing 'at the top' either on a single individual—the prime minister—or the cabinet as a decision-making body, while their public administration colleagues have not had much to say about public sector leadership at all. There is a need to move beyond identifying individuals as leaders by virtue of the positions of authority that they hold and to consider political and administrative leadership from a much broader perspective; there is also a need to bridge the theory and practice of leadership (Kellerman and Webster, 2001; Peele, 2005).

An important first step would be for political scientists and public administration scholars to contemplate exactly what constitutes leadership instead of taking it for granted that those holding a designated office, whether political or administrative, are leaders. While there has been no consistent definition of leadership, which is a central failing of leadership studies (Yukl, 1998; Rost, 1991; Burns, 1978), there are a number of commonly-cited elements which are outlined in the one provided by Rost (1991: 102): '[it is] an influence relationship among leaders and followers who intend real changes that reflect their mutual purposes'. Typically, definitions of leadership will incorporate notions of power and influence (or persuasion) in the context of a group process. And, even though many definitions do not explicitly refer to leadership in the context of followership, they generally recognize that this phenomenon must be understood as a dynamic process of interaction between individuals in an organization. In short, it is difficult to be a leader if no one is willing to follow. While it may be the case that leaders define reality for followers, if the latter are unwilling to accept the articulated vision, leaders will be viewed as weak and ineffectual. Leaders and followers, therefore, are thought to have a symbiotic relationship and are ultimately unable to exist without each other (Kellerman, 2008; Bennis and Nanus, 1985). The definition also accentuates the fact that leaders ultimately deal with change rather than maintaining the status quo.

By putting their minds to this question, those who study political and bureaucratic leadership can break free from the insularity of the approaches that have characterized their research studies to date by integrating the knowledge and insights into the leadership phenomenon that have been developed in other disciplines. More specifically, public sector leadership research needs to give consideration to trait and leadership behaviour theory, to questions of power and influence, the role and impact of charismatic and transformational leadership, the dynamic between leaders and followers and the insights that have emerged from situational theory. As Fielder (1993: 2) noted, 'it is meaningless to talk about leadership outside of the situational context'. Situational or contingency theories attempt to explain leadership in terms of contextual factors such as the nature of the work being performed, specific characteristics of followers or the external environment, or whether certain leader behaviours or trait patterns would be equally effective in all situations—the assumption being that they would not.

In short, what is required is the development of a comprehensive public sector leadership model that is validated through empirical research (Van Wart, 2003). This challenge, while formidable, is not unique to political scientists and public administration scholars. Yukl (1998: 428), for example, wrote: 'Leadership research has been characterized by narrowly focused studies with little integration of findings from different approaches'. More recently, Bruce Avolio, one of the leading minds in the study of leadership, made a strong appeal for more integrative strategies for leadership theory-building. He championed, '… a fuller and more integrative focus that is multilevel, multicomponent, and interdisciplinary and that recognizes that leadership is a function of both the leader and the led and the complexity of the context' (Avolio, 2007: 31). This last requirement, namely, that integrative models must account for the complexity of the context within which leadership operates, is probably nowhere as great as it is in the public sector where politicians and public servants operate in a unique political, social and economic environment characterized by a multiplicity of complex relationships—with each other, the opposition parties, interest groups, the media, citizens and their counterparts from both other levels of government and other countries.

Conclusion

Just as Canadian public administration scholars were recently admonished for their relative neglect of comparative and development administration (Dwivedi and Mau, 2009), so too must they and their colleagues in political science be rebuked for failing to engage in any meaningful way with the theory and practice of public sector leadership. Ultimately, both groups must work towards developing an integrative model or theory of leadership that is appropriate to the public sector, which, despite the shift to managerialism in recent decades, is not analogous to the private sector. The public sector is distinct from the private sector and any integrative model of leadership designed for the public sector must account for that fact. However, prior to even thinking about developing an integrative model of public sector leadership, Canadian public administration scholars must undertake more research to enhance our understanding of how administrative leadership plays out in the context of our parliamentary democracy. Although Van Wart (2003: 225) was writing about the status of the American public administration literature, his words resonate even more strongly in the Canadian context: 'Indeed, no matter where you look in or for this subfield, the needs are great and the research opportunities are manifold'. Scholars who are looking to make an impact with their research agendas could not ask for a better scenario; let us hope that they not only rise to the challenge but also do so forthwith.

References

Adie, Robert and Paul Thomas (1987). *Canadian Public Administration: Problematical Perspectives*. Scarborough: Prentice-Hall.

Aucoin, Peter (1994). "Prime Ministerial Leadership: Position, Power and Politics" in Maureen Mancuso, Richard G. Price and Ronald Wagenberg, Eds. *Leaders and Leadership in Canada*. Toronto: Oxford University Press, 99–117.

Aucoin, Peter (1986). "Organizational Change in the Machinery of Canadian Government: From Rational Management to Brokerage Politics" in *Canadian Journal of Political Science*. XIX: 1, March, 3–27.

Avolio, Bruce (2007). "Promoting More Integrative Strategies for Leadership Theory-Building" in *American Psychologist*. 62, 1. 25–33.

Bakvis, Herman and David MacDonald (1993). "The Canadian Cabinet: Organization, Decision-Rules and Policy Impact" in Michael Atkinson, Ed. *Governing Canada: Institutions and Public Policy*. Toronto: Harcourt Brace, 47–80.

Barker, Paul (2008). *Public Administration in Canada: Brief Edition*. Toronto: Nelson.

Behn, Robert (1998). "What Right Do Public Managers Have to Lead?" in *Public Administration Review*. 58, 3. 209–224.

Bennis, Warren and Burt Nanus (1985). *Leaders: The Strategies for Taking Charge*. New York: Harper & Row Publishers.

Bernier, Luc, Keith Brownsey and Michael Howlett, Eds. (2005). *Executive Styles in Canada: Cabinet Structures and Leadership Practices in Canadian Government*. Toronto: University of Toronto Press.

Blondel, Jean (1987). *Political Leadership: Towards a General Analysis*. London: Sage.

Blunt, Ray (2003). *Growing Leaders for Public Service*. Washington: IBM Centre for the Business of Government, November.

Boase, Joan Price (1994). "Leadership in the Public Service: Renewing an Essential Management Skill" in Maureen Mancuso, Richard Price and Ronald Wagenberg, Editors. *Leaders and Leadership in Canada*. Toronto: Oxford University Press, 190–210.

Borins, Sandford (2002). "Leadership and Innovation in the Public Sector" in *Leadership and Organization Development Journal*. 23, 8. 467–476.

Bourgault, Jacques (2002) "The Role of Deputy Ministers in Canadian Government" in Christopher Dunn, Ed. *The Handbook of Canadian Public Administration*. Toronto: Oxford University Press.

Bryson, John (2004). *Strategic Planning for Public and Non-Profit Organizations: A Guide to Strengthening and Sustaining Organizational Achievement*. 3rd Edn. San Francisco: Jossey Bass.

Burns, James MacGregor (1978). *Leadership*. New York: Harper & Row Publishers.

Cross, William (1996). "Direct Election of Provincial Party Leaders in Canada, 1985–1995: The End of the Leadership Convention?" in *Canadian Journal of Political Science*. 29, 2. 295–315.

Dion, Léon (1968). "The Concept of Political Leadership: An Analysis" in *Canadian Journal of Political Science*. 1, 1, March, 2–17.

Doerr, Audrey (1981). *The Machinery of Government in Canada*. Toronto: Methuen.

Dutil, Patrice, Ed. (2008). *Searching for Leadership: Secretaries to Cabinet in Canada*. Toronto: University of Toronto Press.

Dwivedi, O.P. and Tim Mau (2009). "Comparative and Development Administration: State of the Discipline in Canada" in Dwivedi, O.P., Tim A. Mau and Byron Sheldrick, Eds. *An Evolving Physiology of Government: Canadian Public Administration in Transition*. Ottawa: University of Ottawa Press, 312–57.

Elden, Max and Steven Sanders (1996). "Vision-Based Diagnosis: Mobilizing for Transformational Change in a Public Organization" in *Public Productivity & Management Review*. 20, 1, September, 11–23.

Fielder, Fred (1993). "The Leadership Situation and the Black Box in Contingency Theories" in Martin M. Chemers and Roya Ayman, Eds. *Leadership Theory and Research: Perspectives and Directions*. New York: Academic Press, 1–28.

Hockin, Thomas, Ed. (1971). *Apex of Power: The Prime Minister and Political Leadership in Canada*. Scarborough: Prentice Hall.

Ingraham, Patricia Wallace and Heather Getha-Taylor (2004). "Leadership in the Public Sector: Models and Assumptions for Leadership Development in the Federal Government" in *Review of Public Personnel Administration*. 24, 2, June, 95–112.

——. (2005). "Common Sense, Competence and Talent in the Public Service in the USA: Finding the Right Mix in a Complex World" in *Public Administration*. 83, 4. 789–803.

Ingstrup, Ole and Paul Crookall (1998). *The Three Pillars of Public Management: Secrets of Sustained Success*. Montreal: McGill-Queen's University Press.

Inwood, Gregory (2009). *Understanding Canadian Public Administration: An Introduction to Theory and Practice*. Toronto: Prentice Hall.

Johnson, David (2001). *Thinking Government: Public Administration and Politics in Canada*. Toronto: University of Toronto Press.

Kernaghan, Kenneth and David Siegel (1999). *Public Administration in Canada: A Text*. Scarborough: ITP Nelson.

Kellerman, Barbara (2008). *Followership: How Followers are Creating Change and Changing Leaders*. Boston: Harvard Business Press.

Kellerman, Barbara (2004). *Bad Leadership: What It Is, How It Happens, Why It Matters*. Boston: Harvard Business School Press.

Kellerman, Barbara and Scott Webster (2001). "The Recent Literature on Public Leadership Reviewed and Considered" in *The Leadership Quarterly*. 12, 485–514.

Kent, Thomas (2005). "Leading and Managing: It Takes Two to Tango" in *Management Decision*. 43, 7–8, 1010–17.

Kotter, John (1998). "What Leaders Really Do" in *Harvard Business Review on Leadership*. Boston: Harvard Business School Publishing, 37–60. Originally published in May–June 1990.

Leduc, Lawrence (2001). "Democratizing Party Leadership Selection" in *Party Politics*. 7, 3, 323–41.

Mancuso, Maureen, Richard Price and Ronald Wagenberg, Eds. (1994). *Leaders and Leadership in Canada*. Toronto: Oxford University Press.

Mau, Tim (2009). "Is Public Sector Leadership Distinct? A Comparative Analysis of Core Competencies in the Senior Executive Service" in Jeffrey Raffel, Peter Leisink and Anthony Middlebrooks, Eds. *Public Sector Leadership: International Challenges and Perspectives*. Northampton: Edward Elgar, 313–39.

Mau, Tim (2007). "Public Sector Leadership Development: The Canadian Model Considered" *CSL Leadership Review*. 1, 4, Spring, 267–94.

Michelmann, Hans, Donald Storey and Jeffrey Steeves, Eds. (2007). *Political Leadership and Representation in Canada: Essays in Honour of John C. Courtney*. Toronto: University of Toronto Press.

Mintzberg, Henry and Jacques Bourgault, Eds. (2000). *Managing Publicly*. Toronto: IPAC.

Paige, Glenn (1977). *The Scientific Study of Political Leadership*. New York: The Free Press.

Pal, Leslie (1988). "Hands at the Helm? Leadership and Public Policy" in Leslie Pal and David Taras, Eds. *Prime Ministers and Premiers: Political Leadership and Public Policy in Canada*. Scarborough: Prentice-Hall Canada Inc., 16–26.

Pal, Leslie. and David Taras, Eds. (1988). *Prime Ministers and Premiers: Political Leadership and Public Policy in Canada*. Scarborough: Prentice-Hall Canada Inc.

Peele, Gillian (2005). "Leadership and Politics: A Case for a Closer Relationship" in *Leadership*. 1, 2, 187–204.

Pitts, David (2005). "Leadership, Empowerment and Public Organizations" in *Review of Public Personnel Administration*. 25, 1, 5–28.

Plumptre, Timothy (1991[1988]). *Beyond the Bottom Line: Management in Government*. Halifax: Institute for Research on Public Policy.

Raffel, Jeffrey, Peter Leisink and Anthony Middlebrooks, Eds. (2009a) *Public Sector Leadership: International Challenges and Perspectives*. Northampton: Edward Elgar.

Raffel, Jeffrey A., Peter Leisink and Anthony E. Middlebrooks (2009b). "Introduction" in Raffel, Jeffrey, Peter Leisink and Anthony Middlebrooks, Eds. *Public Sector Leadership: International Challenges and Perspectives*. Northampton: Edward Elgar, 1–32.

Rost, Joseph (1991). *Leadership for the Twenty-First Century*. New York: Praeger Publishers.

Rusaw, Carol (2001). *Leading Public Organizations: An Integrative Approach*. Orlando: Harcourt.

Savoie, Donald (1999). *Governing from the Centre: The Concentration of Power in Canadian Politics*. Toronto: University of Toronto Press.

Schraeder, Mike, Rachel Tears and Mark Jordan (2005). "Organizational Culture in Public Sector Organizations" in *Leadership & Organization Development Journal*. 26, 6, 492–502.

Siegel, David (2010). "The Leadership of the Municipal Chief Administrative Officer" in *Canadian Public Administration*. 53, 2. 139–61.

Smiley, D.V. (1968). "The National Party Leadership Convention in Canada: A Preliminary Analysis" in *Canadian Journal of Political Science*. 1, 4, December, 373–97.

Terry, Larry (1995). *Leadership of Public Bureaucracies: The Administrator as Conservator*. Thousand Oaks: Sage Publications.

Trottier, Tracey, Montgomery Van Wart and XiaoHu Wang (2008). "Examining the Nature and Significance of Leadership in Government Organizations" in *Public Administration Review*. 68, 2, 319–333.

Tucker, Robert (1981). *Politics as Leadership*. Columbia: University of Missouri Press.

Van Wart, Montgomery (with Paul Suino) (2008). *Leadership in Public Organizations: An Introduction*. New York: M.E. Sharpe.

Van Wart, Montgomery (2005). *Dynamics of Leadership in Public Service: Theory and Practice*. New York: M.E. Sharpe.

Van Wart, Montgomery (2003). "Public Sector Leadership Theory: An Assessment" in *Public Administration Review*. 63, 2, 214–28.

Washbush, John (2005). "There is No Such Thing as Leadership, Revisited" in *Management Decision*. 43, 7/8, 1078–85.

Whittington, Michael S. (2004). "The Prime Minister, Cabinet and Executive Power" in Michael Whittington and Glen Williams, Editors. *Canadian Politics in the 21st Century*. Scarborough: Nelson, 31–55.

Wilson, V.S. (1981). *Canadian Public Policy and Administration: Theory and Environment*. Toronto: McGraw-Hill Ryerson.

Wilson, V.S., Lloyd Stanford and O.P. Dwivedi (2004). "From Witchcraft to Proposed Twenty-First Century Reforms: The Ongoing Saga of Training and Development in Canadian Government" in *International Journal of Public Administration*. 27, 3–4, 259–85.

Yukl, Gary. *Leadership in Organizations* (1998). New Jersey: Prentice Hall.

Zussman, David (1989). "Walking the Tightrope: The Mulroney Government and the Public Service" in Michael Prince, Editor. *How Ottawa Spends, 1986–87: Tracking the Tories*. Toronto: Methuen, 250–82.

5

My Land, My Niche and a Lost Home

AMITA SINGH

Land acquisition has been a matter of much discomfort and distress in the last two decades of market-led reforms. Since land constitutes the total ecosystem of a village inhabitant in a manner which provided him or her personal and social security for generations its loss cannot simply be compensated by or reducible to cash and rehabilitation incentives as is generally perceived by policy makers. For an outsider to the village, like the state agencies or multinational companies, land is simply a property or a pot of gold, which could be put to a more profitable use than simply agriculture by building casinos, golf courses, swank high rise office spaces and the shopping malls. The love for this land has led to major battles against the state and has been one of the main reasons for the rise of anti-state and anti-political movements in the last two decades (Moyo and Yeros, 2005: 46). The land connection is an important relationship, which is also an important ingredient into development but the hurriedness of ambitious policies, which have been brought about in India, China and other Asia-Pacific countries, has led to the deepening of the rural-urban divide as never before.

There are some regions in India where the land relationship has been used strategically when some state governments like Gujarat and Tamil Nadu have launched 'sons of the soil policies' (Joseph and Sangita, 1998). It is interesting to study the cultural and sociological connections of land to public policies, which facilitate or obstruct implementation of a rural policy in many ways yet go unrecognized at the formulation stages. Ignorance about these relationships and the policy controls being with the urban elites has turned acquisition of land policies into a nightmare for the villagers. Land is the last frontier of rural and tribal inhabitants and to protect it through whichever strategy possible is understood as some form of chivalry and martyrdom. India, like any other Asian country, is undergoing this turbulence over land where inhabitants witness pots of cash being exchanged for their land and bulldozer flattened homes. Land connections have evoked passions, fears and belligerence not just in Asia but in the USA as well. The anti-immigration laws across many states in USA and Europe have partly been ignited by the large-scale purchase of land by foreign companies in complete defiance of local ecology and communities. In Asia, rural communities have been using the land by virtue of customary rights over small landholdings and any formalization of acquisition and sale involves the potential risks of losing their rights to use the land. Since life for a villager revolves around land most of their community institutions, traditions and festivities are structured in allusion to it. One can even find this in one of earlier surveys by a British Team. Sir Henry Cotton, in his book *New India or India in Transition* (1886: 170), states that even the British House of Commons Report of 1812, during the peak of colonial occupation of India, carried observations about the self-supportive governance system prevailing in Indian villages. Thus, any disruption on this living and functional network within villages entails a serious governance deficit.

The land connection has brought back a large number of non-residents to their ancestral villages in home countries searching for their family history, lost relatives and a desire to compensate for the many injustices of the past. Many scholars (Marsh, 1864; Leopold, 1949; Churchman et al., 1974) writing on land have warned against the market-led development, which subsidizes the value of land and disposes it to developers and realty profit seekers. Land acquisition is changing human geography and geo-physical warnings about catastrophes that would befall due to modifications of physical geography by human action. Continuous and unabated land acquisition and displacement of inhabitants of many regions have broken man's harmonious relationship with nature, weakened commitment to bioethics and human civilization. 'Land' remains central to the development policy debate everywhere in the world but in the Asiatic region, where till today agrarian economy and small landholding farmers dominate policy discourse, land also acquires some form of sacrosanct association ruled by divine providence. Those who have travelled through the Indian countryside, especially the interiors of rural habitats and had the fortune of participating in rural lifestyles, would understand the warmth and belonging which is conveyed in a conversation on land. This land question has also become a long-standing tradition in defense of many customary rights as it provides a traditional social base of all agrarian movements. Peasants have consistently opposed land takeover in the Indian countryside. Gadgil and Guha (1992) documented the history of the conflict over land use, control and acquisition.

Thus, intrinsically the village does not have any such category called 'landless' as the cultural ethics which bonds a village has land as 'commons' or for everyone's use. This land ethics has been carried through history without disruptions by market upheavals in rural areas. Thus, land has never been a commodity but an ecosystem from which everyone got something to survive. At the time when the British landed in India in the pre-19th century their own village commons had almost been devastated. Coleman (1994: 85) has written that this process over common village land called 'enclosure' had also destroyed the commons of Europe. The agonizing displacement of people following 'enclosure' is rooted in the history of violence and Karl Marx's *Capital* (1906: 802) describes how villagers were hunted and shot at while their fields were destroyed and burnt to be converted to pasturage or capital production of dairy products. The loss of the village ecosystem generates an intractable system of poverty and loss of livelihood. Robert Heilbroner (1980: 30) cites the 1820 case of the Duchess of Sutherland, who evicted 15,000 tenants from 794,000 acres of land for creating a pasture for 131,000 sheep. It was found that most of those evicted finally had to settle for a marginalized existence including beggary and prostitution.

State and Land in a Market Economy

Land has undergone many changes in the last two decades where the speed and veracity of acquisition policies has instigated studies that the state would not act for the people and is not altruistic. James Buchanan (1975) suggests that when the state ignores distribution of motivations of other agents in any action, altruistic morality gets caught up in a famous social dilemma, which he calls the 'moral hazard problem' created due to imperfect information. While this analysis may hold itself in perfect unison with the state behaviour in a market economy, it may also highlight the fact that 'welfarism' is likely to create 'welfare parasites' (Wispelaere, 2004: 20) instead of entrepreneurial forces generated over land by virtue of a special motivation produced by working over one's own land. Land acquisition may also be viewed as a symptomatic characteristic of the predatory state oriented towards rapid economic gains in a new market economy. 'If policies that promote economic development (such as building infrastructure and promoting free trade) and good institutions (such as secure property rights and an efficient bureaucracy) are inconsistent with the maintenance of the political status quo, then this gives elites an incentive to be predatory' (Robinson, 2001: 2; Evans, 1989).

The nature of land as a resource for the development of the whole nation has weakened as understanding about the slouching welfare state grew in the context of Pigou's analysis of the welfare state (Pigou, 1954: 1–11). Pigou writes that welfare is a moral activity whereas the later economists of the Virginia School contested the view to suggest that welfare had a dimension in the methodological individualism of Hobbes. James Buchanan, Gordon Tullock and Vincent Ostrom were co-founders of the Public Choice Society as an informal group at the University of Virginia in 1968. The group of economists worked in the area of non-market decision-making or in trying to find an answer to why the government does what it does than to be embroiled in studies on normative taxation principles.

Thus, land acquisition within the framework of neo-liberal policies has stronger connotations to Buchanan's analysis than to Pigou. The philosophy behind land acquisition has been provocative and bereft of alternative ideas or a Plan 'B' approach. The hegemonic capitalistic system, which has been aptly described in Eric Hobsbawm's *How to Change the World* (2011), states that once again the time has come to take Marx seriously as economic and political liberalism, singly or in combination, cannot provide the solution to the problems of 21st century.

Land, Law and Politics

The policy of land acquisition for public purposes was used for land distribution and land reforms in the post-independence era. The acquisition brought to the surface the embedded inequities in land ownerships within the village economy despite the community controls over common land areas. The state started attacking the private ownership of village land instead of providing alongside a more intensive security of commons and its use by the poor in every village. Four decades later this initial neglect helped to consolidate marketization of all village lands.

Given the protection to private property under Chapter III on Fundamental Rights under Article 19(1)(f) and 31 the judiciary and the state remained at loggerheads in many cases some of which can be mentioned here as Kameshwar vs. State of Bihar (1951), Sajjan Singh vs. State of Rajasthan (1965) and the I.C. Golak Nath and Others vs.

State of Punjab (1967). While this intensified the Indian style of socialism it also created a political base of the poverty reduction programmes or the popular 'Twenty-Point Programme' as a 'Garibi Hatao Programme' (Poverty Eradication Programme). The Prime Minister Smt Indira Gandhi explained, 'We have always said that we have our own brand of socialism' (*Statesman*, 25 October 1976). This can be further understood by the fact that the interpretation of Article 31(b) alongside the Ninth Schedule declared that none of the Acts or regulations specified in the Ninth Schedule nor any of the provisions thereof shall be deemed to be void on the ground that they are inconsistent with Part III. This led the government to add many more Acts to it through a series of constitutional amendments(viz., 4th, 17th, 29th, 34th, 39th, 42nd, 47th, 66th and 75th) only to raise the number of total Acts under the IX Schedule to 257. A large number of them are welfare measures for the Scheduled Castes (SCs) and Scheduled Tribes (STs). Even though this redistribution of resources raised constitutional issues and conflicts between the judiciary and the parliament, it nevertheless established 'socialism' as a constitutional principle in Indian politics along with the political gain of interest aggregation, which it brought in favour of the Congress party. This method of redistribution also launched the beginning of inclusive governance, which was stamped with the Constitutional approval of the 73rd amendment in 1992. These amendments enabled the new rural leaders who were also beneficiaries of the distribution of land in the 1960s and 1970s to, now, officially participate in the local decision -making both at the level of their 'Village Panchayats' (Village Councils) but also at the district level. The 73rd amendment created a third constitutional layer of local decision-making. However, the developments over land in the villages have been consistently affecting and weakening the benign nature of village governance. Colonizers and developers in association with the state development agencies identify village land for acquisition for projects and in doing so they only look for the 'financial viability' rather than many more intangible indicators. In many cases the abject poor in the villages are enticed to give away land much before the issue of compensation and rehabilitation is finalized.

In land deals this emboldened defiance of laws by the purchaser of land is possible due to the government's purposeful neglect of avoiding clarifications on 'zoning rules' as a result of which the colonizer/developer starts buying land directly from farmers. The colonizer is set free to buy land in areas where the Change of Land Use (CLU) certificate is not required. Land purchases in controlled areas require a CLU certificate from the District Town and Country Planner, which the land purchased outside the controlled areas does not require.

The role of NGOs also became a matter of concern as they became the legitimate faces of social and philanthropic activities initiated by developers to justify the purchase of land. CAPART as the mother NGO in the Ministry of Rural Development allocated funds directly to NGOs without the consent or knowledge of the district administration. A large number of cases where the development funds have been siphoned out by the IAS promoted NGOs have increased corruption and diverted public funds for development into private pockets (Gaiha and Kulkarni, 2007). The Task Force on Panchayats (2001) admits that since ministries undertake internationally-funded projects, they tend to implement them directly, without any involvement of PRIs. Much of this community land is now with swank multi-specialty hospitals, high class internationally-linked schools and sports complexes for the upper elites while the poor continue to rot in its periphery without schools and public health dispensaries. Even the land contracted to the private developer for the public post offices and banks remain unconstructed by the developer while a neighbourhood shopping mart glitters with prosperity. In one single city Gurgaon alone, the loss of village land is threatening. Panchayats are silenced by the colonizer financed strong men of the village and in many cases the Panchayat itself acts as a mouthpiece of the colonizer. Thus, in the 1991 census there were 688 villages on revenue records with a population of 1,288,365 but ten years later in the 2001 census the number has shrunk to 60 villages and the population halved to 119,901. As these land deals were outside the government's regulatory control many strategies were adopted in defiance of the law to get a compliant Sarpanch elected to the panchayat body so that purchase of common lands or panchayat lands could be facilitated. This blew off the lid over corruption and a barrage of land scams started and it also saw the rags to riches story of many village sarpanchas in new cities. The Sarpanch of Nathupur Village in Gurgaon during his tenure starting in 2004 became a millionaire and the owner of a swank multinational skyscraper over his village common land. His election campaign in 2003 was openly supported by the developer and his tenure is notorious for the highest rate of land acquisition to DLF.

Thus, from the tillers over land to becoming the owners of land, these small and marginal farmers clustered around the Below Poverty Line (BPL) of US$ 1.25/day have once again been uprooted from their land and this time there is no honourable rehabilitation over the same land as the rehabilitation policies have yet to be incorporated in law. The Land Acquisition, Rehabilitation and Resettlement Bill, 2011 is still to be tabled in the parliament.

The rural poor and the government interact on land issues with much distrust which is further exacerbated with the coming of the private commercial interests which is Confederation of Real Estate Developers' Association of India (CREDAI) in the battle. The recent judgment the Allahabad High Court quashed the land notification of three villages in U.P. (Abdullapur, Devla and Chakshahberi) while it provided conditional relief to Patwari village. In the Gajraj and Others vs. State of U.P. and Others (Writ-C No. 37443 of 21.10.2011,1). The Greater Noida and its allottees have been directed not to carry on development (2) Chief Secretary to appoint officers not below the level of Principal Secretary to conduct a thorough inquiry regarding the acts of Greater Noida in implementing Master Plan 2021 without approval of NCRP Board; decision to change the land use; allotment made to the builders; and indiscriminate proposals for acquisition of land and thereafter the state shall take appropriate action in the matter.

The most important issue to be highlighted here is the direction in which the land battles are shaping up in the judiciary from now onwards, which is clearly alleging the state-developer nexus in land grabbing. The Supreme Court in the Case of Greater NOIDA Industrial Development Authority vs. Devendra Kumar & ORS. Case [No. SLP (Civil) 16366/6.7.2011], while striking down acquisition by a state government recently, stated that the authorities were 'subserving' private builders in the name of public interest.

If one goes back to the history of the rise of neo-liberal policies in India starting 1991 with the new economic policy, it would unambiguously demonstrate the shifting of political battles to the rural landscape and in continuity to acquisition involving municipal funds and programmes over these newly-acquired areas.

Land Acquisition and Special Economic Zones (SEZs)

SEZ policy has been the single most potent factor in disturbing the land related to social, economic and ecological dynamics. The Ministry of Commerce of the Government of India brought out the Special Economic Zone Act, 2005, which sought to converge all dispersed directives and notifications into a stable legal framework for export-based industries. This policy, which started in April 2000 as a means to establish some Special Export Promotion Zones within the country, created various units to manufacture goods and render services. At least six states have by now passed their own SEZ Acts. The earlier ones were West Bengal and Madhya Pradesh in 2003, followed by Gujarat (2004),Tamil Nadu and Haryana (2004) and Punjab

(2009). It may be inferred here that investments increase when property rights are secure and there exists an independent judiciary to ensure protection through a firm government. As Mancur Olson (1993: 572) suggests, 'An economy will be able to reap all potential gains from investment and from long-term transactions only if it has a government that is believed to be both strong enough to last and inhibited from violating individual rights to property and rights to contract enforcement'.

Implementation in a stable democracy like India works in favour of global capital investment in a country.

These SEZs have multiplied in the last ten years and since the SEZ Act of 2005 has swept over the rural landscape in a very powerful way. SEZs have become a new face for the new institutional economics demonstrating the priority which material 'growth' has received in competitive global economics by attracting a lot of social science research and media attention both in India and China. A total of 1,006 SEZs have been approved since the SEZ Act of 2005. This includes 582 formally approved, 380 notified and 44 approved in principle. There are several others pre-existing the Act including the older business clusters called the Export Promotion Zones. Considering the need to enhance foreign investment and promote exports from the country and realizing the need that level playing field must be made available to the domestic enterprises and manufacturers to be competitive globally, the government had in April 2000 announced the introduction of SEZ policy in the country, deemed to be foreign territory for the purposes of trade operations, duties and tariffs(see the Ministry of Commerce website http://sezindia.nic.in).

The manner in which land has been acquired and unsuspecting rural inhabitants have been cheated and thrown into homelessness and occupational marginalization has become a new concern for democracy.

By February 2008, the total amount of land acquired for SEZs in Gujarat was 20,800 acres, which is around 40 per cent of the total land under SEZ in the country. However, in some places, it was not so well received. The Goa inhabitants like Singur and Nandigram in West Bengal demonstrated a consolidated opposition to SEZ land acquisition and forced the Centre to cancel all the 18 SEZs in the state. Interestingly, land has a strong emotional value which has not been accounted for in calculating its value. This has resulted in the backfiring of forced land acquisition policies not just for SEZs but for other industrialization purposes also.

Interestingly, the Gujarat government's plea that of the total SEZ land in the state, 45 per cent is wasteland, 43 per cent agricultural land acquired from the farmers and the remaining 12 per cent has been acquired by the Gujarat Industrial Development Corporation (GIDC) much before the birth of the SEZ Act, but later transferred to SEZs. This misinformation about wastelands bypasses the rationale that they serve as 'charagahs' or 'gochars' (grazing grounds) for animals and usufruct sources for the poor in the village. According to the Development Commissioner Ravi Saxena, investment worth ₹ 34,599.44 crore has already been made in Gujarat's SEZs with a total direct and indirect employment of 15,088 persons. However, the amount of Foreign Direct Investment (FDI) coming to Gujarat's SEZ is yet not known even though some of the countries like Japan have expressed willingness to invest in the state. Loss of fundamental resources of life at the cost of creating unreliable wealth for the poor is a policy intervention which raises many questions and doubts.

Haryana has always been in the forefront of progress in various phases of its history since its creation in 1966. This has been due to the ability of its villagers both landed and cattle grazers to reap opportunities during the Green Revolution. Haryana's per capita income has been US$ 862.90, which is much higher than the all-India average of US$ 573.10 (2006). This model of prosperity through an intelligent cultivation over land is now being wound up.

The SEZ Act, under Chapter III 6(1) of Haryana, suggests that the developer would identify the land for SEZ. If land is the focus of SEZ implementation it becomes imperative to understand how smoothly it is allowed to pass out of the hands of villagers. A government appointed Project Approval Committee shall approve, modify or reject any proposal for the establishment of SEZ. It further says that the project approved by the committee shall have precedence over the developmental plan indicating broad land uses. It also gives a substantial relaxation to the developer in various procedures required to look into the issue of land such as the change of land use laws and would also be exempt from the Haryana Development and Regulation of Urban Areas Act 1975 (8 of 1975).

The state also has the highest number of SEZs in the country, eight notified, 29 formally approved and 28 SEZs that have already got in-principle approvals. Reliance Industries Ltd., India's largest private sector company, has inducted ₹ 40,000 crore SEZ project in Haryana to be spread over 25,000 acres and is billed as one of the biggest, multi-product SEZs—with a cargo airport and a 2,000 mw power plant within it. It has a target of giving around five lakh jobs. So far it has only invested just ₹ 3,000 crore in the project and bought around 8,000 acres. The Haryana government is establishing a special economic zone at Garhi Harsaru in New Gurgaon, about 25 km from the international airport in Delhi, adjoining NH 8 and the state highway between Gurgaon and Pataudi. The SEZ would be spread across 3,000 acres and would cost an estimated ₹ 948 crore to build. About 2,400 units are slated to come up in the zone, providing employment to over 60,000 workers and generating exports of around ₹ 42,000 crore. The employment as it arrives is mostly passed over to migrants from Bihar and Bengal rather than to the local people who have given their land.

The issue of reasonable compensation remains unresolved. There is no acceptable methodology to calculate a large amount of intangibles in the transaction, besides the market value of land. These intangibles include the loss of livelihood, mental and physical agony, insecurity, distress, loss or extinction of the ecosystem of communities both human and non-human who shared common spaces but injured or destroyed in panic dispersal and destitution. Almost 80 per cent of the agricultural population owns only about 17 per cent of the total agriculture land. So, where do the others labelled as 'landless' in policy documents get accommodated? The village land belongs to all irrespective of titles, which exist only for those who are agriculturists and have to scientifically monitor crops and its management as a business. Others are free to graze their animals and utilize the usufruct available over village land. Many studies such as the one done by ICRISAT, a Hyderabad-based research institute, found that commons account for 14–23 per cent of the income in poor households and 84 per cent of the poor depend upon it for livelihood. Bina Agarwal also suggests that commons reduce income inequalities (Harris, Guhan and Casen, 1992).

Far more families and communities depend on a piece of land (for work, grazing) than those who simply own it. However, when land is acquired it is only the title over land that becomes an eligible condition to seek compensation. All others are 'uprooted' through a legitimate legal doctrine of treating them as 'landless'. The worst affected are their animals who overnight become 'strays' and hence a sport kill for the new urban settlers. It has also cast in stone the caste divides in India as most landless are dalits and animal-rearing tribes who are never compensated and treated as landless. No part of the country can escape this devastation as India has more than a 5,000-year-old civilization, which nurtures a village everywhere from over the snow-capped mountains and deserts to deep dense forests. Thus, no land is in anyway a wasteland. 'Wasteland' is a term which was brought by the British to convert common rights into private rights (see Singh, 1998: 112). In the first Forest Act of 1865 the government declared forests and wasteland as reserved forests. In the Forest Act of 1878 a system of permits further strengthened private rights on use of this common land. Further, the British passed two draconian Acts, viz., The Cattle Trespass Act 1871 and The Land Acquisition Act 1894. By now, the British were firmly entrenched to divert biomass resources of the poor for commerce and industry.

The most unbearable immediate fallout of land acquisition is the loss of livelihood. Courts have not been radical enough to feel the crumbling of localities where the poor live together on a cost-effective strategy of shared material and labour resources. In N.D. Jayal vs. Union of India 2004, the Supreme Court reiterated a mixed sentiment and anguish on weak rehabilitation policies, even though the priorities are expressively clear, 'the last condition is rehabilitation which is not only about providing food, clothes and shelter, it is also about extending support to rebuild livelihood by ensuring necessary amenities of life' (AIR 2004 SC 867/9SCC 364). Most urban policy makers do not realize the link of land acquisition with the available opportunities for livelihood. A large number of communities survive on the availability of a particular resource, i.e., Kumhars or potters claim mud from the village pond, Gujjars and several other animal-rearing tribes need grasses and wastelands for grazing their animals. This may also ignore the requirements of small and marginal farmers who put up a strong fight to prevent the state from acquiring their land but cannot prevent the drilling out of ground water by a neighbouring industry to leave their land dried out as wasted for agriculture use.

> The land acquisition has usurped ecosystems and destroyed heritage sites which provided natural protection to the village ecosystem. 'Natural resources are the assets of the entire nation. It is the obligation of all concerned, including Union Government and the State Government to conserve and not waste these resources. Any threat to the ecology can lead to violation of the right of enjoyment of a healthy life guaranteed in Article 21 … which should be protected'. (Godavarman Thirumulpad (87) vs. Union of India, 2006, 1 SCC 388)

The Gurgaon story about the complete loss of village ponds and community wells is not unique. Villages in most states have suffered loss of ground water, forest areas and grasslands and the foreign investors have not been made to compensate for this ecological loss through their corporate social responsibility measures. On the contrary, the government extends licenses to them for further destruction, such as the case of the 350 acres of prime land in Wazirabad village near Gurgaon given to DLF for a recreation and leisure park for ₹ 1,700 crore. This prime forest area was successfully rehabilitated from the degraded community lands of 294 villages in southern Haryana in a span of less than a decade with the support of the European Union. Nearly 38,000 hectares was rehabilitated through planting and natural regeneration in the Aravalli region. Satellite imagery reveals that the forest cover of this region, which was around 10,000 hectares in 1990, increased to 42,000 hectares in 1997. Environmental experts and land developers are shocked that the prime land was sold in callous disregard to environmental laws laid down by the Supreme Court regarding the Aravalli Plantation Scheme, in an attempt to restore the forests of the fragile hill range *(Tehelka Magazine,* 2011*)*.

Rise of New Administrative Agencies and Land Scams

To implement the central and state SEZ Acts the older administrative system in districts proved ineffective and outdated. Thus, a set of new developmental agencies with special regulatory powers over land were brought about. They were expected to be jointly implementing the new urbanization projects, which involved the process of change of land use, allocation and demarcation of land for specific activities, issuing licenses to conduct a particular business and providing land for specific infrastructural schemes on subsidized rates or with tax holidays. Most of these new public agencies were occupied by the Indian Administrative Service and with the autonomy which they enjoyed and the accountability which they lacked due to unclear jurisdictional boundaries, it became much easier for them to emerge as new power centres in the district. For example, land identification and subsequent allocation to parties involves Municipal Corporation, working with DTCP, District Planning Board, Urban Development Authority and the District Magistrate. The traditional role of the District Commissioner (DC) is much reduced in the new set up as all these new agencies have taken out the steam from his office by controlling the land management issues. Due to the multiple agency set up and dispersed authority of the DC, corruption and land scams are more frequent. The case of the Bangalore District Magistrate T.M. Vijay Bhaskar's Report (http://www.daijiworld.com/news/news) on land grabbing and violations of Karnataka Land Reforms Act and The Revenue Act is worthy of mention here. The report indicted the Minister S.A. Ramdas along with other political leaders and land developers. The Senior Revenue Official, Baladev Krishna, indicted many higher officials but politicians were left scot free and the report was also finally clamped and the officials transferred.

All the above administrative changes and amendments in the District Administration setup and in the State Panchayat Acts respectively restricted the role of panchayats as a deliberative peoples' institution (Singh, 2004). The report of the Task Force on Panchayats, constituted in 2001 under the chairmanship of K.B. Saxena, had pointed out certain grave factors that prevented people's access to the planning process. 'It is observed that a number of Ministries of the Central Government have not taken any concrete steps to integrate PRIs in their strategy of planning and implementation of various programmes which essentially fall in their jurisdiction' (2001: 1). It further stated that 'PRIs do not really figure in this strategy of implementation and in fact there is not even a conceptual recognition of it. NGOs are operating in areas and on subjects which belong to the PRIs and therefore are expected to work in tandem with them' (ibid.). The land acquisition, which started as a blizzard over some states, has usurped many villages and weakened panchayats. Gurgaon and Bangalore have particularly reported instances of colonizer-controlled panchayats. DLF as the major beneficiary runs a parallel government in the new township which has the world's top 20 highest profit-making IT companies brought in from USA, UK, Europe and even China and Malaysia.

The record of most state governments on the use of land has been one of forceful acquisition by mischievously invoking the 'urgency clause' for rushing projects. The Delhi High Court and the Allahabad High Court have whiplashed the Delhi and Uttar Pradesh governments for their claim of 'urgency' in land acquisition. B.S. Yeddyurappa, the Chief Minister of Karnataka, has already been jailed for the infamous land denotification scam. A large number of administrators and company directors have been jailed for land grabbing. In 1999, the Supreme Court had to issue notices to the District Magistrate of Faridabad for filing false affidavits regarding three court directives in 1983, 1991 and 1996 on the rightful use of land for workers [Bandhua Mukti Morcha vs. Union of India 1999, SCC (L&S) 656].

However, the state does have a right to acquire land and displace people under the law of eminent domain. This law of eminent domain is an attribute of sovereignty of every state within which it could take property for public use without owner's consent upon making just compensation [Coffee Board vs. Commissioner of Commercial Taxes (1988) 3 SCC 263]. This has been a choice instrument of the socialist state since the early decades of post-independence India even though CJ Patanjali Shastri in the State of Bihar vs. Kamleshwar Singh (AIR

1952, SC 252) clarified that under the law of eminent domain, the state cannot take away the property of its subjects unless there is a public purpose and an obligation to pay just compensation. This was carried through B.D. Sharma vs. Union of India (1992, SCC 93) and N.D. Jayal vs. Union of India 2004 (AIR 2004, SC 867/9 SCC 364), which strongly suggested that, 'those ousted or displaced from the area have a right under Article 21 to a decent life and earn livelihood in rehabilitated locations ... oustees should be adequately compensated by minimum possible disturbance to their life source and lifestyles'. A similar sentiment was expressed in Narmada Bachao vs. Union of India (10 SCC 664, AIR 2000 SC 3751), 'the effect is to see that on their rehabilitation at new locations they are better off than what they were ... to have more and better amenities than which they enjoyed in their tribal hamlets. The gradual assimilation in the mainstream of the society will lead to betterment and progress' (para 62). However, it is also clear that most judicial benches have treated rehabilitation as a last priority to economic development. The judgment delivered in Jayal vs. UOI (2004) reiterated that for the state '... the last condition is rehabilitation ...'. This anthropogenic judicial inclination had caught attention of Justice P.N. Bhagwati and Justice Krishna Iyer when historic words passed out of the judgement in the case of the State of Kerela vs. Gwalior Rayon and Silk Manufacturing (Wvg.) Co. Ltd. (1973, 2 SCC 713 and AIR 1 SCC 671). The analysis was in the context of agrarian reforms yet it expressed for the first time an acknowledgement about the dynamics of village economy, which is intrinsically ecological. In this context it observed, 'The Indian Constitution is a social instrument with an economic mission and the strength and sweep of its provisions must be gathered by judicial statesmen on a seminal footing'. The judgment was encompassing and could have been a torch bearer for a sturdier ecologically designed Indian economy by invoking the doctrine of 'public trust'. This doctrine of 'public trust' found way in Godavarman Thirumulpad (87) vs. Union of India, 2006 (1 SCC 388) where it was explained as 'a doctrine which looks beyond the need of the present generation and also suggests that certain resources are invested with a special nature. We are trustees of natural resources which belong to all including the future generation as well. The public trust doctrine has to be used to protect the rights of this as also the rights of future generations' (para 88–89). This understanding was further reiterated in M.C. Mehta vs. Kamal Nath 1997 (1 SCC 388).

Thus, in the policies of land acquisition and rehabilitation, the Supreme Court has not been able to clarify location of land use policy in the overlapping domains of public interest and public trust. The judiciary has now to play a pro-active role as a third branch of governance to set the disturbed house in order on land acquisition, displacement and rehabilitation. Sustainability of economic and social advancement cannot be ensured without this intervention.

Conclusion

Land is one of the most sensitive resources of governance. Land acquisition ought to be sensitive to the concerns of the poor in villages who are dependent upon common lands. SEZs have become a new concern for governance because of the reorganization and reshuffling of local life as they encroach into the niche of village life. The displacement and the sufferings, which follow even in SEZs, are still treated in an ad hoc manner with deficient political sops from projects. The issue of locals getting a share in local employment, capacity enhancement programmes to be employed locally for the land they have given for development is not being addressed to absorb local villagers in the development process. Despite judicial sympathy towards the woes of the displaced, i.e., the six month condition has been prescribed in the case of B.D. Sharma vs. UOI (SCC 93, 1992) for rehabilitating oustees, this is less followed in practice.

A sustainable development cannot arrive in defiance of the requirement and participatory motivation of people who have their livelihoods based upon land in the villages.

References

Churchman, C. West, Rosenthal, Albert H. and Smith, Spencer H. (1974). *Natural Resources Administration,* Boulder: Westview Press.

Coleman, Daniel A. (1994). *Ecopolitics: Building a Green Society,* New Brunswick, N.J.: Rutgers University Press.

Cotton, Henry (1886). *New India or India in Transition: British House of Commons Report.* 1812, quoted in London: Kegan Paul and Trench, Truber and Co. Ltd. (revised 1905).

Gadgil, Madhav and Guha, Ramachandra (1993). *This Fissured Land: An Ecological History of India,* Berkeley: University of California Press.

Gaiha, Raghav and Kulkarni, Vani S. (2006). Common Interest Groups, Village Institutions and the Rural Poor in India: A Review of the District Poverty Initiatives Project, 19 *Contemporary South Asia,* Volume 15, Issue 1: 15–34.

Government of Haryana (2007–2008). *Haryana Economic Survey,* Government of Haryana Press, Haryana Special Economic Zone Act, 2005, Chandigarh: Government of Haryana Press.

——. (1975). *Haryana Development and Regulation of Urban Areas Act* (No. 8 of 1975), Chandigarh: Government of Haryana Press.

Harris, Barbara, Guhan S., and Casen R.H. (1992). *Poverty in India: Research and Policy,* New Delhi: OUP.

Heilbroner, Robert (1980). *The Worldly Philosophers,* New York: Simon and Schuster.

Hobsbawm, Eric (2011). *How to Change the World,* London: Little Brown.

Joseph, T.M. and Sangita, S.N. (1998). Preferential Policies and "Sons-of-the-Soil" Demands: The Indian Experience, *Ethnic Studies Report*, Vol. XVI, No. 1, January.

Leopold, Aldo (1949). *A Sand Country Almanac,* New York: OUP.

Marsh, G.P. (1864). "Man and Nature" in Charles Scribner, 1965, *Physical Geography as Modified by Human Action,* Cambridge: Becknap Press of Harvard University.

Ministry of Panchayati Raj (1998). *Task Force on Panchayati Raj Institutions,* 2001.No P-12025/5/98–RD. 20 December 1998. Report. Vide Notification. No P-12025/5/98–RD. 20 December 1998. New Delhi: Government of India.

Moyo, Sam and Yeros, Paris, Eds. (2005). *Reclaiming the Land: The Resurgence of Rural Movements in Africa, Asia, and Latin America, African* Institute for Agrarian Studies, London: Zed Books.

Olson, Mancur (1993). "Dictatorship, Democracy, and Development", *The American Political Science Review*, Vol. 87, No. 3 (September): 567–76.

Pigou, A.C. (1954). "Some Aspects of the Welfare State," *Diogenes* 7: 1–11 (Summer).

Robinson, James A. (2001). When is the State Predatory? CESifo Working Paper Series No. 178, Available at SSRN: http://ssrn.com/

Singh, Amita (1998). *Public Administration: The Grassroot Concerns,* New Delhi: Mittal.

——. (2004). "Deliberate Democracy and Electoral Fallacy: The Logic of Coexistence, A Comparative Study of Two Globalizing Cities in India" in Jak Jabes, Ed., *The Role of Public Administration in Alleviating Poverty and Improving Governance*. Manila: ADB.

Statesman, 25 October 1976 and 28 October 1976.

Tehelka Magazine (2011). Vol. 8, Issue 5, February 2005.

Wispelaere, Jurgen De (2004). "Altruism, Impartiality and Moral Demands" in Seglow, Jonathan, Ed., *The Ethics of Altruism*, Great Britain: Frank Cass.

6

The Diasporic Identity and Globalization

New Cultural Politics in Hindi Cinema

REETA CHOWDHARI TREMBLAY

In *Dilwale*, Baldev Singh's statement to his daughters, *dhobi ke kutai, na ghar ke na ghat ke* (a washerman's dogs belong neither to the household (whose laundry he washes) nor to the river bank (where he plies his trade) is a declaration of the liminality and marginality of the South Asian diaspora in Great Britain. While expressing the diasporic anxiety associated with a threshold state of ambiguity and indeterminacy regarding power and status in their adopted homeland, this film is a prime example of the assertion of a subsuming Indian identity (to be read as Hindu identity). Rejecting this liminal region as their only dwelling place, home has come to be redefined in relation to the culture and the social community of their past. This has resulted in a recent trend in popular Bombay cinema, exploring the social interaction between the diasporic Indian community and the home (*desi*) culture. The latter is celebrated in contrast to 'vice, crime and high sex drives' in the West. Bombay cinema, a post-colonial border crosser, while consistent with cultural globalization, exposing an Indian audience to consumerism and the virtual West, also addresses the trans-ethnicity and the transnational experiences of the migrant. It joins yet subverts the West by asserting the authenticity and primacy of Indian culture and its values. This cinema revives the fifties' traditional versus modern/western dichotomy, which, reflecting Indian modernity, it had abandoned in the seventies and the eighties. While the fifties' cinema typically called upon a good traditional, *sari*-clad Indian woman to rescue an Indian male seduced by the glitter of the city, modern/western values, drinking and bare-legged cabaret dancers, the nineties' Bollywood cinema, ranting about an America 'where women are kidnapped and morals are loose' introduces the figure of an Indian male, brought up in the West, but certain about his Indianness. In this cinema, the potent West can only be tackled by the male, professing 'what it means to be Indian' to other misguided migrants, particularly confused young migrant Indian women who have been unable to reconcile their in-betweenness and are pushed simultaneously by the liberating experience of individualism of the West and the sanctity of traditional Indian values propagated by their fathers. The Bombay cinema, along with temples, processions and the replication and re-invention of traditions such as *yagyas* (these are prayers according to Vedic traditions, performed on all occasions—for individuals, families, organizations) becomes an innovative instrument for the diasporic community to assert its authenticity.

Bollywood: Globalization and Isomorphism

It is pivotal to note that Indian authenticity is equated with a subsuming Hindu culture—absorbing India's minorities into a specific construction of 'masculine' self and an intolerant cultural/religious community. Major themes explored by the most popular films coming from Bollywood in the last decade have espoused this concept of Indianness (what it means to be Indian and an absolute silence on the place of minority communities, particularly the Muslims) and the situation of the Indian diaspora in North America and Europe. The huge success, extending beyond India's borders into the West, of films such as *Dilwale Dulhaniya Le Jayenge* (Love Bride), *Pardes* (The Foreign Land), *Aur Pyar Ho Gaya* (And Then We Fell in Love) and *Aa Phir Laut Chalain* (Then Let's Return) has been attributed by both the Indian media and the Bombay Film industry in part to lucrative overseas markets (film music sales abroad make up 10–15 per cent of total sales) and to a growing nostalgia among the Indian diaspora for the homeland. In this essay, I suggest that this cinema acts as a symbolic construct in structuring social relations and represents the pan-Indian homogeneous nationalist project, constructed and constantly reinforced in light of the majoritarian community and religious politics in India. This hegemonization of the nationalist project, where repeated reference is made to a monolithic and a unified identity, has its roots, in particular, with the new language of cultural politics in India and, in general, with 'the spatial hardening of states' and ideas in response to the marginalization of states within the global economy and their reduction to 'cartographic illusions'. Mac culture, the global invasion of the television waves through MTV and *The Bold and the Beautiful,* and the invasive transnational consumer industry are being concurrently complemented by a conscious and concrete effort on the part of the political classes of states with developing economies to establish political control over their cultural politics. The concepts of an indigenous Indian (read: Hindu) community and of a home (India) are being played out simultaneously in the recent Bollywood cinema to respond to the internal needs and the construction of a new cultural politics in India, to the displacement of the diasporic Indian community abroad and to the exigencies of globalization. In other words, what is being suggested here is two-fold: First, while, in responding to globalization, states and their political leadership participate in the dismantling of their control over the economic domain, they consciously assert their autonomy over the cultural domain. Particularly in a democratic polity where the maintenance of political legitimacy is essential for the elected leadership, the cultural arena provides an avenue for mobilizing the population towards a national project of unity against the evil forces of the 'foreign'.

Second, the construction of any cultural project (in this case the construction of an 'Indian' identity and the concept of 'home') is indeed a political project. The institutional order and patterns of institutional development directly impact upon the conflation of the cultural and the political project. In other words, institutions structure politics as they internalize elements of the cultural and normative contexts. Any action on the part of the actors is not only shaped by the institutional context within which they operate but it is also embedded in it. To put it simply, Bollywood as a cultural institution is an integral part of the Indian institutional framework and its autonomy might severely be constrained by the logic of institutional development and reproduction. The most obvious explanation for this logic of reproduction is that actors adapt their behaviour to existing institutional frameworks, thereby legitimizing and favouring institutional continuity. This institutional continuity produces repetitive behaviour on the part of the actors.

The new language of cultural politics takes its cues from and is structured in India's material and non-material institutions. While the material institutions include, among others, India's constitution, its party and electoral systems, and the structure of relationships between branches of government, the non-material institutions can be defined as beliefs, values and scripts. Though the latter might emerge as cognitive scripts outside the formal structures, most often norms and values are a function of the material institutions from which they emanate. Bollywood, a booming commercial enterprise, is a significant cultural institution in India and the development of cognitive scripts in the texts and sub-texts underlying the popular films is directly associated with that of the political institutions of the Indian state and the normative ordering used in mobilizing the citizenry. India's popular Hindi cinema has, indeed, played a significant role in constructing or confirming nationalism, whether of the inclusive secular kind as in the early fifties and sixties or of an exclusive nature as during the last two decades, involving group differentiation and providing identity markers as a mechanism of inclusion and exclusion. The roots of these contradictory nationalist projects to a large degree lie in the material institutions of India. The fifties' cinema not only reflected the newly independent India's secular democratic constitutional principles and a hope for progress, based on the principles of growth and justice, it also acted as an agent for institutional reproduction. The Indian popular cinema adapted its behaviour to the existing institutional framework of secularism and socialism, thus legitimizing independent India's newly formed institutions (its constitution, the Congress party's rule and political agenda). In short, one can suggest that through its nationalist, inclusive discourse, the cinema of the fifties and sixties both favoured and legitimized institutional continuity. However, starting with the late 1960s and the early 1970s, the rupture in the Indian political system—the deinstitutionalization of the Congress party, the crystallization of Indian identities (the scheduled castes and tribes) in response to the affirmative action provisions in the Indian constitution, the playing of the Hindu card initially by Mrs Gandhi of the Congress party and later by the Hindu nationalist party, the BJP, the Mandal Commission Report (proposing a 27% reservation of seats in educational and government institutions for backward castes known as OBCs), the Shah Bano case (Rajiv Gandhi and his government's confirmation of the Muslim personal law to an alimony case against the Supreme Court judgment and the subsequent fury of the Hindu nationalists) and the Masjid-Mandir catastrophe (the destruction of the Babri mosque by the Hindu nationalists)—brought about a distinct change in the Indian state—both in the government and the nature of the party system. The party system, dominated by two national parties and a score of regional parties, generated a political discourse that favoured the development of distinct identities and the transformation of politics toward favouring different and competing versions of nationalism—the dominant version entailing a Hindu identity and a Hindu state. Instead of acting independently of the state institutions, Bollywood, the cultural institution, realigned and adjusted itself to this emerging dominant cognitive script. One can understand this kind of transformation in an institution through the concept of legitimacy. Institutions attempt to change themselves when they perceive that they are not in tune with the dominant social and cultural codes. This kind of isomorphism is a conservative strategy adopted by co-existing institutions which maintain their alikeness despite the differences in their environment. Both legitimacy vis-à-vis the citizenry and long-term institutional survival are achieved through this process of maintaining an isomorphic relationship.

The Cultural Project

Dilwale and *Pardes*, two of the films under discussion here, from the very start lay the framework of the cultural project with their articulation of the anxiety of a displaced Indian, the glorification of India as home and its values of affection and generosity. In the opening of the film *Dilwale*, Chaudhary Baldev Singh, on his way to his convenience store in London, stops in a downtown square to feed pigeons and compares his homelessness and the necessity to make a living with the self-centred and nomadic life of the pigeons. He says, 'This is London—the world's largest city. I have been living here for 22 years. Everyday I pass by this street and everyday this street asks me my name, who is Chaudhary Baldev Singh, where has he come from and why he is here. What should I say? After spending half of my life here, this land is foreign to me and I am foreign to this land. Nobody knows me except these pigeons because they are like me. They do not have a country. They go wherever there is grain and once they have eaten to their fill, they fly away'. Baldev Singh asks, 'When will I fly away?' He declares that although necessity has restricted him to this foreign land, 'but I will certainly go back to my country, to my Punjab'. In the film *Pardes*, the multi-millionaire businessman Kishori Lal, who has lived in the United States for 35 years, rejoices over his return to his country, to his home. On a trip 'home', he introduces India to Western friends by saying, 'whenever I return to India, every pore of my body is thrilled. I feel as if I have returned to my mother's lap. It does not matter whether my Bharat has anything, but it has affection. My dear American friends, in the West there is give and take. But in India it is give, give, and give'. Kishori Lal sings, 'I have seen London, Paris and Japan. I have seen Michael and Elvis. But there is nothing like India. This is my India. I love my India.'

Although the concept of the West vis-à-vis Indian culture, in terms of the construction of the 'Other', has been a recurrent theme in the popular Hindi cinema for the past five decades, it is only recently that the homogeneous and villainous 'Other' has been dichotomized and that the Indian identity has been liberated from the specificity of place. In other words, the narrative of the recent cinema is that the Indian identity is both strong and authentic and that it 'instinctively' and 'naturally' endures, irrespective of where one resides, at home or abroad. The notion that there is an 'immutable' link between culture, people, and identity, on the one hand, and specific and delimited territory, on the other hand, has given away to the emerging reality of a diasporic population 'who are enmeshed in circuits of social, economic and cultural ties encompassing both the mother country and the country of settlement' (Lavie and Swedenburg 1996: 14) and they are constantly negotiating and renegotiating their identities and their cultural spaces, depending upon the politics of their location.

While the global cultural economy forms the backdrop where globalization, in the form of large-scale migrations and flows of foreign capital and culture, has weakened those local structures which reinforce local identities and shield them from external structures and processes, it is the Indian legal structures which have acknowledged and reinforced the Indian diaspora's intercontinental identities. In the 1970s, the Indian state formally acknowledged the existence of Indians abroad and laid claim to them, in particular to their wealth, by giving them the legal designation of Non-Resident Indians (NRIs). For the NRIs, this was not only recognition of their Indianness, but also of their affluence and of an unofficial higher ranking in stratified Hindu society. This class of the upwardly mobile, westernized, prosperous and educated, whose Indian accents were modulated with foreign intonations, was to become, unofficially, a caste above the Brahmins. The Foreign Exchange Regulations Act of 1973 transformed this diaspora from 'overseas Indians' to 'persons of Indian origin irrespective of their current nationality'. In exchange for their financial capital, the Indian state was to provide them with a sense of belonging. The regulation defines: 'A person shall be deemed to be of Indian origin if he, at any time, held an Indian passport; or he or either of his parents or any of the grandparents was an Indian and a permanent resident of undivided India at any time'. The designation, however, was not gender neutral: while an Indian male married to a foreign woman can claim NRI status for himself and his family, an Indian female married to a foreign male cannot do so. Shashi Tharoor suggests in his work that the NRIs (in his gloss of the acronym, those who Never Relinquished India) 'are the prodigal sons of a motherland they have left but not forgotten, clinging to a sense of nationhood they cannot define but will not surrender' (Tharoor, 1997: 158). India's major initiative to give the NRIs a sense of belonging when in January 2003, the Ministry of External Affairs joined with the Federation of Indian Chambers of Commerce and Industry to organize *Pravasi Bhartiya Divas*, the first-ever major conference to consult with prominent members of the Indian diaspora. Prime Minister Vajpayee informed delegates that during the forthcoming budget session of parliament, the government intended to introduce legislation allowing NRIs to hold dual citizenship. This decision was based on the recommendation of a committee established in 2002 under the chairmanship of India's former high commissioner to Britain L.M. Singhvi. It found that there were persistent demands from overseas Indians (particularly those in North America and Europe) for dual citizenship. The 1955 Citizenship Act stipulates that a person loses his or her Indian citizenship if he or she voluntarily becomes a citizen of another country. The Government of India introduced legislation in Indian Parliament in May 2003 and passed it unanimously in December 2003. The concept of dual citizenship, now phrased as 'overseas citizenship', grants overseas citizenship to persons of Indian origin belonging to 16 specified countries (Australia, Canada, Finland, France, Greece, Ireland, Israel, Italy, Netherlands, New Zealand, Portugal, Republic of Cyprus, Sweden, Switzerland, United Kingdom and United States of America). No wonder the Indian cinema has fully taken advantage of the diasporic theme, where the glitter and consumerism of the West is virtually brought to the Indian masses and where the virtue of being Indian and the accompanying values of respect for elders and the institution of arranged marriage are reinforced among the confused American-born *desis*.

Identity Formation

Bombay cinema's new emphasis on the diasporic Indian identity is reflective of the new public discourse on 'Indianness', which, though the concept has been consistently espoused by the Hindu nationalist groups such as the RSS and the Bhartiya Jan Sangh since the inception of India, has only gained large-scale momentum in the last two decades. This has come about largely as a result of the serialization by Indian television, *Doordarshan*, of the Hindu epics *Ramayana* and *Mahabharata*, and the emergence of the *Ram Janam Bhumi* issue, supported by the BJP, the Vishva Hindu Parishad and the *Sangh Parivar*. A new political era may be said to have been ushered in with the successful implementation of symbolic politics. BJP leader Advani's

Rath Yatra (pilgrimage) from Somnath to Ayodhya in September 1990 in order to mobilize the masses' support for rebuilding the temple in Ayodhya that had been destroyed centuries earlier by the Muslim invaders, was a mission undertaken to restore the national honour, overcome caste differences and unify the Hindu (which should be read 'national' in BJP terms) community. The chariot carrying Advani was reminiscent of those portrayed in epics serialized on the television over the preceding three years. Although Advani did not actually don religious garb, images of Ram and the Ayodhya temple adorned the chariot and formed the large background in front of which he stood, with folded hands, as large numbers of saffron-clad volunteers followed the procession. Advani made stops in nine states and did road-side *puja*, wearing a crown, once again invoking the image of epic leadership. Advani categorically stated that this *yatra* had no political motives and was fundamentally an act of devotion to Lord Ram, thus equating *Ram bhakti* to *Lok bhakti*. In other words, religious goals were made co-terminus with national goals and Hindu identity with national identity. National television, through a shift in its policy of broadcasting religious programming in serializing the Hindu epics, had already brought the Hindu rituals and myths into the public arena and identified them with the general culture. In conformity with the Indian state's goals of secularism or equi-distance from all religions, the television allocated a half-hour to devotional music, representing all the communities. However, during the emergency, the information and broadcasting Ministry had allowed the broadcasting in northern India of Tulsi's *Ram Charitmanas*. The broadcasting of *Ramayana* was defended by the retired Secretary of the Ministry as cultural and not contradicting the goals of secularism. However, he maintained that 'the fact of the matter is that the Hindus constitute 83 per cent of the country's population and the Indian ethos is predominantly Hindu and *Ramayana* is its centre-piece' (*The Times of India*, August 8, 1988). Not only was the Hindu epic brought into the public space, the equation of Hindu values with the national values (India was in essence largely Hindu) and the associated gendered social relations became the implicit hallmarks of the new public discourse. A woman's virginity, purity, morality, faithfulness and obedience were underscored in the epic story and epitomized in the event of *agni pariksha*, where Sita enters the fire to prove to Ram and society the indestructibility of her virtue. Although the public domain was expanded to include religious and political female leaders to espouse the cause of the temple, women's traditional roles were reinforced. For example, the BJP's newspaper *Organizer* states how young women traditionally carried *kumbh* on their head to greet the *rath* (while male devotees pull the chariots in a *yatra* (procession) through the streets, it is the women who greet the chariot and the procession, perform *puja* and pray to the Lord to steer the chariots of their daily lives). Interestingly, the Hindu community in North America has actively supported the new public discourse. The support of the local chapters of the VHP and the *Overseas Friends* of the BJP to the success of the *Ram Janam Bhumi* movement is evident in the fact that the BJP has included the concerns of the NRIs in their party platform.

While the films of the fifties clearly underlined the dichotomy between the traditional (rural/Indian) and the modern (urban/Western) where conflict between the two was resolved in favour of the traditional, the films of the sixties and the seventies celebrated the fusion and intermingling of *desi* and *videsi*. The earlier symbols associated with villain and villainess—whiskey, disco-dancing, skirt-wearing females, cigarettes and the glittering seductive powers of the city (all of which distracted the good Indian male protagonist who would typically finally be liberated by a *sari*-clad, good Indian woman) —were largely abandoned in favour of an Indian modernity, capable of indigenizing values which it had picked and chosen from the West. In the new hybrid culture where 'the Other' was indigenized and subversively appropriated, disco-dance and whiskey came to co-exit with the *desi* values of arranged marriages and the priority of the requirements of the collectivity over those of the individual (Tremblay, 1996). However, the nineties' cinema with its prominent diasporic themes has effectively reintroduced the 'Indian-versus-the-Other dichotomy'. While the fifties' cinema binaries clearly revealed an anxiety about the West and its corrupting influences, the recent films show a self-confident assertiveness of Indianness and its privileging over the West. In the newly articulated dichotomy of 'us versus them', there is no place for liminality and hybridity. Baldev Singh in *Dilwale* is relieved that his daughters are well schooled in the Indian/Hindu values while being brought up in London and are not stuck in an in-between culture. He refers to the diasporic youth as *dhobi ke kutai, na ghar ke na ghat ke* (the washerman's dog who belongs neither to the home nor to the river bank). This assertiveness not only corresponds to a shift in the political discourse and the success of the BJP in conflating Hindu identity with the national identity, but is also reflective of the self-confidence of the Indian middle classes for whom the exoticism of West has been fading as accessibility to Western consumer culture becomes a reality. Ashis Nandy in his recent work on Indian cinema uses the metaphor of the slum to describe the cinema as a major political statement and as the language for a new form of politics. The metaphor refers to the lower middle class' rising expectations from its exposure to the global market and its constant anxiety about slipping back into the life of the slum never to reemerge. For Nandy, this numerous lower middle class upon whom the political class (the upper-middle class) is dependent for their electoral success constitutes the ideological basis of Indian politics. The political class/upper-middle classes, in turn, maintain 'continuities with the lower-middle class in political and cultural tastes'. Nandy suggests that the political and cultural self-expression must be contexualized within the psychological state and the material expectations of the large lower-middle class. For him, the language of the slum in India is the lower-middle class reading of the culture of the *haute bourgeoisie* into which it breaks in fantasy, memories of a peasant or rural past serving as a pastoral 'paradise' from which it has been banished, fears about the urban-industrial jungle into which it feels it has already strayed, and anxieties about the 'amoral' frame of modern life into which it fears it might any day slip. It is a psychological existence at the margins of at least two utopias, one of them located—as with all utopias—in the future and the other paradoxically in the past (Nandy, 1998: 5). The Indian cinema represents, reaffirming these lower-middle class sensibilities, 'the low-brow version of the values, ambitions and anxieties of Indians who are caught between two cultures, two lifestyles, and two visions of a desirable society' (ibid.: 6).

In *Dilwale* and *Pardes*, the theme of the land is the background within which the binaries of good and evil are played out. It is the countryside which is the repository of the traditional values and a summary statement of 'what is India/Bharat' and 'what is Indianness'. Very often the referent is *desh ki mitti* (soil of the country) and its beautiful smell. In *Pardes*, the young protagonist Arjun wants to sanitize the big country house and clear of it of the odours of the countryside and the animals, cows and buffaloes who occupy space with the family so that Rajiv, the corrupt westernized Indian son of Kishori Lal, would come to like India and agree to marry Ganga, his father's choice. Ganga convinces Arjun to bring the animals back by saying, 'In order to make relationships, we do not break the old ones.' The countryside is presented as an organic entity. On the other hand, money and wealth also figure prominently in the cinema. The West is portrayed largely via its tourist spots, casinos in Atlantic City and Las

Vegas and Disney Land and by the wealthy lifestyle of the diasporic Indian community. The characters constantly negotiate and renegotiate two utopias, of the past and of the future. In *Aa Phir Laut Chalain*, when Rohil receives his first salary, he buys tickets to India for the mistreated elderly parents of his Indian friend (who strayed away from the path of duty and respect for parents and uses them as his servants in his motel). He also buys two television sets, one each for Iqbal and Sardar, his two benefactors in New York City, so that they can watch cricket matches between India and Pakistan on their respective TV sets. Rohil can thus fulfil the desired Indian values yet at the same time indulge in the consumerist desires of his two friends.

In *Pardes*, Kishori Lal, a US-based NRI who has made good, comes to India in search of a suitable bride (a virgin imbued with good Indian values) for his son, Rajiv. He finds this paragon in the person of Ganga and sends his son, Rajiv, and adopted son, Arjun, to India to check her out. The film balances the rural first half with a Los Angeles-based second half. Anyone familiar with the Indian cinema and its practices can probably imagine parts of the story line. Ganga is the Ganges, symbol of purity and Arjun is the brave warrior in the epic *Mahabharata* who has been entrusted to save the honour of the Pandavas. *Pardes*' village belle, Ganga, who accompanies her in-laws to their Los Angles home and is waiting to be married, refuses to have pre-martial sex with her fiancé. Arjun is Ganga's saviour in the US, where she knows no one. Repeatedly throughout the film, Rajiv constantly questions India and its value structures. 'Is Indian society all about segregating men and women before marriage?' He cannot understand the concept of chastity and virginity. He expresses both astonishment and disgust when he adds: 'Yet, the minute they marry they create one of the most populated nations on this planet.' Arjun, on the other hand, instinctively recognizes his duty as a male, to protect Ganga. The film dwells on tradition, culture and the need for conformity, entrusting the fate of the protagonists in the hands of their elders. Interestingly, one of the film's main settings is the Red Fort, Fatehpur Sikri, in Haridwar, constantly reinforcing the linkage between Indian cultural and national identity. Similarly, in *Dilwale*, the father disapproves of his daughter's choice of her lover as her husband (although he is an Indian whom she meets in Switzerland during her holidays) and sends her to India where a marriage is arranged for her. Her lover, the NRI hero, comes to India and the whole story revolves around his attempts to win over the father before the arranged ceremony can take place. In these films, the NRIs are the ones who move back and forth, between India and the West, reassured and reassuring about traditional values. While the NRI adds value to the culture by endorsing it (he has succeeded in terms of material wealth but still retains his Indian values), he nevertheless leaves home only to discover the essential Indianness.

In *Aur Pyar Ho Gaya* (1997), Aashi's marriage has been arranged to a rich, international, garment businessman. Since Aashi's friend just died, supposedly due to her arranged marriage, Aashi, with the help of her grandfather, convinces her over-bearing father to let her spend some time in Switzerland. This urbane Indian heroine sets out to meet her prospective bridegroom, an NRI, and ensure that he has proper Indian values. She assumes a fake identity, falls in love with another part-time NRI who pretends to be her fiancé. This ensues a tale of mistaken identity and deception, but as expected, Aashi eventually falls in love with him. Meanwhile, her father causes problems in the couple's wedding plans. When she discovers her true love to be an imposter, she leaves him. He finally wins her back for his courageous display of his love. Here the hero subscribes to all Indian values—purity, chastity/virginity, protection of an unmarried woman in the public space.

In *Aa Phir Laut Chalain*, Raj, an unemployed young man, comes to New York in search for a job. His childhood friend, an NRI, refuses to provide him assistance. Raj is given shelter and assistance by the local Indian community, particularly by two taxi drivers, Iqbal (a Sikh) and Sardar (a Pakistani Muslim from the North-West). Simran who had come from India to visit her brother leaves her brother's office after she discovers that her brother and sister-in-law had arranged her marriage to an older rich white American in exchange for money. Raj, Iqbal and Sardar offer her home. Raj, obsessed with getting a green card, allows himself to be linked with an NRI Indian girl who has completely lost her Indian values and drinks, gambles and is not concerned about her chastity and purity. Simran is the saviour who not only makes Raj see the value of her love but unites him with his father. Both return to home/India and to the Indian values where they reunite Raj's estranged father with his mother. What is notable in this film is that, India in New York is defined in terms of an unpartitioned India and the nostalgia of the diasporic community is for the old, not the new India. Although Iqbal is called Hindustani and Sardar Pakistani and though they often fight during the Indo-Pakistan cricket matches (they have collected the broken TV sets which, over the years, each had broken when his country lost the match), they subscribe to the good old Indian values where affection, loyalty, generosity and brotherhood constitute the moral framework. The cinema problematizes the notion of a singular identity and a singular home. The golden past/home is pre-partitioned India, a safe place which denies exclusion, power relations and difference. The dislocation felt by Iqbal and Sardar is doubly troubling for them—dislocation resulting from the pre-partitioned India and the dislocation from their exile to the West.

All the four films discussed above emphasize the major themes of Indianness as a return to traditional values such as marriage, chastity, purity, honour, respect for elders underlying the traditional rural structures. It is interesting to note that the cinema parallels the male-centric Hindu nationalist project. Gender and community interests intersect in the production of an irreducible and an essentialist identity where women emerge as important signifiers of differences between groups. The Indian/Hindu identity is defined through the conduct of women within the narrow social spaces as articulated in the customary strictures of tradition. Women are not only the repositories of traditional values of *dharam* and *maryada* but through their positioning in the private realm of the household are also the passive enforcers of customs and religious prescriptions. Radhakrishnan aptly notes that 'by mobilizing the inner/outer distinction against the "the outernes" of the West, nationalist rhetoric makes "woman" the pure and ahistorical signifier of "interiority". In the fight against the enemy from the outside, something within gets even more repressed, and "woman" becomes the mute but necessary allegorical ground for the transactions of nationalist history' (Radhakrishnan, 1996: 192). In order to reintroduce the dichotomy between the public and the private spaces, the potent male must liberate the private from newly introduced immorality of the public/western domain. The male hero is privileged and moves easily between the two domains. Raj in *Dilwale* arranges Simran's Indian household, helps in the preparation of the wedding and its rituals. Home must be brought back to its true Indian self—characterized by purity and represented by women. This realignment of the private space is essential to the construction of Indianness. Women are safe and protected within their domestic spaces. Once they move out the boundaries of these protected spaces, they are responsible for whatever happens to them. In the Indian cinema's new cultural project, the Indian women have unwittingly allowed the foreign, public values into their private domain, thus denying themselves the safety of home and exposing themselves to the danger presented by the corrupt values of the West. And, therefore, gender codes need to be re-established and private spaces must be separated from public spaces.

All four films centre around the male members of the household while the females are the passive instruments and showpieces through which the value of Indianness is constituted and reinforced. The older male (In *Dilwale*, Baldev Singh and in *Pardes*, Kishori Lal) sets the framework of the Indian identity and the younger male (Raj in *Dilwale* and Arjun in *Pardes*) articulate these values and perform a didactic role. The younger male who 'instinctively' knows these values never deters from the 'right' path. Raj refuses to elope with Simran, even when her mother requests him to do so. He can only wed Simran when her father is convinced of his good values and true Indianness. Similarly, in *Pardes*, Arjun's staunch adherence to authentic values and his right conduct have to be acknowledged by Ganga's father and his own adopted father before he marries Ganga. Indianness is constantly defined in terms of chastity and virginity and the marriage as the final destiny of the girl. The traditions of marriage and respect for elders are the recurring themes in these movies. In *Aur Pyar Ho Gaya*, the father convinces his daughter to get married and states that 'it is our tradition that a father is only the caretaker of the treasure that is a girl, he looks after "it" for somebody else'. While the Indian females can get distracted in the West, the good NRI male is very confident of his Indian values and thereby saves the female from making grave mistakes. In an interesting incident where three foreigners (whites) attack and try to molest the Indian heroine in Switzerland, the Indian hero chases them and saves her chastity. In another scene, when she walks in her sleep (which she does regularly) she is guided by the hero to his room in the hotel where he watches over her protectively all night. She wakes up the next morning and is panicky and aghast to find herself in his bed. This panic is related to the notions of loss of chastity/virginity. This notion has an even more emphatic resonance in *Dilwale* where there is a whole conversation between the two leads, linking Indianness to the importance of woman's chastity. Simran who gets drunk on a college trip to Europe and who wakes up in Raj's bed and Raj's shirt is immediately worried about her virginity. Raj convinces her that he is a true Indian and would never do anything which is against the Hindustani values. In *Pardes*, again this notion is explored in a relatively significant episode in the movie. Ganga finally leaves her fiance, Rajiv, the westernized son of Kishori Lal, when in a Las Vegas hotel, he tries to rape her after being told by Ganga that there could be no sex before marriage. That's Ganga's final breaking point. Uptil that time, she tolerates Rajiv's vices such as drinking, smoking and having sex with North American girls. Chastity and virginity, the ultimate traditional moral codes of the Hindu society, can under no circumstances be compromised. Similarly, in another crucial cinematic moment in *Aur Pyar Ho Gaya*, the heroin's woollen top gets caught in a branch and she only realizes this after a few seconds by which time, her top has unravelled enough to expose a fair bit of skin. In a modern replay of the Draupadi scene from the *Mahabharata* where Krishna protects Draupadi's virtue, the hero in this film rolls her back towards the branch and re-covers her body/modesty/chastity.

Where are the Minorities?

Is it a coincidence or has there been a conscious choice not to have any non-Hindu characters in all the four movies? Absence of the Muslim characters, except the role of Sardar in *Aa Phir Laut Chalain*, suggests the denial of plurality, divisions and differences in inventing authenticity and an all-embracing homogeneous identity. The role of Sardar is made possible within the context of loyalties to a pre-partitioned India. And, moreover, Sardar is supposed to be a Pathan, just like *Kabuli Wallah* (the film is based on a Rabindranath Tagore's 1916 story where a fruit seller from Kabul develops a loving friendship with a five-year-old girl. It is a story about love and family relationships) for whose values of honour and loyalty, the Hindu India had great admiration. In the over-arching Indian identity, Pathans' values are those of the united India. As mentioned above, in the newly articulated dichotomy of us versus them, there is no place for liminality and hybridity. 'Us' does not include minority cultures and denies them a space for the articulation of their identity. What amazes the reader of these films is that there is a complete silence about the minorities, as if these do not exist. By not acknowledging their presence, they become marginalized to the discourse. Khilani confirms this silence: 'a strong Muslim aesthetic impress on the Indian cinema is undeniable; but it is much harder, for instance, to see any distinctively Muslim political presence in the Indian cinema, nor has it proved possible to establish a distinct Muslim voice. In this sense, Muslims remain as unrepresented here as they are in the political arena' (Khilani, 2002). This silence about minorities is reflective of the consolidation of Hindu nationalism. While in the initial stage, it felt the need to define *hindutva* and the place of minorities within it, as over the years, the hegemonic ideology has become embedded in Hindu psyche, it has chosen to ignore the question of minorities. The Gujarat elections in 2002 provide an excellent example of this 'silence'. In Gujarat, the site of a brutal carnage of some 2,000 Muslims, the BJP's Narendra Modi and other Hindu leaders decided to work on Hindu feeling and kept the

Godhra incident (in which 58 Hindus had been killed) a consistent theme in election speeches. Even the Congress party, after castigating Narendra Modi for the Gujarat killings, decided to adopt a soft *hindutva* line. It chose as its leader Shankersingh Vaghela, the man who had helped launch Advani's *Rath Yatra* in 1991 from Gujarat. The Indian popular cinema has reinforced this dominant language of politics.

Are we seeing a shift in this silence? In one of the recent popular films, *Kal Ho Naa Ho* (2003) where the plot of individualistic West versus community-oriented Indian society is played out in New York city, there is an espousal of Indian values (Hindustani) of patriarchy, marriage, extended families and there is an attempt to generate a multiethnic identity based on Hinduism, Sikhism and Christianity. Though space for Muslims still remain undefined in this film, it is possible that the institutional transformation in India has begun with a change in political power at the central level? In a Punjabi/Christian family, Naina (Preity Zinta), has the responsibilities of taking care of her younger brother and sister, as well as helping her mother, Jennifer, handle the family's unsuccessful restaurant business. The film's hero, Aman (Shahrukh Khan), arrives in New York to take care of his deteriorating medical condition, although he hides this from all. He moves into Naina's small Indian neighbourhood, and with him he brings his joyfulness and charming personality. He helps solve everyone's problems and helps them face the obstacles and challenges that life usually has in store. Although Naina is in love with him (and he with her—a fact she is not aware of), Aman forces her to marry their common friend Rohit (Saif Ali Khan). It is interesting to note that the hero in this film uses the term 'Hindustani' to define the Indian identity. In encouraging Jennifer, the mother, to remodel her restaurant and convert it into an ethnic Indian restaurant, he describes the values of the Hindustani society and culture. He says, 'We must bring Hindustan here, spread it'. 'Hindustan is our advantage' and 'Hindustan can achieve anything, anytime'. Indeed, in this film, 'Bharat' is replaced by Hindustan signalling a plural, multi-ethnic India. However, the Hindustani values portrayed in the film maintain continuity with the gendered, masculine cultural project of 'what constitutes Indianness'. It would stand to explain that there is neither visible tensions within India's institutional landscape (Indian political institutional normative framework) nor are any shifts in the external environment of these institutions (both the Indian diaspora and the Indian civil society are consuming enthusiastically the gendered and a Hindu version of Indianness) to bring forward a change in Bollywood's cultural project.

References

Khilani, Sunil (2002). "A New Cultural Lexicon" *The Hindu*, September 1. http://www.hinduonnet.com/thehindu/lr/2002/09/01/stories/2002090100080100.htm

Lavie, Smadar and Swedenburg, Ted (1996). "Introduction: Displacement, Diaspora, and Geographies" in Smadar Lavie and Ted Swednburg (Eds.), *Displacement, Diaspora and Geographies of Identity.* Durham and London: Duke University Press.

Nandy, Ashis (1998). "Introduction: Indian Popular cinema as a Slum's Eye View of Politics" in Ashis Nandy (Ed.), *The Secret Politics of Our Desires: Innocence, Culpability and Indian Popular Cinema*. New Delhi: Oxford University Press.

Radhakrishnan, R. (1996). *Between Home and Locations: Diasporic Mediations*. Minneapolis: University of Minnesota Press.

Tharoor, Shashi (1997). *India: From the Midnight to the Millennium*. New Delhi: Viking, Penguin Books India.

Tremblay, Reeta Chowdhari (1996). "Representation and Reflection of Self and Society in the Bombay Cinema" *Contemporary South Asia,* 5:3, 303–18.

7

Research and Development in Central Public Sector Enterprises

A Macro Analysis

R.K. MISHRA

The basis for the establishment of public sector enterprises (PSEs) in India is the socialist philosophy which believes in the role of government as an agent for change and entrepreneurial function (Srivastava et al., 2006). Friedmann (1954) termed 'public enterprise' as an institution operating a service of an economic or social character on behalf of the government but as an independent legal entity. Though

---

This chapter has been written for incorporation in the felicitation volume of Dr O.P. Dwivedi on his 75th Birthday. Dr Dwivedi is known as an original thinker, an academic who has extended the boundaries of public policy and public administration and made these relevant and topical to the present-day socio-economic and administrative problems. My relationship with Dr Dwivedi has several facets. I have benefited from Dr Dwivedi's contributions for the last 40 years in the field of environment, governance, energy, ethics and morality and performance management in government. Dr Dwivedi's stint as Advisor (Environment) to Prime Minister, Mrs Indira Gandhi has given a basic building block to develop environmental administration in India. Dr Dwivedi played a key role in introducing me to the International Institute of Administrative Sciences, Brussels and its affiliate International Association of Schools and Institutes of Administration (IASIA), Brussels. On Dr Dwivedi's suggestion, I have been representing India as Vice President of IASIA. It was Dr Dwivedi who appreciated the idea of internationalizing research on energy, environment, food security and well being. In appreciation of his ideas, IASIA set up a Working Group on Energy, Environment and Food Security. Dr Dwivedi's contribution as Expert on Public Administration to the United Nations is held very high. Dr Dwivedi has contributed in various ways to my growth, learning and professional development. His divine blessings will always guide me in all situations in future.

responsible to the public through government and parliament and subject to some direction by the government, the public enterprise has an independent and separate fund of its own. The public sector in India could be sub-divided into three categories: (i) departmentally owned and managed establishments; (ii) public corporations; and (iii) governmental enterprises established under the Companies Act, 1956. These governmental enterprises could be further divided into two categories; (a) Central Public Sector Enterprises (CPSEs); and (b) State Level Public Enterprises (SLPEs).

CPSEs in India have undergone a very turbulent phase in the past, which led to the initiation of public sector reforms through de-regulation and de-reservation. During the early 1990s, the Indian economy passed through the most difficult time with huge imbalances in the internal and external accounts. These unfavourable developments led to a severe external liquidity crunch, which turned into a crisis of unprecedented dimensions. It was against this backdrop that the Government of India initiated the reform process by launching 'Stabilization and Structural Adjustment Programmes' for reviving the existing public sector enterprises both at the central and state levels. It was also identified that the thrust should be to foster sustainable economic and social development and a competitive market economy that encouraged investment, employment and trade. In this process, some of the enterprises were identified for privatization as a multi-prolonged strategy to mobilize funds from healthy CPSEs or SLPEs and to reduce the financial legacies of the chronically sick entities (Mishra, Kumari and Kiranmai, 2010).

The success of a nation is deeply intertwined with its 'capabilities' for innovation of technologies that compete in the world market. Development of capabilities is a long-term process, which requires a country to pass through different phases of learning, creating the required physical infrastructure, human capital, institutions that support these activities, and creating interlinkages among them (Bhattacharya and Lal, 2008). In other words, the forces of globalization, liberalization, privatization, and technology are combining to make life harder than ever for public sector enterprises in this globalizing world. Therefore, use of technology and competitiveness are becoming the key to survival of public enterprises in an open and market-driven economy. For this purpose it is necessary to enquire whether Indian CPSEs are technologically competitive or not?

In recent years, the increasing involvement of the public sector is an important phenomenon in the industrialization of developing countries. Over the past two to three decades, the CPSEs have played a key role in accelerating the growth of Indian economy. The Government of India has consistently emphasized the importance of technology development and technology upgradation in the CPSEs and has viewed it as an engine for rapid industrialization and in catching up with advances in technology. In the absence of critical inputs, particularly technology, however, the strong position the state has assumed is inadequate to meet the objective of rapid and widespread industrialization of the country. Given the technological gap in the product structure, the import of critical inputs like technology and capital from developed countries was found to be expedient (Pillai, 1978).[1]

As far as spending on research and development (R&D) and technological development are concerned, a number of empirical studies have highlighted its importance and impact on productivity and the profitability of enterprises in various sectors (manufacturing and services), both at the firm level and industry level. Liu and White (1997) have explored the relative contributions of technology and domestic inputs to innovation and concluded that, in developing economies, innovation is driven by the synergy between the absorptive capacity of the R&D personnel and investment in sources of new knowledge embedded in foreign technologies. Hu et al. (2005) found that technology transfer—whether domestic or foreign—affects productivity only through its interactions with in-house R&D. For developing countries like India, Schware (2000) has highlighted the application of technology to improve public sector performance.

The Present Research

The present research is an effort to study the role played by technology in the process of uplifting and maintaining growth performance in CPSEs amidst competition, the R&D investment scenario in Indian CPSEs, and growing innovativeness in selected CPSEs. The paper is divided into three sections. The first section examines international R&D investment trends in major industrialized and emerging economies. The international investment provides a benchmark for Indian R&D investment. The second part of the paper examines R&D investment by selected CPSEs. The analysis has been done for the years from 2005–06 to 2009–10. The data on investment by CPSEs on R&D, expenditure on royalties, technical know-how fees, investment on software development, Information Technology and other professional services, were analysed to find a pattern of investment trends and their competitiveness. The final section sums up the research findings and offers policy conclusions.

Data and Research Methodology

The research draws its foundation from published information sources and a number of interviews with officials from selected CPSEs. The analysis uses both quantitative and qualitative source materials and information obtained from both primary and secondary sources. Primary sources include information collected through a structured questionnaire. The questionnaire deals with innovation in public sector enterprises with a focus on the following topics: R&D policy, innovation activities and expenditures, information channels for innovation activities, and benefits from innovative practices. Secondary sources include annual reports of the CPSEs, Central Statistical Organization (CSO), Centre for Monitoring Indian Economy's (CMIE) *Prowess* database, Department of Science and Technology (DST), Government of India, etc. CMIE's *Prowess* database has been extensively used to analyse the CPSE's expenditure on technology. A simple OLS regression technique has been used to understand how expenditure on R&D and technology is impacting the profitability of the CPSEs.

The present research divided the CPSEs into two broad categories, viz., manufacturing and services. Again, in each category enterprises have been divided into three categories on the basis of their technology content: low technology-based, medium technology-based and high technology-based (Table 1).[2]

Table 1

Sectoral Technology Capabilities

Sector	*Technology Capability Level*
Metal forming and forging	Low technology-based
Steel	Medium technology-based
Machine tools	Low technology-based
Pharmaceuticals	Medium technology-based
Chemicals	Low technology-based
Electrical and electronics	Low technology-based
Automotive	Medium technology-based
Auto components	High technology-based
Information technology	High technology-based
Telecommunication	High technology-based
Petrochemicals	Medium technology-based
Light engineering	Low technology-based
Power	Medium technology-based
Transport	Low technology-based
Fertilizers	Medium technology-based

Source: UNIDO (2005); IPE Databank on CPSEs 2010.

The analysis is based on the data taken from the CMIE *Prowess* database and the annual reports of selected CPSEs. The time series data of 70 CPSEs (comprises Maharatna, Navaratna, Miniratna I and Miniratna II enterprises)[3] obtained in the above said sectors for an in-depth examination of their technological soundness. The scope of present research does not include technology mapping related issues in the private sector enterprises.

Literature Review

In the literature on R&D in public enterprises innovation, implementation and dissemination of technologies and practices are recognized as highly vital to economic growth and development. Over the last two to three decades researchers have shown considerable interest in various aspects of technology in enterprises for formulation of strategies to planning and implementation of technology in organizations (Bakos and Treacy, 1986; Grover et al., 1993; King and Sethi, 1993; Venkatraman, 1994; Yetton et al., 1994). There has been a shift in focus from technology being conceived as a means of improving the efficiency of processes (Ein-Dor and Segev, 1978; Nolan, 1979; Rockart, 1979) to its use as a strategic tool in the hands of management and enabling re-engineering and transforming the ways enterprises do business (Galliers, 1993; Venkatraman, 1994). Through the adoption of newer, more advanced technologies and practices, industries in general and enterprises in particular, can increase their production capabilities, improve productivity, and expand lines of new products and services (Earl, 2002). Ferrantino (1992) investigated the effects of expenditure on R&D and purchase of technology on costs in the Indian manufacturing sector using firm-level data. The research found that expenditures for R&D, royalties and technical fees potentially induced the efficiency. The effects of expenditure on technology are found to vary by industry, by type of expenditure and by domestic or foreign origin of the seller.

Kumar and Siddharthan (1994) found that technological activities of enterprises from India to be important in explaining their export performance. The estimated Tobit models predicted that in developing countries like India, an enterprise's technological activity favourably influences its export behaviour only in medium and low-technology industries. Katrak (1985) found that enterprises in the countries like Brazil, India and South Korea, recognizing the importance of technical progress for improving their enterprise performance, have been following a strategy of using imported and indigenous technologies.

The major reason for turning to imported technologies in the first instance is that they involve lower uncertainty and/or a more favourable time-cost trade-off than indigenous technologies. However, the subsequent R&D is required because the imported technologies are often not entirely appropriate to the domestic consumers' tastes, market size, factor prices, etc.

Li, in his current research, empirically investigates the effect of three types of investment in acquiring technological knowledge (in-house R&D, importing foreign technology, and purchasing domestic technology) on the innovation output of Chinese firms in high-tech industries based on the data set of the National Bureau of Statistics of China (NBSC). The research found that investing in foreign technology does not enhance innovation in domestic enterprises, unless it is coupled with an industry's own in-house R&D effort. Literature on technology mapping of public enterprises argues that despite the potential offerings by globalization and liberalization, the benefits of international technology transfer can only be delivered with parallel indigenous innovation efforts by the domestic enterprises and the presence of modern institutional and governance structures that are conducive to innovation systems (Fu et al., 2010). Technology is no longer considered as merely a supportive tool for existing organizational processes, but is perceived as an integrating tool for initiating business changes and shaping structures in enterprises in tune with business needs (Kanungo et al., 2001).

The existing literature emphasizes two sources of innovation in enterprises, viz., internal development and external collaborations. Teece (1992) averred that state-of-the-art technologies are often developed from tacit knowledge that is built internally through investments or 'learning by doing'. However, recent research has suggested that an enterprise level of innovation can and should be evaluated by considering internal research efforts jointly with external R&D collaborations (Fabrizio, 2009). Fleming and Sorenson (2004) suggest that an enterprise must clearly understand the directions intended for internal research and use external R&D to complement it. In recent years, open innovation has been changing the way enterprises function, which also help them in increasing their revenues by working closely with the customers and developing new products (Chesbrough, 2011).

Indian CPSEs and Spending on R&D

The expenditure on R&D by an enterprise is the most important indicator of innovation, i.e., the extent of investments in future directed efforts on new products/processes, new designs, novel solutions/discovery, new packaging, etc., or on improving the quality of the services or goods (Kshitij et al., 2008). Enterprises in developing countries have, essentially, two sources for their technological requirements. The first source is from its own in-house R&D centres and the second one is from external sources, which are either from within the country or from abroad. There is of course a relationship between the two sources. Very often enterprises first purchased technology from external sources and then adapted it to local conditions by performing in-house R&D efforts. The literature reviewed (Katrak, 2002) shows that in-house R&D and technology acquisition efforts to be complementary in nature. Mani (2009) averred that in-house R&D expenditures have increased tremendously since 1991and since public enterprises have a freer access to external sources of technology in the wake of liberalization of the conditions governing the importation of technologies from abroad. According to Mohan (2008), based on data from Reserve Bank of India, most Indian enterprises import technology from abroad through the employment of consultants.

Over the years there has been a cyclical increase and fall in the number of Indian enterprises reporting having R&D. The years 1997

Figure 1

Average R&D Expenditure, 2005–2009 (₹ in crores)

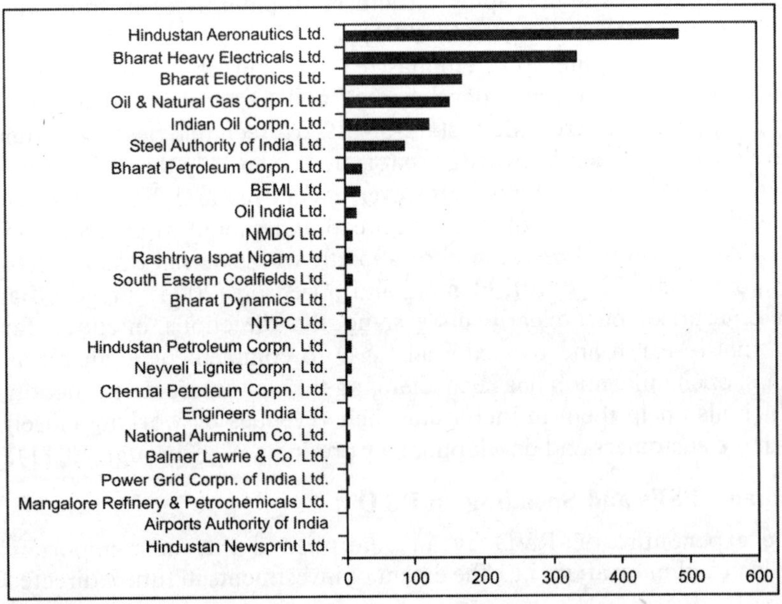

Figure 2

Top CPSEs Expenditure on Royalties, Technical Know-how, Fees, etc.
(₹ in crores)

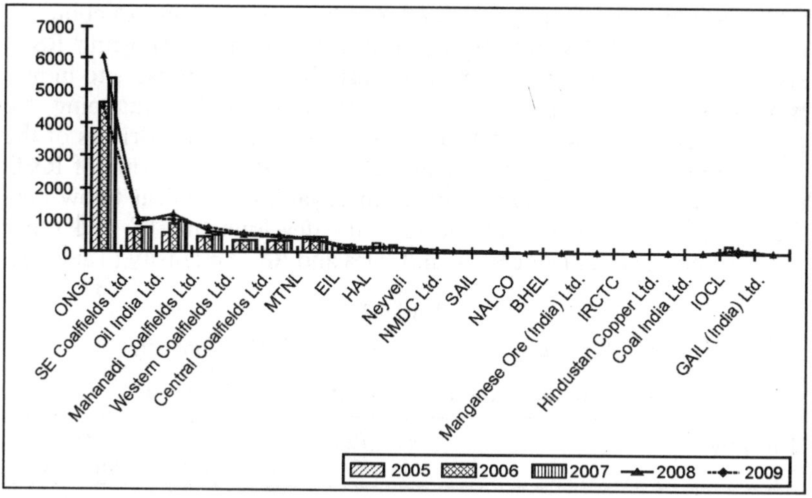

Figure 3

Top CPSEs Average Expenditure on Software Development, IT and other Professional Services 2005–2009 (₹ in crores)

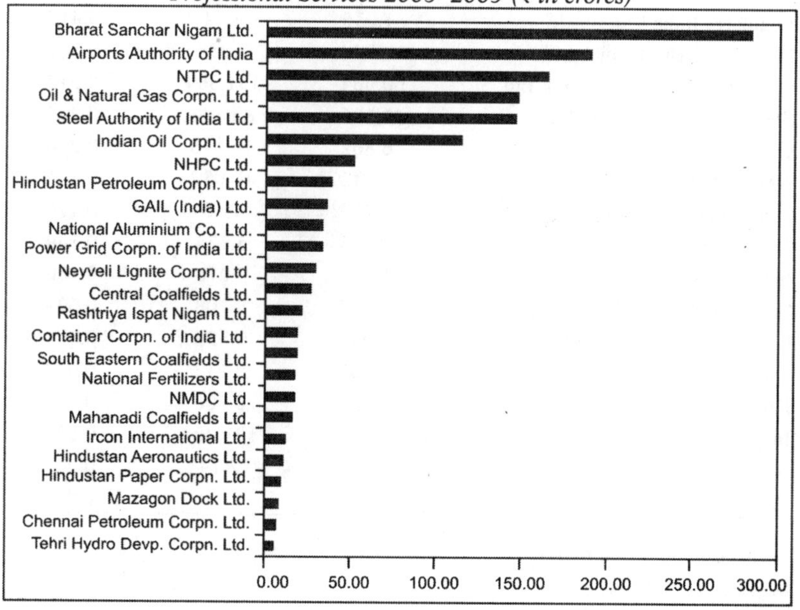

and 2004 had the maximum number of R&D reporting companies. More importantly, this table exhibits the fact that companies doing R&D have under them most part of the market, close to 60 per cent, and this share rose from a little under 50 per cent in 1995 to about 60 per cent by 1998 (Kshitij et al., 2008). The sectors reporting R&D spanned from drugs and pharmaceuticals, dry cells, fertilisers to industrial machinery, marine foods, etc. In terms of technology mapping, the present study observed 70 CPSEs. To observe the major drivers of the above trends, the paper investigated the top CPSEs in terms of R&D investment (Figure 1), expenditure on royalties, technical know-how fees (Figure 2), investment on software development, IT and other professional services (Figure 3), and sales and R&D intensity (Table 2).

Table 2

Top CPSEs Sales, R&D Investment and R&D Intensity

(Average Sales and R&D Investment, 2005–2009)

Enterprise	*Sales (Rs in crores)*	*R&D Investment*	*R&D Intensity**
Hindustan Aeronautics Ltd.	8,621	485.528	5.632
Bharat Electronics Ltd.	4,091	170.04	4.156
Bharat Heavy Electricals Ltd.	20,143	336.582	1.671
BEML Ltd.	2,547	21.062	0.827
Engineers India Ltd.	1,035	4.34	0.419
Manganese Ore (India) Ltd.	728	2.238	0.307
Oil and Natural Gas Corpn. Ltd.	60,964	151.564	0.249
Steel Authority of India Ltd.	41,186	85.886	0.209
Oil India Ltd.	6,862	14.146	0.206
NMDC Ltd.	5,142	10.032	0.195
Hindustan Paper Corpn. Ltd.	785	1.38	0.176
Neyveli Lignite Corpn. Ltd.	3,425	5.774	0.169
Balmer Lawrie & Co. Ltd.	1,425	2.278	0.160
South Eastern Coalfields Ltd.	8,757	8.708	0.099
Rashtriya Ispat Nigam Ltd.	9,956	9.392	0.094
Hindustan Newsprint Ltd.	303	0.232	0.077
KIOCL Ltd.	1,355	0.706	0.052
Indian Oil Corpn. Ltd.	24,2781	121.464	0.050
National Aluminium Co. Ltd.	5,850	2.74	0.047
Power Grid Corpn. of India Ltd.	4,574	1.636	0.036

* Expenditure on R&D/sales.

Source: CMIEs *Prowess.*

It is clear from the above figures and tables that over the years, the CPSEs investment in R&D and allied activities have grown rapidly. The central and state governments together spent about ₹ 30,000 crore on R&D in 2009. About 10 per cent of the government agencies such as the Defence Research Development Organization (DRDO), Department of Atomic Energy, Council for Scientific and Industrial Research (CSIR) and the Ministry of Non-Renewable Energy, account for about 85 per cent of the central R&D expenditure. During 2009, it has been observed that there was a slowdown in the R&D spending in the enterprises of engineering and capital goods, oil and gas, iron and steel as compared to the previous year, whereas the enterprises in mining, power and fertilisers have shown a remarkable increase in expenditure on R&D and allied activities. The CPSEs in the capital goods sector, like Bharat Heavy Electricals Ltd., Bharat Electronics Ltd. and Hindustan Aeronautics Ltd., are the major spenders on R&D among the CPSEs as a whole. Interestingly, mining enterprises like National Mineral Development Corporation (NMDC) have shown a remarkable increase of more than 100 per cent in 2009 in terms of investment in R&D.

India's Top R&D Spenders

The R&D investment patterns in India more or less mirror global trends. The computing, electronics and semi-conductor industries account for almost a fourth of global R&D, followed by pharma, healthcare and auto. In the absence of a large manufacturing base for semiconductors or high-end electronics, pharmaceutical companies account for one-third of India's R&D expenditure (Vivek, 2010). Due to the global financial crisis of 2008–09, worldwide investments in R&D declined to 3.5 per cent, but according to a study by ET Intelligence Group (STIG), R&D expenditure of the top 100 Indian companies increased by 9 per cent to ₹ 11,582 crore in 2009–10. The study also stated that as enterprises cut down their R&D investments, the centre of gravity for R&D gradually shifts to developing countries. STIG also suggested that Indian enterprises now look for 'in-house' technology developments to further accelerate their growth. The number of patents filed is good dipstick measure of the R&D health of a nation. According to Thomson Reuters, there are two CPSEs in the top list of R&D spenders in India in 2009–10: Bharat Heavy Electricals Limited (BHEL) is at number two and Bharat Electronics Limited (BEL) at number 11. The list is compiled by global management consulting firm Booz & Co. In 2009, BEL ranked 590 in the top 1,000 R&D spenders in

Table 3
The Patent Leaders (2007–09)

Company	*No. of Patents*
Bharat Heavy Electricals Limited	433
L&T	296
Data Steel	273
Steel Authority of India Limited	230
Data Motors	212
TVS Motors	151
Infests Technologies	119
Compton Greaves	98
Data Consultancy Services	72
Baja Auto	66
Maser Baer	57
Mahendra & Mahendra	55
Godrej & Boyce	54

Source: Thomson Reuters, 2009.

the world. The CPSEs like BEL with 433 patents between 2007 and 2009 is leading the list and Steel Authority of India Limited (SAIL) (230) is also setting the pace in this area (Table 3).

Over the last three decades, the relationship between R&D and patenting has been broadly analysed in the literature. Pakes and Griliches (1984) argue that patents indicate successful R&D and separate the intermediate R&D outcome from the profit generating part of the innovative process. The literature also highlights that patents are mainly considered indicative of how up-to-date the enterprises are. Hall et al. (1986) analysed the lag structure between R&D expenditure and patenting. They confirm the result of Pakes and Griliches (1984) that there is the strongest weight on the contemporaneous relationship between R&D expenditure and patenting, and they further conclude that the contribution of the observed R&D history to the contemporaneous patent applications is quite small.

Data Analysis

The regression equation was estimated using the data from CMIEs *Prowess* and the constructed dataset contains the data of 70 CPSEs. Most satisfactory results were obtained with the data. The variables like expenditure on R&D, consultancy fees, payments for software development, technical know-how fees, license fees, and royalty fees were considered for multiple regression analysis to explain their impact on the profitability (net profit) of the selected CPSEs. The Beta coefficients of the royalty fees, payments for software development and expenditure on R&D were positive and significant as expected and are consistent with the literature. It can be concluded from the analysis that expenditure on R&D, royalty fees and investment in IT have significant impact on the CPSEs' innovation inputs, outputs, productivity and profitability. These results underscore the specific significance of a component in technology usage in R&D in Indian public sector enterprises. The introduction of technology and allied activities, if supported by a good technology policy of the government, could increase the competitiveness and profitability significantly, and make Indian CPSEs globally more competitive.

While there is technology adoption witnessed in a big way in many of the CPSEs, a precise technology mapping process is not currently available in a documented fashion. Hence, as a part of the project, it was decided to circulate a questionnaire to scientifically study the technology mapping process, i.e., technology policy, technology handling and implementation issues, technology management along with budgets approved and spent, benchmarking practices, technology sourcing and upgradation process and foreign technological collaborations. This also included taking the opinions of CPSEs in terms of government's policy support for enhancing their activities related to technology. The technology mapping process of each of the above mentioned CPSEs are detailed below:

Table 4

Technology Mapping Process at Selected Indian CPSEs

Enterprise	*Technology Mapping Practices*
Oil and Natural Gas Corporation	• The user groups at the institutes and operational areas constantly track the technology availability and also the evolving technologies. • There is regular technology scanning through interactions with technology providers for suitability. • Continuous technology scouting is done in the international market place. • ONGC initiated an R&D pilot project for shale gas and has seen encouraging results in the form of flowing shale gas on surface for the first time in India, which has opened up new frontiers for exploration of unconventional hydrocarbon.

Cont'd...

...Cont'd

Oil India Limited	• Scouting: Technology Management Team will be responsible for scouting of technology and passing on the relevant information to the user team. • Innovations that can be implemented using in-house capabilities. • Technologies that are established in the oil industry but not inducted in OIL. • Emerging technologies that could add value in OIL's operations. Technologies that can give better returns that the existing ones, i.e., addressing obsolescence.
Indian Oil Corporation Limited	• For identifying best available technology licensors in respective process area, views of the various consultants are sought over and above IOC's own in-house experience/data bank. Licensors across the globe are invited to present their technology and capabilities along with the latest developments/R&D efforts. • IOCL refineries have undertaken various improvement measures through hardware changes, heat integration, automation, state of the art-technologies, etc., for minimising fuel consumption and production loss.
Bharat Petroleum Corporation Limited	• BPCL identifies and assesses projects for immediate and future benefits. • Prioritize the identified projects based on their competitive advantage, customer satisfaction and increasing scientific knowledge and excellence. Once such projects are identified, it looks both internally and externally for suitable partners. • Assess them for their capability, expertise, experience and financial ability. • While finalizing business plans for the year initiatives for technology upgradation are discussed at length in the respective business units and accordingly a plan is developed as per the requirements.
Hindustan Petroleum Corporation Limited	• The technology is sourced to meet the requirement of new specifications of fuels and lubricants and to increase secondary processing capacity and collaborative R&D projects. • Technology licensors are shortlisted across the globe and technology is selected on a competitive bidding basis. • Process consultants and licensors supply the various refinery technologies and upgradation of these technologies is generally their agenda as driven by the raw material availability, product pattern/quality requirements and economic considerations.
National Aluminum Corporation Limited	• Various technological issues, viz., innovation, modification, upgradation and improvements pertaining to alumina refining and aluminium smelting are generally sourced from the parent company who has supplied NALCO the technology for the same.

Cont'd...

...Cont'd

	• The same is being upgraded through continued technical assistance agreement over the years. Further, some of the technological upgradation has been developed through in-house R&D efforts. • Technology in NALCO is sourced by inviting expression of interest, competitive bidding and evaluating various criteria.
BHEL	• Absorb and indigenize the energy efficient technologies. • Use judicious mix of acquisition of technologies and in-house developments and leveraging capability to develop product variants to meet market demand. • Attain leadership in selected products. • Pursue in-house R&D to become self-reliant in identified products by focusing on application development. • Establish Centres of Excellence to foster expertise (design, optimization, manufacturing, application development, processes) building and bridge engineering/R&D infrastructure gaps and are supported by 24 labs at corporate R&D centre as well as various BHEL units. • Collaborate with national/international institutions of excellence, academia and research laboratories to supplement in-house R&D efforts. • Acquisition of companies having strong intellectual property and technical expertise in areas of business growth. • Currently for technology sourcing BHEL is adopting four-pronged approach, namely, Technology Transfer Agreement (TTA), Business Sharing Agreement (BSA), joint working with the technology holder and acquisition of companies having Intellectual Property Rights (IPRs) for the technology.
BEL	Technological issues are handled by the Technology Planning Group at Corporate Office, whose primary functions are as follows: (a) Identification of technology gaps in the core areas of business, by assessing the market/customer's futuristic requirements, current technology levels at national/global levels and technology available within the company. (b) Formulation of a technology road map, identifying the action plan, responsibility and method of acquisition of technology. (c) For each business segment, R&D committees are constituted to identify the nodal responsibility for developing each technology module where competencies are spread over multiple locations. (d) In case of ToT from foreign collaborator, Strategic Planning and Licensing Departments from Corporate Office will handle all issues, related to ToT agreements, in consultation with respective Business Heads and Technology Planning.

Cont'd...

...Cont'd

	There are various sources of technology for Bharat Electronics Ltd., viz., (a) In-house technologies developed at BEL. (b) Technologies developed at DRDO labs and adapted at BEL. (c) Technologies developed at ISRO, C-DoT and other R&D centres of the country and adapted at BEL. (d) Technologies developed through private sector design houses and academic institutions. (e) Technologies developed in collaboration with foreign OEMs.
Bharat Dynamics Limited	• The necessity of transfer of technology from foreign sources is intended to induct high-end technologies of missile systems that are not readily available or not yet matured in the country and to facilitate speedy induction of the weapon systems into service. • The technologies associated with the manufacture of weapon systems are basically imparted through Transfer of Technology (ToT) agreements from overseas Original Equipment Manufacturers (OEMs) for license production and DRDO for the indigenous weapon systems. • The technology assimilation is well established in case of license production, with manufacturing activities spread over various phases of production, namely, Fully Formed (FF), Semi Knocked Down (SKD), Completely Knocked Down (CKD), and Indigenous Manufacture (IM).
Electronics Corporation of India Limited	• Product developments/upgrades in a proactive manner in anticipation of customer needs. • Joint development works in association with R&D organizations like BARC, DRDO and ISRO. • Joint development in association with Institutes of Higher Learning like the IITs. • MS by research programme with universities to take up actionable research. • Product development in association with major clients like Election Commission of India for Electronic Voting Machines and Registrar General of India (for National Population Register). • Promoting inter-PSU synergy for providing technology development support for projects like National Population Register. Sourcing of technologies in ECIL is a three-step process: 1. Identifying 'technology gaps' vis-à-vis the mission and objectives. 2. Determining the availability of the technology within the organization and the possibility of developing it in-house. 3. Environmental scanning for the requisite technology with the R&D laboratories and reputed academic institutions.

Cont'd...

...Cont'd

Powergrid Corporation Limited	• Technology & Development Department aims to provide the necessary impetus for the need to aggressively pursue R&D initiatives and channelize the efforts and outcome to benefit Indian power sector. • To steer the technology initiatives in POWERGRID and achieve these objectives, POWERGRID has formed an advisory body consisting of national institutions. The technological development activities include a mix of in-house activity and project-managed outsourced activity with various international and national institutes and others.
National Buildings Construction Corporation Limited	• NBCC relies on design consultants for technology sourcing for a particular project. Once the technology is identified, vendor identification is carried out and shortlisted, where NBCC is functioning as a project implementing agency including designs and estimates, etc. • NBCC carries out technology option reviews and thereafter the most suitable technology is adopted at the design state itself with feedback from various vendors/manufacturers of equipment, client's requirements, etc. The enterprise has not attempted any bench marking with other CPSEs/private enterprises and MNCs for this purpose. • On a priority basis, the company is arranging training programmes for engineers on particular technology, study tours/awareness programmes for new technologies/materials available in the market.

Source: Author's own compilation.

Conclusions and Policy Recommendations

The CPSEs in India have taken considerable efforts in investing in technology in the industrial sector to enhance innovative practices in the respective enterprises. This has shown some significant increase in their performance during the post-reform period as indicated by the profitability levels and market capitalization. The enterprises in the high-tech industries like capital goods, electronics, aerospace, etc., contributed over 5 per cent to the national GDP. It can be observed from the data that innovative activities and spending on technology and allied activities are dominated by a few enterprises in the high-tech industries. Increasingly, MNCs operating from India are also contributing to enhancing the country's innovative performance. This is the very likely consequence of ever increasing FDI in R&D. Most of the MNCs patents are in the IT industry. In short, it may not be incorrect to draw the conclusion that India's pharmaceutical and IT industries are becoming innovative although domestic enterprises are more active innovators only in the former industry while it is the MNCs that are active in the latter industry. The integration of Indian economy with rest of the world has opened up a number of opportunities which seems to have been capitalized by the CPSEs. The main recommendations are as follows:

- Expenditure on R&D is important for enterprise growth and profitability. Enterprise R&D has high spillover effects, which enhances the ability of the sector to absorb technology coming from abroad or from government and various universities, institutions at home.
- Government should provide sufficient funding for R&D performed in the public sector enterprises, which has a substantial impact on economic development in the long run.
- The government should provide the right framework for encouraging relationships between public and private research, so that knowledge flows more easily between the sectors.
- Successful international enterprises (IBM, GE, 'Chaebols' in Korea, etc.) have implemented a deliberate strategic management process to create and share explorative and exploitative technological knowledge among affiliated companies.
- Modern management techniques should be applied in project selection, investment decision, planning, monitoring and control of R&D projects.
- Adoption of collective learning based approach on specific organizational mechanisms.
- Performance evaluation should be given importance in R&D and suitable criteria should be evolved for evaluating the performance of R&D personnel, projects and enterprises.
- Centralization of knowledge management approach to integrate technological resources accumulated by individual enterprises to undertake breakthrough innovations.
- The CPSEs, government and research institutions should interact with each other for various sources of information. The better the interaction, better will be the access to relevant competencies and partners, which will help them in their learning processes, and enhance the chances for their innovation processes to succeed.
- The government should ensure access to foreign technology, through flows of goods, of people or of ideas, and ensure that enterprises have the absorptive capabilities needed for making the best of foreign technology.

- Countries that spend more on R&D also take more advantage of foreign technology, free riding (i.e., by waiting for other countries to develop the new technology and just trying to imitate when it is ready) would be ineffective.

By and large, the paper points to the competitive advantage of firms when investment in technology is made and the resultant impact on productivity, profitability and economic growth. The results obtained also show the strong interactions between the various channels and sources of technology, which underline the necessity for government to have a broad and coherent innovative policy. Future studies could focus on the examination of performance measures in R&D both at enterprise as well as national level to evaluate the government's efforts of fostering R&D activities.

Notes

1. During 1955 to 1970, about 233 foreign technological collaboration agreements were made with public sector enterprises in India. The industry-wise distribution of the agreements indicates that electrical goods and mechanical tools accounted for the largest number of collaborations followed by chemicals and transport equipment. The United Kingdom accounted for largest number of collaborations followed by United States and West Germany. The share of Russia and other Eastern European countries is as low as 10 per cent of total agreements.
2. Technological capabilities can be best described in terms of three levels: the low technology-based level involves the ability to operate and maintain a new production plant based on imported technology; the medium technology-based level consists of the ability to duplicate and adapt the design for an imported plant and technique elsewhere in the country or abroad, while the high technology-based level involves a capability to undertake new designs and to develop new production systems and components in-house.
3. The Government of India (GoI) had identified nine CPSEs as Navratnas in July 1997 on the basis of their potential to emerge as global giants. These enterprises were provided with enhanced autonomy and delegation of powers to incur capital expenditure, enter technology joint ventures/strategic alliances, and affect organizational restructuring, to create and wind up board level posts and raise capital from domestic and international markets. Further, in October 1997, the GoI granted autonomy to another set of profit-making CPSEs to make them more competitive and efficient. These companies are known as Miniratnas in two categories I and II. The criteria for Miniratna are: (a) the CPSE

should be profit making for the last three years continuously and should have positive net worth; (b) should not have defaulted in repayment of loans/interest; and (c) should not depend upon budgetary support or government guarantee, etc. The CPSEs which made pre-tax profits of ₹ 300 million or more in at least one of the three years will be given Category I Miniratna while others get Category II.

References

Bakos, J.Y. and Treacy, M.E. (1986). "Information Technology and Corporate Strategy: A Research Perspective", *MIS Quarterly*, Vol. 10, No. 2, pp. 107–19.

Bhattacharya, Sujit and Lal, Kashmiri (2008). Industrial R&D in India: Contemporary Scenario', S&T and Industry, India, Science and Technology: 2008, NISTADS/CSIR, India.

Chesbrough, Henry (2011). "Bringing Open Innovation to Services", *MIT Sloan Management Review*, Vol. 52, No. 2, pp. 85–90.

CMIE (2011). *Prowess Database*, Centre for Monitoring Indian Economy.

Earl, Louise (2002). "Innovation and Change in the Public Sector: A Seeming Oxymoron", Cat. No. 88F0006XIE02001, Science, Innovation and Electronic Information Division, Statistics Canada, pp. 1–35.

Ein-Dor, P. and Segev, E. (1978), 'Strategic Planning for Management Information Systems', *Management Science*, Vol. 24, No. 15, pp. 1631–41.

Fabrizio, Kira R. (2009). "Absorptive Capacity and the Search for Innovation," *Research Policy*, Vol. 38, No. 2, pp. 255–67.

Ferrantino, Michael (1992). "Technology Expenditures, Factor Intensity, and Efficiency in Indian Manufacturing", *Review of Economics and Statistics*, Vol. 74, No. 4, pp. 689–700.

Fleming, Lee, and Sorenson, Olav (2004). "Science as a Map in Technology Search," *Strategic Management Journal*, Vol. 25, No. 8–9, pp. 909–28.

Friedmann, Wolfgang (1954). *The Public Corporation.* London: Stevens.

Fu, Xiaolan, Pietrobelli, Carlo, and Soete, Luc (2010). "The Role of Foreign Technology and Indigenous Innovation in Emerging Economies: Technological Change and Catching Up", Technical Notes No. IDB-TN-166, Inter-American Development Bank, Washington, D.C., USA.

Galliers, R.D. (1993). "IT Strategies: Beyond Competitive Advantage", *The Journal of Strategic Information Systems*, Vol. 2, No. 4, pp 283–91.

Grover, V., Teng, J.T.C. and Fiedler, K.D. (1993). "Information Technology Enabled BPR: An Integrated Planning Framework", *Omega International Journal of Management Science*, Vol. 24, No. 4, pp. 433–47.

Hall, B.H., Griliches, Z. and Hausman, J.A. (1986). "Patents and R&D: Is There A Lag?", *International Economic Review*, Vol. 27, pp. 1029–54.

Kanungo, Shivraj, Sadavarti, Sanjeev and Srinivs, Yedlapati (2001). "Relating IT Strategy and Organisational Culture: An Empirical Study of Public Sector Units in India", *Journal of Strategic Information Systems*, Vol. 10, No. 1, pp. 29–57.

Katrak, Homi (2002). "Does Economic Liberalisation Endanger Indigenous Technological Developments?: An Analysis of the Indian Experience", *Research Policy*, Vol. 31, No. 1, pp. 19–30.

King, W.R. and Sethi, V. (1993). "Developing Transnational Information Systems: A Case Study", *Omega International Journal of Management Science*, Vol. 21, No. 1, pp. 53–59.

Kshitij, Avinash, Sinha, Bikramjit, and Banerjee, Parthasarathi (2008). "Pattern of Innovation and R&D in Select Sectors of Listed Companies of India", S&T and Industry, India, Science and Technology, NISTADS/CSIR, India.

Kumar, N. and Siddharthan, N.S. (1994). "Technology, Firm Size and Export Behavior in Developing Countries: The Case of Indian Enterprises", *Journal of Development Studies*, 31 (2), pp. 289–309.

Li, X. (forthcoming). "Sources of External Technology, Absorptive Capacity and Innovation Capability in Chinese State-Owned High-Tech Enterprises", *World Development* (Special Section).

Mani, Sunil (2009). "Is India Becoming More Innovative Since 1991? Analysis of Its Evidence and Some Disquieting Features", Working Paper Series 58, Institute of Public Enterprise, Hyderabad, India.

Mishra, R.K., Lakshmi, Kumari and Kiranmai, J. (2010). *Globalising Public Enterprises*. New Delhi: Excel Books.

Nolan, R.L. (1979). "Managing the Crises in Data Processing", *Harvard Business Review*, Vol. 57, No. 2, pp. 8–27.

Pakes A. and Griliches, Z. (1984). "Estimating Distributed Lags in Short Panels with an Application to the Specification of Depreciation Patterns and Capital Stock Constructs", NBER Working Paper 0933, National Bureau of Economic Research, Cambridge.

Pillai, Mohanan P. (1978). "Foreign Collaboration in Public Sector", *Economic and Political Weekly*, Vol. 13, No. 21, pp. M48–M55.

Rockart, J.F. (1979). "Chief Executives Define their own Data Needs", *Harvard Business Review*, Vol. 57, No. 2, pp. 81–93.

Schware, Robert (2000). "Information Technology and Public Sector Management in Developing Countries: Present Status and Future Prospects", *Indian Journal of Public Administration* (available at: www1.worldbank.org/publicsector/egov/Schware.pdf).

Teece, David J. (1992). "Competition, Cooperation, and Innovation: Organisational Arrangements for Regimes of Rapid Technological Progress," *Journal of Economic Behavior & Organization*, Vol. 18, No. 1, pp. 1–25.

Venkatraman, N. (1994). "IT Enabled Business Transformation: From Automation to Business Scope Redefinition", *Sloan Management Review*, Vol. 35, No. 2, pp. 73–87.

Vivek, T.R. (2010). "Searching for Scale", *The Economic Times*, December 27, p. 6.

Yetton, P.W., Johnston, K.D. and Craig, J.F. (1994). "Computer Aided Architects: A Case Study of IT and Strategic Change", *Sloan Management Review*, Vol. 35, No. 4, pp. 57–67.

8

Rural Development and Women Empowerment in India through MGNREGA

Opportunities and Challenges

DEEPTIMA SHUKLA

A History of Employment Programmes in India

India has three decades of experience in implementing employment generation programmes. The concept of creating employment in public works is therefore not new. It was first in 1970s that the National Rural Employment Programme and the Rural Landless Employment Programme were adopted. They not only provided employment opportunities during lean agricultural seasons but also in times of floods, droughts and other natural calamities. The then Prime Minister Rajiv Gandhi integrated the two schemes into one in 1989 and it was decided that delivery would occur through the Panchayati Raj Institutions (PRIs, village-level elected institutions). This scheme was called Jawahar Rozgar Yojana (JRY). The bureaucracy was bypassed and funds were planned to be deposited in the accounts of each village institution responsible for planning development activities used to create employment creation, and overseeing implementation. The scheme began but it was never given a chance to succeed.

In 1990, V.P. Singh promised to guarantee an employment scheme for all. The subsequent, Narasimha Rao-led, government diluted what existed. In 1993, JRY received little political leadership or attention. It was agreed that the scheme, controlled by people's representatives, was leading to increased corruption and inefficiency in delivery by government servants; therefore, it needed revamping.

In 1993, the Employment Assurance Scheme (EAS) was launched covering 1,778 drought prone, desert, tribal and hill area blocks. It was later extended to all the blocks in 1997–98. The EAS was designed to provide employment in the form of manual work in the lean agricultural season. The works taken up under the programme were expected to lead to the creation of durable economic and social infrastructure and address the felt-needs of the people. Through this scheme it was decided that half the allocated funds for rural employment would be channelized through the bureaucracy, not the PRIs. The budget allocated was roughly ₹ 2,000 crore per year.

The Food for Work Programme was started in 2000–01 as a component of the EAS in eight notified drought-affected states of Chhattisgarh, Gujarat, Himachal Pradesh, Madhya Pradesh, Orissa, Rajasthan, Maharashtra and Uttaranchal. The programme aims at food provision through wage employment. Food grains are supplied to states free of cost. However, lifting of food grains for the scheme from Food Corporation of India (FCI) godowns has been slow. In April 2002, renaming took place and two schemes JRY and EAS were merged to form Sampoorna Gramin Rozgar Yojna (SPRY). Its spending was, too, divided between the PRIs and administration. During the period of National Democratic Alliance (NDA) government the name JRY had been changed to the Jawahar Gram Samridhi Yojna (JSGY). A component of SGRY provided food grain to calamity-stricken states for relief work. The budget now increased to about ₹ 4,000 crore per year.

Launching of MGNREGA (Mahatma Gandhi National Rural Employment Guarantee Act)

In late 2004, the National Food for Work Programme (NFWP) was launched in 150 backward districts of India. These districts were identified through a task force set by ministry of rural development, which used three variables to compute 'backwardness'—agricultural productivity per worker, agricultural wage rate and the scheduled caste and scheduled tribe population in the district. The programme was implemented through the district administration and a menu of 'labour-intensive projects' would be prepared, to be undertaken over a five-year period. In 2005–06 budget, the allocation was enhanced; NFWP got ₹ 6,000 crore in addition to the SGRY's ₹ 4,000 crore. The NFWP remains the programme design for NREGA (National Rural

Employment Guarantee Act). In December 2004, National Rural Employment Guarantee Bill was tabled in parliament and in August 2005, the parliament unanimously passed the Act. In February 2006, the NREGA, now called the MGNREGA, was launched in the 200 most backward districts of India. As a component of the United Progressive Alliance (UPA) government's Common Minimum Programme, its intention was to create waged work during the lean agricultural season through a public works programme available on demand and guaranteed by the Act.

Rural Wage Employment Programmes in India

1980	*1983*	*1989*	*1993*	*1999*
National Rural Employment Programme (NREP) launched to use unemployed and underemployed workers to build community assets.	Rural Landless Employment Guarantee (RLEG) launched to provide 100 days of guaranteed employment to one member from each rural, landless household.	Jawahar Rozgar Yojna launched combining NREP and RLEG.	Employment Assurance Scheme (EAS) launched to provide employment during the lean agricultural season.	Jawahar Gram Samridhi Yojna (JGSY) launched; dedicated to development of demand-driven rural infrastructure.
ALLOCATION	ALLOCATION	ALLOCATION	ALLOCATION	ALLOCATION
6th Plan	**6th Plan**	**7th Plan**	**8th Plan**	**9th Plan**
1980–1985: ₹ 980 crore	1983–1985: ₹ 500 crore	1985–1990: ₹ 2,100 crore	1993–1994: ₹ 600 crore	1997–1998: ₹ 2,077 crore
			1994–1995: ₹ 1,200 crore	1998–1999: ₹ 2,095 crore
7th Plan	**7th Plan**	**8th Plan**		
1985–1990: ₹ 1,682 crore	1985–1989: ₹ 2,412 crore	1992–1993: ₹ 2,546 crore	1995–1996: ₹ 1,570 crore	1999–2000: ₹ 2,095 crore
		1993–1994: ₹ 3,306 crore	1996–1997: ₹ 1,970 crore	
		1994–1995: ₹ 3,855 crore	1997–1998: ₹ 1,970 crore	
		1995–1996: ₹ 3,862 crore	1998–1999: ₹ 1,990 crore	
		1996–1997: ₹ 1,865 crore	1999–2000: ₹ 1,700 crore	

2001	*2004*	*2006*	*2009–10*
Sampoorna Gramin Rozgar Yojna (SGRY) launched, merging EAS and JGSY.	Food for Work Programme (FWP) launched to generate additional supplementary wage employment and create assets.	Mahatma Gandhi National Rural Employment Guarantee Scheme (MGNREGS) launched to provide 100 days of guaranteed employment to one member from each rural household and create community assets.	MGNREGA provided employment opportunities for more than 4.47 crore households in 2008–09. ₹ 39,100 crore was allotted for MGNREGA in the year 2009–10, which marks an increase of 144 per cent over 2008–09 budget estimates. In 2010–11, MGNREGA scheme allocation raised to ₹ 41,000 crore. This marks increase of 15 per cent over 2009–10 budget estimates.
ALLOCATION	ALLOCATION	ALLOCATION	
9th Plan	**10th Plan**	**10th Plan**	
2000–2001: ₹ 2,950 crore	2005–2006: ₹ 6,000 crore	2006–2007: ₹ 11,300 crore	
2001–2002: ₹ 3,250 crore			
10th Plan			
2002–2003: ₹ 4,440 crore			
2003–2004: ₹ 4,900 crore			
2004–2005: ₹ 5,100 crore			
2005–2006: ₹ 4,000 crore			
2006–2007: ₹ 3,000 crore			

Source: Natural Resource Management and Livelihood Unit Centre for Science and Environment, New Delhi, 2010.

Objective of the Act and Goals of MGNREGAs

The main aim of the Act is to enhance livelihood security in rural areas by providing at least 100 days of guaranteed wage employment in a financial year to every household whose adult members volunteer to do unskilled manual labour.

The first Millennium Development Goal (MDG) of 'Eradicating Extreme Poverty and Hunger' aims at reducing the proportion of people whose income is less than $1 between 1990 and 2015 by half. India's 11th Five-Year Plan, reiterating the country's commitment the MDGs, has set socio-economic targets for inclusive growth and development. These include, reducing the headcount ratio of consumption poverty by 10 percentage points, raising real wage rate of unskilled workers by 20 per cent and creating seven crore new work opportunities.

According to National Sample Survey Organization (NSSO), 30 crore Indians live in extreme poverty. The poor faces absence of basic capabilities to function in society and lack of opportunities such as access to public infrastructure and income earning. A majority of them earn their livelihood through unskilled, casual manual labour and exploitation of the natural resource base. This dependence makes them more vulnerable to crises, like climate shock, natural disaster or ill-health, all of which adversely impact their employment opportunities and reduces their ability to move out of the poverty trap.

The Indian government has adopted a holistic development plan to promote economic growth and also address the needs of the poor by ensuring their basic rights. In this context, workfare programmes have been important interventions. Through short-term employment, these programmes provide income transfers to poor households during critical times such as lean agricultural seasons, and enable consumption smoothening. Over time, this will facilitate the transition of the village economy from subsistence to self-sustenance by increasing agricultural productivity and creating durable assets for the regeneration of the natural resource base. The infrastructure will not only lead to market linkages but also create further employment opportunities.

With an aim to fight poverty more effectively, MGNREGA with its legal framework and rights-based approach sets a goal of enhancing livelihood security and sets certain goals to help in poverty alleviation. These goals can be summed as:

- Strong social safety net for the vulnerable groups by providing a fallback employment source, when other employment alternatives are scarce or inadequate.
- Growth engine for sustainable development of an agricultural economy. Providing employment to address poverty caused due to drought, deforestation and soil erosion, the Act seeks to strengthen the natural resource base of rural livelihood and create durable assets in rural areas.
- Empowerment of rural poor through the processes of rights-based law.

- New ways of doing business, as a model of governance reform anchored on the principles of transparency and grassroots democracy.

Thus, MGNREGA fosters conditions for inclusive growth ranging from basic wage security and recharging the rural economy to a transformative empowerment process of democracy.

Salient Features of MGNREGA

This clearly indicates that MGNREGA maximizes work opportunities and thus helps in livelihood security. Besides, it augments household income, savings and investment. The objective of MGNREGA is to regenerate natural resources and address growing concerns of food security with emphasis on water and soil conservation. MGNREGA is seen as investment in climate change for poor. Climate change is happening and will increasingly affect the poor who are most vulnerable to it by reducing access to drinking water, negatively affecting the health of poor and posing a real threat to food security. Among the poor vulnerability may also vary, since some groups are more lacking in the financial, social and political means of securing alternative livelihoods less exposed to risk than others. Women, for example, who may be constrained by social and cultural reasons, are the most affected in terms of livelihood security. Thus, MGNREGA aims at increased public participation, which results in a deepening of democracy. For this purpose the Act sets up certain distinct features such as:

- Adult members of a rural household, willing to do unskilled manual work, may apply for registration in writing or orally to local Gram Panchayat.
- The Gram Panchayat issues a job card within 15 days of application. The Gram Panchayat after due verification will issue a job card. The job card will bear the photograph of all adult members of the household willing to work under MGNREGA and is free of cost.
- A job card holder may submit a written application for employment to Gram Panchayat, stating the time and duration for which work is sought. The minimum days of employment have to be at least fourteen days.
- The Gram Panchayat will issue a dated receipt of written application for employment, against which the guarantee of providing employment within 15 days operates.
- In case employment is not provided within 15 days of the application, then the state has to pay an unemployment allowance.

- Work should be provided within a 5 km radius of the village. Beyond that 10 per cent extra wages are to be paid for transportation.
- Wages are to be paid according to the Minimum Wages Act, 1948 for agricultural labourers in the state. Presently, the wage is ₹ 100 per day.
- Equal wages are to be paid to both men and women.
- At least one-third of the beneficiaries shall be women.
- Worksite facilities such as crèche, drinking water, and shade have to be provided.
- Planning of the project will be recommended by the Gram Sabha and approved by Zilla Parishad.
- Permissible works mainly include water and soil conservation, afforestation and land development works.
- At least 50 per cent of works will be allotted to Gram Panchayats for execution.
- A 60:40 wage and material ratio has to be maintained. No contractors or machinery is allowed.
- Social audit has to be done by Gram Sabha.
- All accounts and records relating to the scheme should be available for public scrutiny.
- Grievance redressal mechanisms have to be put in place for ensuring a responsive implementation process.

In this way MGNREGA marks a paradigm shift from all precedent wage employment programmes as:

- MGNREGA provides a statutory guarantee of wage employment.
- It provides a rights-based framework for wage employment.
- There is a 15-day time limit for fulfilling the legal guarantee of providing employment.
- The legal mandate of providing employment in a time-bound manner is underpinned by the provision of unemployment allowance.
- MGNREGA is demand-driven.
- MGNREGA has extensive in-built transparency safeguards such as document-related, processes-related, etc.

Employment Guarantee and Women Empowerment

As perceived above, the MGNREGA is one of the most progressive pieces of legislation enacted since independence. Its significance is evident from a variety of perspectives. It is no doubt a bold and unique experiment in the provision of rural employment; it is also a first law of its kind, which entitles the right to work. Apart from being a rights-based and demand-driven employment programme, the MGNREGA makes special provisions for women's empowerment. More women than men work under the national programme that guarantees employment to rural people. In the financial year 2010–11 women availed more than 50 per cent of employment created under MGNREGA. Women's participation in MGNREGA points at some unique and interesting aspects. States not known for women's participation in the workforce are reporting a high number of women joining the programme. For example, Kerela accounts for about 15 per cent of the women workforce but under MGNREGA it takes up 79 per cent of the employment created. Similarly, Rajasthan and Tamil Nadu, with a low share of women in workforce have 69 and 82 per cent workers under the Act. On the other hand, a poor state with greater casual labour potential, like Orissa, Uttar Pradesh and Bihar, only 22–33 per cent of women participation is reported. Nevertheless, the Act provides many opportunities to rural women.

- The Act stipulates that wages will be equal for men and women. Thus, by generating employment for women at fair wages in the village, MGNREGA plays a substantial role in the economic empowerment of women. Women take up this opportunity as economic freedom.
- Employment at MGNREGA worksites has raised enthusiasm and expectations among women workers. MGNREGA wages are far higher than the wages that are otherwise available in villages. The economic empowerment of women has served as a basis for greater self-esteem and independence among women.
- The provision is made that a minimum of one-third of the beneficiaries will be women, i.e., 33 per cent of the workers shall be women. Government figures indicate impressive participation of women in MGNREGA.
- Participation of women is above 33 per cent in almost all the states. Tamil Nadu and Kerala show highest participation followed by Andhra Pradesh and Rajasthan. Government records (2nd February, 2011) stipulate that almost 47 per cent of total workers in MGNREGA are women.
- The Act provides worksite facilities for women, i.e., water, shade, crèche, transportation, etc. In Rajasthan, MGNREGA worksites have good facilities for women and children. In Kerala, the management of worksites and other logistics for implementation is placed in the hands of women self-help groups under the poverty eradication mission—Kudumbshree.

- More than 90 per cent of women workers are farm labourers or cultivators. A substantial part of their labour is unpaid because they work in their own farms. MGNREGA has changed this. Now parts of women's non-paid jobs, like levelling and digging a pond in their farms, are paid for.
- Putting cash income in their hands, MGNREGA has created a greater degree of confidence among women. With the increased participation of women in household income generation a positive contribution to gender relations could be made.
- Survey data suggest that women workers are more confident about their roles as contributors to family expenditure and their work decisions.
- MGNREGA has brought a significant change in the life of villagers as a whole as in the life of women. This is because employment is being provided within their village, generating community assets and enhancing their spending capacity.
- Evidently, MGNREGA employment has encouraged women to take the decision to enter the sphere of the cash economy (more than 65 per cent women also decided the worksite on their own).
- Women workers receive their wages in person, rather than through husbands or other proxies. Women collect their own wages.
- Women workers spent their wages on regular food and consumer goods. The increased income has helped them to repay small debts and keep themselves away from the clutches of local money-lenders.
- Children's education and healthcare sector has improved due to employment through MGNREGA. Women's labour and functions previously had been made invisible due to lack of monetary remuneration, but by putting cash in hand MGNREGA has made women wage earners.
- MGNREGA has also marked a positive impact on migration patterns. Whereas earlier entire families would migrate, now only one or two persons tend to leave for seasonal work in cities and neighbouring states. This has had good effect on women in particular as they suffer most in shifting households.
- Studies suggest that women are now more able to take decisions on their own. As such their decision to work under MGNREGA has been their own.

- In Kerala, Tamil Nadu and Rajasthan, the history of women mobilization for schemes and campaigns seems to have contributed to their higher participation. In Rajasthan, the campaign for social audits, in which women play major role, has contributed to enhance awareness and increased participation under MGNREGA.
- MGNREGA seems to have created reasons and opportunities for people to work and remain in their own villages. The strengthening of this perception in rural areas can have significant impacts on questions of security, health and children's education, all of which are often compromised, in one way or another during migration.

In a holistic manner it can be said that there seems to be the beginning of a marked shift from the previous role of women in a society. Women have contributed as farm and non-farm labour and thus been a vital component in the functioning of rural households, but their contribution remained invisible due to lack of monetary earning. MGNREGA has put cash remunerations in the hands of women workers and thus it has both increased and extended their contributions to households as wage earners as well.

Challenges

- There seems to be lack of awareness about the provisions of MGNREGA, especially among the disadvantaged community and this includes women. Women are not aware of the minimum wage that they should get against the work done.
- Though women are aware that under the Act each household is guaranteed 100 days of work in a year yet they seem to be less aware regarding operational guidelines, household registration, the job card distribution process, work application and entitlements such as worksite facilities and unemployment allowance.
- Women, being illiterate, generally apply orally or give their names when asked whether they wanted a job card. Very few women are aware of the work application process and apply for work themselves.
- The low level of awareness and generating awareness regarding MGNREGA work clearly constitutes one of the key challenges for authorities, NGOs and popular movements.
- Poor worksite facilities such as safe drinking water, shades for periods of rest, first aid and childcare facilities at times are found missing from worksites. Though funds are provided for the same.

- MGNREGA is designed to be largely implemented through PRIs. Gram Panchayats and Gram Sabhas play crucial role in the implementation and selection of works. Gram Sabhas also conduct social audit and therefore, participation of people at large and women in particular in these institutions and assemblies is, then, critical to realizing the participatory potential of the Act. It is seen that women workers did not generally take part in Gram Sabhas mainly due to lack of awareness about the significant role they can play in making shelf of projects and conducting social audit.

Summing up

Despite many problems and challenges it can be said that MGNREGA is a programme that has started to make difference in the lives of women. Furthermore, women are willing to do more work under MGNREGA if possible. The overall impact of MGNREGA on women's lives is quite positive in many ways, whether it is by enhancing their economic independence and self-confidence, contributing food security, helping to reduce distress migration or fostering better awareness of minimum wages.

As a progressive legislation for excluded groups—women, scheduled castes, scheduled tribes and others—MGNREGA can help to reclaim the lost faith in the possibility of pro-people governance and grassroot democracy.

References

Ambasta, P., P.S. Vijay Shankar and M. Shah (2008). Two Years of NREGA: The Road Ahead, *Economic and Political Weekly*, 43 (8): 41–50.

An Ecological Act: A Backgrounder to the National Rural Employment Guarantee Act (NREGA): Draft Paper Prepared by Natural Resource and Livelihood Unit, Centre for Science and Environment, New Delhi.

Comptroller and Auditor General (2008). Performance Audit of Implementation of National Rural Employment Guarantee Act, 2005 (NREGA). Performance Audit Report No. 42. New Delhi, India: Comptroller and Auditor General.

Critical Issues for Fullfilment of NREGA Objectives, http://ranchi.nic.in/Critical_Issues_%20in_NREGA.pdf

Drèze, J. and R. Khera (2008). From Accounts to Accountability. *The Hindu*, December 6. <http://www.sacw.net/article382.html>. Accessed March 21, 2009.

Jandu, Navjyoti (2008). Employment Guarantee and Women's Empowerment in Rural India: Paper Presented at a National Seminar on NREGA at Vigyan Bhawan.

Narayanan, S. (2008). Employment Guarantee, Women's Work and Childcare. *Economic and Political Weekly*, 43 (9): 10–13.

National Rural Employment Guarantee Act (NREGA), Some Reports from the Field, 2006–07, Ministry of Rural Development, Government of India, New Delhi.

National Rural Employment Guarantee Act 2005 (NREGA), Operational Guidelines, 2008, Ministry of Rural Development, Government of India, New Delhi.

NREGA (National Rural Employment Guarantee Act). 2005. No. 42 of 2005. <http://www.commonlii.org/in/legis/num_act/nrega2005375>. Accessed on September 5, 2008.

PACS-CSO (Poorest Area Civil Society—Civil Society Organization). 2007. Status of NREGA Implementation: Grassroots Learning and Ways Forward. 2nd Monitoring Report (April 2006 to March 2007). Delhi, India: Poorest Area Civil Society (PACS) Programme.

Rohatgi, V.D. (2009). Introduction to National Rural Employment Guarantee Act (NREGA), Sumit Enterprises.

Shah, M. (2008). Governance Reform Key to NREGA Success. *The Hindu*, March 14.

Siddhartha and A. Vanaik (2008). CAG Report on NREGA: Fact and Fiction. *Economic and Political Weekly*, 43: 39–45.

Sudarshan, Ratna M. India's National Rural Employment Guarantee Act: Women's Participation and Impacts in Himachal Pradesh, Kerala and Rajasthan. http://www.ids.ac.uk/files/dmfile/ResearchReport06FINAL.Pdf

UNDP (United Nations Development Programme) (2009). Employment Guarantee Quickening India's March Towards MDGs. Report on An International Seminar on Rural Poverty: Key Initiatives in Achieving Millennium Development Goals and the Role of NREGA, January 21–22, 2009, National Agricultural Science Centre, New Delhi. New York: United Nations Development Programme. < http://undp.org.in/node/213>. Accessed on March 14, 2010.

PART II

Environment and Society

9

Governance and Water

Integrated Water Resource Management

BRUCE MITCHELL

Governance is a key component for successful water management. Indeed, without an appropriate governance system, the scientific and technological aspects of water-related work are unlikely to be effectively implemented at the policy and management levels (Tropp, 2007: 19–20). Systematic and explicit research on water governance, however, is relatively recent (Mehan, 2010).

Link between Governance and Water Management

A range of views exists related to 'governance' and 'governance for water'. Regarding governance, Tortajada (2010: 298) has observed:

> It embraces the relationships between governments and societies, including laws, regulations, institutions, and formal and informal interactions which affect the ways in which governance systems function, stressing the importance of involving more voices,

---

It is a privilege to contribute a chapter to this felicitation volume to honour O.P. Dwivedi. We have known each other for decades, and it has been my pleasure to have him as a nearby neighbour at the University of Guelph, a 30 to 40 minute drive east of the University of Waterloo. I have observed with respect and admiration his significant research programme over decades focused on governance and protection of the environment, especially his work regarding environmental policy in both developed and less-developed countries. His various initiatives to provide educational and health care facilities in the communities in which he grew up as a youngster in India have also been inspirational. Through his scholarship and humanitarian roles at a global scale, he is a wonderful role model for all, but especially for the students who have had the good fortune to be taught or supervised by him. If the world had more OPs, it would be a better place.

responsibilities, transparency and accountability of formal and informal organizations associated in any process.

Furthermore, she argued, 'Broadly speaking, water governance should consider both inter-sectoral concerns such as those from the energy, agricultural or environmental sectors' (Tortajada, 2010: 304).

Olsson (2007: 269) provided a similar interpretation that,

> ... governance is the process of resolving trade-offs and providing a vision and direction for sustainability, management is the realization of this vision, and monitoring provides feedback and synthesizes the observations to a narrative of how the situation has emerged and might unfold in the future.

The World Water Assessment Programme (2006: 47–48) of the United Nations provides a clear statement of the relationship between, and the significance of, governance and water. In its view,

> Governance addresses the relationship between organizations and social groups involved in water decision-making, both horizontally across sectors, and between urban and rural areas, and vertically, from local to international levels. Operating principles include downward and upward accountability, transparency, participation, equity, rule of law, ethics and responsiveness. Governance is therefore not limited to 'government' but includes the roles of the private sector and civil society. The character of relationships (and the formal and informal rules and regulations guiding such relationships) and the nature of information flow between different social actors and organizations are both key features of governance.

The above discussion provides some definitions and interpretations of governance, and indicates how it connects to water management. In the following section, attention turns to the significance of 'water governance'.

Significance of Water Governance

Increasing attention is being given to 'water governance', and, indeed, arguments are made that governance is critically important. For example, Lautze, de Silva, Giordano and Sanford (2011: 1) commented that,

> ... water governance has emerged as perhaps the most important topic in the international water community in the 21st century. The 2001 Bonn International Conference on Freshwater, a precursor to the 2002 Johannesburg World Summit on Sustainable Development

... identified water governance as the first of three areas for priority action. The second World Water Assessment report [in 2006] highlighted the central role of water governance in improving water resource conditions and boldly stated that 'the world water crisis is a crisis of governance—not one of security'. The World Bank has also recognized the importance of key governance trends, such as accountability, in all its efforts to reduce the impact of water scarcity.

The hyperbole of a 'world water crisis' does not have to be accepted to appreciate the strength of views being expressed about the need for more attention to governance. The image of a 'crisis' has undoubtedly been invoked to draw attention to governance, but evidence is rarely presented to verify what the nature of the 'water crisis' is.

Along with calls for more attention to 'water governance', suggestions have been offered regarding explicit principles or criteria against which to assess different water governance models. In that regard, Rogers and Hall (2003), in a report prepared for the Global Water Partnership (2002), identified 12 principles for water governance: (1) open, (2) transparent, (3) participative, (4) accountable, (5) effective, (6) coherent, (7) efficient, (8) communicative, (9) equitable, (10) integrative, (11) sustainable, and (12) ethical. Such principles provide an evaluative lens through which to view characteristics of different water governance models, as well as what happens when a specific model is put into practice.

Importance of 'Integration' Related to Water Governance

The motivation to ensure water governance facilitates an 'integrated approach', which is straightforward. Water is a system which interacts with other natural and social ecosystems. To illustrate, some water problems begin on the land (non-point pollution), but just as many problems on the land (flooding) begin with water. Therefore, to try to resolve water problems without attention to land issues is unlikely to lead to effective solutions. In a similar way, managers frequently have to deal with surface and groundwater, requiring expertise and attention regarding both. In addition, decisions and activities in upper parts of catchments have implications for downstream areas. And, often, the downstream areas are under different political or administrative authority, requiring capacity and competence to manage the catchment as a single management unit. Managers also must be able to determine the needs of humans and other species, in order to determine how water should be allocated to support economic, social and ecological services, especially in situations where potential need exceeds available supply (Conca, 2005; Mitchell, 2005, 2006; Mollinga et al., 2006; Kemper et al., 2007). These aspects are highlighted by Mehan's (2010: 14) comment regarding practice in the United States:

> For too long, water quality management has been characterized by compartmentalization and the creation of artificial boundaries among and between various aspects of what should be a unified approach to water quality in terms of the chemical, physical, and biological integrity of the nation's waters. It has tolerated—even encouraged—a bifurcated approach, allowing unnecessary polarities to dominate policy and practice: water quality versus quantity; land versus water; surface water versus groundwater; point versus non-point sources; energy versus water; and supply-side versus demand-side management.

Institutional arrangements often have reflected the 'silo' approach noted above by Mehan, with various government agencies each receiving responsibilities for specific aspects of water systems but without any provision for effective coordination processes or mechanisms. As a result, one agency might be responsible for water quantity and other for water quality, making decisions with regard to only its own responsibility. However, the reality is that both need to be viewed together to address 'water security' problems. Or, one agency might be responsible for water, while others are responsible for agriculture and wildlife, even though decisions taken by any one of them often impact the responsibilities of other agencies.

Various individuals have highlighted the importance of using an integrated perspective to overcome a silo or fragmented approach. Falkenmark et al. (2004: 305) stated that,

> Irrespective of the hierarchical structure of the institution arrangements, an integrated approach has to be taken to water, land use and ecosystems to secure an optimal use of both water and other water-dependent resources. IWRM is essential for securing a proper overview of all the activities that depend on the same resource and which are internally linked by the mobility of water, from the water divide to the river mouth.

They continued, elaborating about Integrated Water Resource Management (IWRM):

> ... a distinction has to be made between IWRM and coordination and execution of sector activities. IWRM secures compatibility and

> overall effectiveness, whereas specific sector activities and their coordination refer to implementation and service delivery. The notion of IWRM is quite broad and it should be seen as a necessary framework and guiding principle for sector-specific activities and competence and not as a substitute. (Falkenmark et al., 2004: 306)

In another publication, Falkenmark (2004: 279) provided further insight:

> ... the challenge is how to advance from today's single-component approaches—separately discussing water quantity, water quality, water for human water supply, water for food security, water for downstream aquatic ecosystems, water-related disease vectors, etc.,—to integrated approaches to catchments keeping both biophysical and societal processes in focus.

The above comments highlight why and how 'governance' is viewed as a key building block to achieve 'integration' and thereby to realize effective, efficient and equitable water management decisions. In the next section, the concept of IWRM is reviewed in more detail.

Integrated Water Resource Management

As already noted, the concept of IWRM, has been promoted in the belief that water policies and water management should be designed and implemented on the basis of an ecosystem approach, requiring explicit and systematic coordination and collaboration (Mitchell, 1990).

The most frequently cited definition of IWRM is the one by the Global Water Partnership (2000: 22): 'a process which promotes the coordinated development and management of water, land and related resources, in order to maximize the resultant economic and social welfare in an equitable manner without compromising the sustainability of vital ecosystems'. This definition reflects all the key concepts identified in the previous sections about outcomes expected from effective 'integration'.

Jaspers (2003: 78) provides specific insight about both benefits from and key components of an integrated approach,

> To prevent or remedy problems or conflict and to meet social and natural demands, integrated approaches are indispensable. Basic elements of these integrated approaches are a basin-wide planning scope, attention to management of surface and subsurface water and to water quantity, water quality and environmental integrity as an inseparable entity. Further, there should be an emphasis on the

relations between land use and water resources and to the integration of natural limitations, social and economic demands, and legal, political and administrative processes.

With reference to experience in Mexico, Garcia (2008: 32) concluded that, for water management to be integrated, the following processes should be addressed when solving problems: (1) soil-water and water-vegetation relationships, (2) economic, social and environmental aspects, (3) actions from all levels of government and stakeholders, (4) surface and groundwater, (5) water volume and water quality, (6) supply and demand-oriented actions, and (7) uses and/or users, that compete for the same water body or source.

No one has ever suggested that implementing IWRM would be easy, as an ecosystem approach poses many challenges, not the least is presence of diverse stakeholder interests, making achievement of agreement about overall directions and setting priorities a formidable task (Weale, 1992; Conca, 2005). Thus, it is not surprising that criticisms have arisen about IWRM (Braga, 2001: 586; Molle, 2008; Chéné, 2009; Butterworth et al., 2010; Tortajada, 2010).

Common criticisms have been that (1) there is no accepted definition for the concept of IWRM, making it difficult to apply or assess, (2) if an ecosystem approach is to be taken, how many other systems beyond water need to be considered because of their interrelationships with water (energy poverty)? (3) there is normally an uneven distribution of power among stakeholders in a catchment or watershed, meaning some interests are consistently under represented, (4) collaborative effort requires engagement by an active citizenry, but achieving genuine engagement often is challenging, (5) where there is inadequate infrastructure, political will, or corruption, attempts to achieve integration have little prospect of being successful, and (6) there are few examples of successful implementation of IWRA (Biswas, 2004, 2008a, 2008b; Rahman and Varis, 2005; Koehler and Koontz, 2008).

Hierarchies of IWRM

Garcia (2008: 28–29) suggests that different levels of IWRM can be viewed as a hierarchy. In his view, at least three different hierarchies should be considered when designing an IWRM approach:

1. *Constitutional*: Creating and applying basic water legislation and IWRM policies and strategies to establish the necessary enabling environment. Achieving this level requires commitment from key

political and management leaders. This level has attracted the most attention and effort.

2. *Associative*: Creating the means to facilitate a river basin or watershed approach, including design and implementation of river basin organizations with functions to allocate water flows, determine assimilative capacity, and facilitate ecosystem maintenance.
3 *Operational*: Ensuring funding for aspects such as water supply and sanitation, irrigation and drainage, and hydropower projects in order to meet demands and needs.

The above three levels related to IWRM provide a helpful framework to guide design of an integrated approach for any given situation.

IWRM and Arrangements for Governance

Regarding governance arrangements for IWRM, Jaspers (2003: 83) suggested following essentials: (1) management based on hydrological boundaries, (2) an organizational structure involving river basin and sub-basin authorities with their respective by-laws to incorporate decision-making at the lowest appropriate level, (3) a planning system oriented to production of integrated river basin plans, (4) mechanisms to facilitate stakeholder involvement in decision-making, and (5) a system of water pricing and cost recovery.

With specific regard to organizational structures, Jaspers (2003: 84) noted that the public sector has three options:

1. *De-concentration*: Assigning executive tasks and competencies to regional offices of a central authority or to lower levels within a central authority structure, but with basic authority and responsibility remaining with the central institution.
2. *Delegation*: Assigning executive tasks and competencies to some other public or private organizations, but without irreversible transfer of authority.
3. *Devolution*: Assigning executive tasks and competencies to other administrative organizations on an ongoing basis and with a complete shift of both responsibility and authority.

The three hierarchical levels proposed by Garcia and the three organizational options provided by Jaspers, along with the principles or criteria identified earlier, provide a template against which different water governance configurations can be considered. These ideas will be revisited later in this chapter, after considering experience with water governance in China.

China: Experience with Water Governance and an Integrated Approach

China has a long history regarding water management, especially related to watersheds or catchments. He and Chen (2001: 368) explain that China established water conservancy organizations for its major rivers starting in the late 1920s and early 1930s. At that time, conservancy organizations were created for the Huai, Yellow and Yangtze rivers. Later, during the 1950s, new river basin commissions were put in place for each of the seven major rivers: Yangtze, Yellow, Pearl, Huai, Hai, Songhua and Liao. He and Chen (2001: 368) state that 'These organizations ushered in a new era of integrated watershed management in China'. While several of the organizations were disbanded between the mid-1960s and mid-1970s, they were re-introduced in the late 1970s. Furthermore, in the mid-1990s, water pollution management was introduced on a 'whole-of-basin' basis for the Huai river and Taihu lake.

By the end of the 20th century, governance-related challenges had been identified related to the Chinese experience with water management. Major limitations include:

1. The river basin commissions, created by the central government, were focused on flood mitigation, sediment and drought control, and water pollution along sub-basin borders. However, each province also had a water resources bureau with 'equivalent power within its provincial boundary and considers watershed management planning only for its own provincial benefits'. One outcome was that, 'The commissions have little authority over administrative and economic issues in each basin, and there is little coordination of water issues with provincial water resources bureaux, environmental protection agencies and other agencies involved' (He and Chen, 2001: 169).
2. The Ministry of Water Resources, a central government agency, with responsibility for water quantity, had overlapping duties with the National Environmental Protection Agency, responsible for water quality protection and management. The MWR also shared roles with other agencies, such as those responsible for agriculture, forestry and transportation.

The main problems from such governance arrangements were identified by He and Chen (2001: 370–71) to be:

> The separation of water quantity management and pollution control, and the fragmentation of national and local agencies are regarded as

the main institutional issues in the water sector in China; in particular, river basins are separated by administrative boundaries with overlapping roles. This multi-agency sharing of water resources management leads to a situation where all agencies are partly responsible for their respective interests but none is readily liable for the damage.

> ... no acts or laws integrating resources development with environmental protection have been formulated for any particular river basin. In addition, rules of organization regarding river basin organizations are absent, which implies that there is no legal base for the stability, responsibilities and missions of river basin commissions. In this respect, another serious problem is the absence of any procedural laws related to public participation or community involvement.

The above assessment was reiterated by Yan, Daming and Kinne (2006). They characterized the administrative framework for water resources as the 'nine dragons', referring to nine separate government agencies: Ministry of Water Resources (MWR), State Environmental Protection Administration (SEPA), Ministry of Construction, Ministry of Agriculture, State Forestry Bureau, State Development and Reform Commission, State Electric Power Company, and Ministry of Communications. The intent of this mix of agencies was to create a 'combined force' to increase the efficiency of management and administration, However, as Yan, Daming and Kinne (2006: 292) commented,

> ... the fact that, along with the rapid and sustained economic development of China, the water situation continues to deteriorate, points to some problems in water administration. More specifically, policies on water in different departments weaken their power and reduce the efficiency of water resource management. In addition, the responsibilities of each department are not clearly defined making it difficult to realize that everyone [is] doing their best according to their responsibility. Furthermore, there is lack of coordination between industry management and administrative regional management.

They were particularly concerned about serious overlap in responsibilities and authority between the MWR and SEPA related to water resource protection and administration. Specifically, they noted,

> Disputes over trans-boundary water pollution between upstream and downstream users, or between/among different administrative areas in the same watershed are frequent and difficult to resolve. SEPA has both administrative authority and the responsibility to guide and

> coordinate the trans-regional environmental problems and the environmental pollution disputes between provinces. However, because trans-boundary water pollution disputes usually occur in a watercourse, the MWR, as the administrative department entrusted with watercourse management, has the power to management and coordinate the disputes. (Yan, Daming and Kinne, 2006: 297)

The above concerns are re-iterated by Wang, Gu and Higano (2006) based on their analysis of management for Lake Taihu, the third largest freshwater lake in China and located on the southern extent of the Yangtze River delta. In their view,

> In the Lake Taihu basin, for example, the main philosophy of environmental management still remains command-and-control, the legacy of the planned economy. Therefore, administrative entities are usually vertically, horizontally, and functionally fragmented. Public involvement in the management process is far from adequate .... To promote cooperation among different administrative entities, it is urgently necessary to establish a basin authority that is powerful enough to be responsible for overall planning, implementation, monitoring, and evaluation of environmental protection programs. (2006: 585)

Given the above assessments of governance arrangements at the national, state and municipal levels, it is instructive to examine experiences in two specific places: the Biliu river basin, Liaoning province, and the Hongze lake and Gaoyou lake, Jiangsu province.

Biliu River Basin, Liaoning Province

The Biliu river basin is situated in northeast China in Liaoning Province. The river is the largest (156 km long, 2,814 km^2) in the southern part of the province, and is the primary water source for Dalian Municipality, with a population of well over 6 million people. The upper portion of the basin is within Yingkou municipality, while the mid and lower portions are within Dalian Municipality, creating a shared jurisdiction for the basin.

Gong et al. (2010) analysed management approaches in the basin. In their view, while the Biliu river basin is relatively small, it faces many challenges associated with split and overlapping jurisdictions. Thus, although all national environmental regulations apply to it, the local municipalities have flexibility to develop policies and practices that reflect the local context. The outcome is that each of Yingkou and Dalian has developed and implemented its own regulations, creating difficulties to harmonize upstream-downstream interrelationships. As Gong et al. (2010: 176) observed,

> Both of the water and environmental bureaus have power within their municipal boundary and consider watershed management planning only for their own benefit. The dilemma is that although each city has relevant agencies to manage its water issues within its territories, none of these agencies are subordinate to one another, nor can any of them play a leading role in watershed management. Consequently, cross-regional and cross-departmental issues always exist.
>
> ... both cities have little coordination of water issues with each other, and with the provincial water resources bureau, environmental protection bureau and other agencies involved. As a result, the fragmented responsibilities among watershed management organizations have led to several unsatisfactory outcomes, such as lack of a legal framework for managing water resources between watershed boundaries, increased water pollution, and ineffective and inefficient water resource allocation.

Another challenge is that the two municipalities have had difficulties in enforcing their regulations. To illustrate, regulations exist related to water quality, with special orders providing ability to ensure capacity of treatment facilities, suspend production and even close a non-complying facility. Nevertheless, over a five year period, only 50 warnings, fines and revocation of water permits had been issued. The main reasons were viewed to be a strong, pro-growth philosophy of local leaders, pro-development attitudes of enforcement officers, a well-entrenched culture (guanxi) that ensures influence based on the strength of relationships and personal reciprocity, and inadequate enforcement capacity due to minimal allocation of resources and development of management skills.

Hongze Lake and Gaoyou Lake, Jiangsu Province

Hongze and Gaoyou lakes are sources of water for the Grand Canal as well as for the eastern route of the South-to-North Water transfer project. Hongze lake is the fourth largest freshwater lake in China, with a surface area of 1,960 km^2. Gaoyou lake is smaller, with an area of 674.7 km^2. Monitoring indicates that the water quality of both lakes is poor, and does not meet many national environmental standards.

Some issues experienced in the Biliu river basin also occur with regard to the two lakes. For example, many provincial, municipal and county agencies are involved in water management, ranging from bureaus of water resources, environmental protection, fisheries, land resources, tourism and transportation. Li, Wei and Mitchell (2010: 7) state that the Bureau of Water Resources of Jiangsu Province (BWRJP), the agency mainly responsible for management and development of water quantity, has overlapping responsibilities with the Environmental Protection Agency, which is responsible for water quality protection and management. The BWRJP also shares responsibilities with agencies dealing with agriculture, fisheries and transportation. A further organization in this area is the Huaihe River Commission (HRC), established in 1990 and directly under the central Ministry of Water Resources. The HRC is primarily responsible for flood control and distribution of water resources, but has little authority related to pollution control. Furthermore, it concentrates on the Huaihe river, and is not involved with lakes outside of its watershed. As a result of these institutional arrangements, there are ongoing challenges related to coordination and collaboration.

Li, Wei and Mitchell (2010: 8) also note that, while stakeholder participation is a component of best practice in water management, 'In China, environmental issues have largely been tackled by government officials in a "top-down" manner. The public has little access to planning and management processes'. However, various pilot projects have been undertaken in Jiangsu province, and it is stated under General Rules that government units are to ensure both experts and the public participate actively in environmental assessment and management processes. Despite such a directive, there still often are gaps between intent and action, with the result that public participation is still often uneven and limited. Thus, opportunity exists for improvement related to stakeholder engagement or public participation.

China: Implications Moving Forward

The experiences documented above highlight that separation of water quantity and pollution management, along with fragmentation of national and local agencies, hinder the management of water in China. To overcome such governance issues, the following initiatives are frequently endorsed by researchers:

1. *Legislation* to confirm both the missions and functions of river basin commissions (He and Chen, 2001: 372), which is also Garcia's *constitutional* requirement. Yan, Daming and Kinne (2006: 299) elaborated upon what should be included in laws, suggesting that it would be desirable '... to build cooperative

relationships between the departments into the water laws to make cooperation one of the legal principles upon which water management is based'.

2. *River Basin Agencies* should be either created, rebuilt or improved 'to satisfactorily address the integration of water resources development and protection' (Gong et al., 2010: 177), reflecting Garcia's *associative* requirement and Jaspers' *devolution* option. Yan, Daming and Kinne (2006: 300) suggested a further feature to allow collaborative administration of water management in river basins. In their view, it would be desirable '... to set up unified collaboration/negotiation institutions at the state and river basin levels to facilitate negotiation between the relative departments of water administration, to confirm water policies and to coordinate and mediate water resource disputes'. In addition, Wang and Gao (2002: 347) have urged that basin agencies need to advance 'local economic development and co-ordination in the basin and unified planning [for] water utilization in the upper, middle and lower reaches ...'.
3. *Attributes for River Basin Commissions*, as outlined by He and Chen (2001: 372). These are: (a) comprehensive administrative authority regarding economic and social development within each catchment, (b) significant independence regarding both watershed management and administrative expenditures, and (c) strong coordination functions and capacity (Garcia's *associative* and *operational* requirements). Furthermore, these recommendations urge the adoption of Jaspers' *devolution* model by assigning to the river basin commissions executive tasks and competencies on an ongoing basis and with a complete shift of both responsibility and authority to them.
4. *Community-based Watershed Management*: As outlined by Gong et al. (2010: 178), the use of a community-based approach adds value from local knowledge and also promotes openness and transparency. However, they also observed that '... such an approach would be unique in China, since public participation on public affairs is still limited and weak'. Encouraging and facilitating public participation is also proposed by He and Chen (2001: 371).

If the above four initiatives were advanced, governance arrangements for water management would evolve, and move closer to what is advocated internationally as best practice for an integrated or systems approach.

Implications

At the outset of this chapter, it was observed that increasing attention is being given to governance issues in order that the management of water resources can be improved. Some argue that 'governance' may be the most critical aspect. In that context, IWRM has received considerable attention in the last two decades, as it is one of the means to overcome basic challenges related to compartmentalization, fragmentation, silos, and polarities among organizations and interests involved in water management. Such challenges are exacerbated due to the interrelationships of water with other natural and human systems.

IWRM is not a panacea or silver bullet to resolve the above problems, and the difficulties in achieving coordination and cooperation are well highlighted by the challenges experienced in China. It is not surprising that problems are encountered with initiatives to implement an integrated approach. Factors such as ongoing change, complexity, uncertainty and conflict are non-trivial, and need attention in all planning and management situations (Mitchell, 2002).

It is relatively easy to identify weaknesses in the concept of IWRM and with specific IWRM experiences. However, I suggest that criticism unaccompanied by constructive alternatives to achieve coherent, coordinated and collaborative approaches to water management are not helpful. More specifically, if IWRM and associated governance arrangements are found wanting to resolve the water problems encountered in most parts of the world, it would be helpful to have alternatives put forward related to how to deal effectively with: (1) upstream and downstream issues in catchments; (2) relationships between surface and ground water; (3) interconnections between water quantity and quality; (4) achieving balance among aspirations for economic development, ecological integrity, and cultural sensitivity; (5) connections of water with other biophysical ecosystems, such as land or forests; and (6) relationships of water with other systems such as energy, health and poverty. All these matters are significant, and highly likely to endure. Ongoing dialogue and development of constructive options will facilitate progress for all of these at local, regional, national and international scales.

References

Biswas, A.K. (2004). "Integrated Water Resources Management: A Re-assessment", *Water International*, 29(2): 248–56.

——. (2008a). "Integrated Water Resources Management: Is It Working?", *Water Resources Development*, 24(1): 5–22.

——. (2008b). "Current Directions: Integrated Water Resources Management: A Second Look", *Water International,* 33(3): 274–78.

Blanco, J. (2008). Integrated Water Resource Management in Colombia: Paralysis by Analysis? *Water Resources Development,* 24(1): 91–101.

Braga, B.P.F. (2001). "Integrated Urban Water Resources Management: A Challenge into the 21st Century", *Water Resources Development,* 17(4): 581–99.

Butterworth, J., J. Warner, P. Moriarity, S. Smits, and C. Batchelor, C. (2010). "Finding Practical Approaches to Integrated Water Resources Management", *Water Alternatives,* 3(1): 68–81.

Chéné, J.M. (2009). "Integrated Water Resources Management: Theory Versus Practice", *Natural Resources Forum,* 33(1): 2–5.

Conca, K. (2005). *Governing Water: Contentious Transnational Politics and Global Institution Building,* Cambridge, Mass.: MIT Press.

Falkenmark, M. (2004). "Toward Integrated Catchment Management: Opening the Paradigm Locks Between Hydrology, Ecology and Policy-making", *International Journal of Water Resources Development,* 20(3): 275–82.

Falkenmark, M., L. Gottschalk, J. Lundqvist and P. Wouters. (2004). "Towards Integrated Catchment Management: Increasing the Dialogue Between Scientists, Policy-makers and Stakeholders", *International Journal of Water Resources Development*, 20(3): 297–309.

Garcia L.E. (2008). "Integrated Water Resources Management: A "small" Step for Conceptualists, A Giant Step for Practitioners", *Water Resources Development*. 24(1): 23–36.

Gong, Y., B. Mitchell, F. Tsuyoshi and T. Nakayama (2010). "Perspectives on Small Watershed Management in China: The Case of Biliu", *International Journal of Sustainable Development and World Ecology*, 17(2): 172–79.

Global Water Partnership (2000). *Integrated Water Resources Management*. Technical Advisory Committee Background Paper No. 4, Stockholm: Global Water Partnership.

——. (2002). *Introducing Effective Water Governance*. GWP Technical Paper, Stockholm: Global Water Partnership.

He, D. and J. Chen (2001). "Issues, Perspectives, and Need for Integrated Watershed Management in China", *Environmental Conservation,* 28(4): 368–77.

Jaspers, F.G.W. (2003). "Institutional Arrangements for Integrated River Basin Management", *Water Policy,* 5: 77–90.

Kemper, K.E., W. Blomquist, and A. Dinar (Eds.) (2007). *Integrated River Basin Management though Decentralization.* Berlin: Springer-Verlag.

Kidd, S. and D. Shaw (2007). "Integrated Water Resource Management and Institutional Integration: Realizing the Potential of Spatial Planning in England", *Geographical Journal*, 173(4): 312–29.

Koehler, B. and T.M. Koontz (2008). "Citizen Participation in Collaborative Watershed Partnerships", *Environmental Management*, 41(2): 143–54.

Lautze, J., S. de Silva, M. Giordano and L. Sanford, L. (2011). "Putting the Cart Before the Horse: Water Governance and IWRM", *Natural Resources Forum*, 35(1):1–18.

Li, S., W. Guo and B. Mitchell (2010). "Evaluation of Water Quality and Management of Hongze Lake and Gaoyou Lake along the Grand Canal in Eastern China", *Environmental Monitoring and Assessment*. Published Online at DOI 10.1007/s10661–010–1590–5

Mehan, G.T. (2010). "A Symphonic Approach to Water Management: The Quest for New Models of Watershed Governance", *Journal of Land Use and Environmental Law*, 26(1): 1–33.

Mitchell, B. (1990). "Integrated Water Management", in B. Mitchell (Ed.), *Integrated Water Management: International Experiences and Perspectives*. London and New York: Belhaven Press, pp. 1–21.

——. (2002). *Resource and Environmental Management*. Harlow: Prentice Hall.

——. (2005). "Integrated Water Resource Management, Institutional Arrangements and Land-use Planning", *Environment and Planning*, 37(8): 1335–52.

——. (2006). "IWRM in Practice: Lessons from Canadian Experience", *Journal of Contemporary Water Research and Education*, 135: 51–55.

Molle, F. (2008). "Nirvana Concepts, Narratives and Policy Models: Insights from the Water Sector", *Water Alternatives*, 1(1):131–56.

Mollinga, P.P., A. Dixit and K. Athukorala (Eds.) (2006). *Integrated Water Resource Management: Global Theory, Emerging Practice and Local Needs*, Vol. 1, London: Sage Publications.

Olsson, P. (2007). "The Role of Vision in Framing Adaptive Co-management Processes: Lessons from Kistianstads Vattenrike, Southern Sweden", In D. Armitage, F. Berkes and D. Doubleday (Eds.), *Adaptive Co-management: Collaboration, Learning and Multi-level Governance*. Vancouver: University of British Columbia Press, pp. 168–85.

Rahman, M.M. and O. Varis (2005). "Integrated Water Resources Management: Evolution, Prospects and Future Challenges", *Sustainability: Science, Practice and Policy*, 1(1): 15–21.

Rogers, P. and A.W. Hall (2003). *Effective Water Governance*. TEC Background Paper No. 7, Stockholm. Sweden Water Partnership.

Tortajada, C. (2010). "Water Governance: Some Critical Issues", *International Journal of Water Resources Development*, 26(2): 297–307.

Tropp, H. (2007). "Water Governance: Trends and Needs for New Capacity Development", *Water Policy*, 9(1): 19–30.

Wang, Q.G., G. Gu and Y. Higano (2006). "Toward Integrated Environmental Management for Challenges in Water Environmental Protection of Lake Taihu Basin in China", *Environmental Management*, 37(5): 579–88.

Wang, X., and Q. Gao (2002). "Sustainable Development and Management of Water Resources in the Hei River Basin of North-west China", *International Journal of Water Resources Development*, 18(2): 335–52.

Weale, A. (1992). "Implementation Failure: A Suitable Case for Review?" In E. Lykke (Ed.), *Achieving Environmental Goals: The Concept and Practice of Environmental Performance Review.* London: Belhaven, pp. 43–63.

World Water Assessment Programme (2006). *Water, A Shared Responsibility*, The United Nations World Water Development Report 2, Paris: United Nations Educational, Scientific and Cultural Organization, and New York: Berghahn Books.

Yan, F., H. Daming and B. Kinne (2006). "Water Resources Administration Institution in China", *Water Policy*, 8(4): 291–301.

10

The Trajectory of Environmental Justice in India

Prospects and Challenges for the National Green Tribunal

KIRIT PATEL AND KATHRYN DEY

The Indian judiciary entered a new era of environmental jurisprudence with the official notification of the National Green Tribunal (NGT) on October 18, 2010. The NGT is a specialized environmental court with a mandate to provide effective and expeditious disposal of cases relating to environment, to enforce any legal right relating to the environment, provide relief and compensation for damages caused to person and property and for dealing in matters connected therewith or incidental thereto (Government of India, 2010: 1). The creation of the NGT has come at a time of accelerated economic growth in India marked by an average GDP increase per year of 7.2 per cent between 1994 and 2010 (World Bank, 2011). The economic surge has, however, been clouded by widespread environmental degradation, income inequality and rising poverty. In spite of profound ecological consciousness and values rooted in its ancient culture (Dwivedi, 1997: 224), massive deforestation, soil erosion, overgrazing, loss of

It is a privilege to contribute a chapter to this felicitation volume to honour Dr O.P. Dwivedi. I have known Dr Dwivedi for over a decade and this chapter draws inspiration from his pioneering research on India's environmental policy, governance, justice and ethics for four decades. As a graduate student at Guelph, I had the opportunity to work with Dr Dwivedi in his various research projects and assisted him in teaching his most popular course at Guelph on Environmental Policy Formulation and Administration. Dr Dwivedi is an exemplary scholar, teacher, mentor, philanthropist, and human being of a stature beyond my ability to express in words.

biodiversity and pollution from industrial effluents and vehicular emissions are growing at an alarming pace. Approximately half of India's population continues to live in multidimensional poverty (UNDP, 2011). The majority of the rural poor rely directly on the already degraded natural resources for their livelihood while their counterparts in overpopulated cities experience unprecedented risk to their health due to rampant pollution in places where they work and live. In this context, the proclamation of the NGT brings high hopes for mitigating the complexities of the environment versus development debate with the help of specialized judges and environmental experts.

The year 1972 marked a defining era in the history of environmental policy making in India (Dwivedi, 1997: 54). It was the year when India established the National Committee for Environmental Policy and Coordination (NCEPC) that eventually became the Ministry of Environment and Forests (MoEF) in 1985. Further, it was in 1972 at the United Nations Stockholm Conference on Human Environment that Prime Minister Indira Gandhi alerted the global leadership to the fact that issues pertaining to the natural environment could not be separated from the grim poverty confronting large numbers of people in the developing world. This essay presents a trajectory of environmental justice in India over three periods: (i) post-UN Stockholm Conference (1972–1992); (ii) post-Rio Conference (1992–2009); and (iii) the creation of the National Green Tribunal (NGT) (2010–2011). The chapter then discusses the important features of the NGT from the following perspectives: (i) structure and appointment process; (ii) jurisdiction and access for the poor; and (iii) compensation for environmental externality. In the last section, the chapter examines challenges faced by the NGT under the neo-liberal policy environment and growing marginalization of the poor.

Post-Stockholm Conference (1972–1992): Beginning of Green Justice

There was no mention of the natural environment and environment-related rights in the original Constitution of India endorsed by the parliament in 1950. Until the establishment of the NCEPC in February 1972, the environment did not receive significant attention from Indian policy makers, administrators or the judiciary. Then, as a signatory to the Stockholm Declaration in 1972, India's legislative and executive branches responded with an array of environmental laws. A series of legislative foundations for environmental protection were enacted during this period beginning with the Wildlife Protection Act of 1972 and the Water (Prevention and Control of Pollution) Act of 1974. Through the 1980s to early 1990s, the Indian government enacted the Forest Conservation Act (1981), the Air (Prevention and Control of Pollution) Act (1986), the National Forest Policy (1988), the Environmental Protection Act (1986), the Public Liability Insurance Act (1991) and the Wildlife Protection Amendment Act (1991) to initiate a wide range of regulatory instruments. Despite having several important environmental Acts in place within a decade of the Stockholm Conference, the executive branches lacked the resources, capacity and the political will to enforce them (Dwivedi, 1997).

The Stockholm Declaration expected signatory nations to include environmental rights within the fundamental human rights embraced by their highest constitutional authority. This became a challenge for India as it was in political turmoil leading up, in March 1975, to the declaration of a National Emergency under Article 352 of the Constitution.[1] Though most of the constitutional amendments introduced just before or during the Emergency period were strongly criticized as anti-democratic, some amendments made positive contributions towards environmental protection. The 42nd amendment, for example, enacted by the captive parliament in 1976, included several important provisions for environmental protection in the sections on Directive Principles for State Policy (Article 48A) and fundamental duties of citizen [Article 51A(g)]. The amended Article 48A of the Constitution directed provincial governments to protect and improve the environment and to safeguard the forests and wildlife of the country. Similarly, the amended Article 51A(g) expects every citizen, as a part of their constitutional duty, to protect and improve the natural environment, including forests, lakes, rivers and wildlife. Irrespective of strong nationwide protest and democratic backlash toward the overall 42nd amendment to the Constitution, it earned distinct international honour for India in the environmental policy arena. India became the first country in the world to amend its Constitution to include environmental protection in accordance with the Stockholm Declaration. On the other hand, constitutional and legal experts described the 42nd amendment as one of the most draconian Acts of independent India because it established the supremacy of parliament and curtailed the powers of the judiciary, especially the Supreme Court and High Courts. The new government that came into power after the end of Emergency period in 1977 introduced several amendments to remove most of the provisions of the 42nd amendment and restored the *status quo ante* to revive the power and independence of the judiciary.

The courts became important actors in the protection of the environment in India because institutions overseeing the enforcement of various environment-related laws were weak and because constitutional provisions related to citizens rights, in lieu of their duties stipulated in Article 51A(g), to a healthy or wholesome environment were ambiguous. The constitutional and political challenges created in the mid-1970s provided several opportunities for the judiciary to assert its independence from legislative wings and its power to introduce legal innovations for protecting parliamentary democracy and the fundamental rights of citizens (Baar, 1990). At the end of the Emergency, these legal innovations played a critical role in addressing socio-economic inequality and environmental degradation. The judiciary entered a creative phase of constitutional interpretation throughout the 1980s in an effort to protect the environment and provide access to the courts for the poor. In a series of unprecedented rulings, the Supreme Court institutionalized the expansion of basic human rights by its broad interpretation of the right to life and liberty provisions made under Article 21 of the Constitution. The apex court's initial motivation for the interpretation of the right to life provision was in protecting basic human or socio-economic rights of prisoners, bonded labourers, child labourers and pavement dwellers.[2] The Supreme Court, in a landmark judgment, in *Subhash Kumar* v. *State of Bihar* [AIR (1991) 420], held that the right to life guaranteed under Article 21 of the Constitution includes the right to the enjoyment of pollution-free water. Though the court dismissed the appeal for recourse on another grounds, the judgment became a crucial case law for seeking court intervention to protect the environment and seek redress for any violation of individual citizens' rights to a wholesome environment, including the right to air and water free of pollution.

In the post-Stockholm Conference era, the cause of environmental justice made significant progress as a result of the Supreme Court's innovative interpretation of the Constitution to relax requirements for *locus standi*.[3] After the landmark ruling of Justice P. N. Bhagwati describing the significance of public interest litigation (PIL) in *S.P. Gupta* v. *Union of India* (1982 SC 149), the courts faced a huge influx of cases with environment-related issues. Further, the apex court relaxed the rules of filing PILs and introduced epistolary jurisdiction where a simple letter or postcard to the court constitutes a writ petition for PIL. These decisions created the legal space for any citizen, acting in good faith on behalf of another disadvantaged person, to petition the court without paying any fees for court proceedings. It brought a new era of activism in India by providing a legal instrument and legitimacy for non-governmental organizations (NGOs) and activists to seek the court's intervention for protecting the environment and socio-economic rights of the poor. In summary, the innovative role played by the judiciary through the provision of PIL and creative interpretations of the Constitution during the two decades after the Stockholm Conference made significant contributions to the environment, democracy, and the realization of the socio-economic rights of citizens.

Post-Rio Conference (1992–2009): National Environmental Tribunal, Appellate Authority and Green Benches

The UN Conference on Environment and Development held in Rio de Janeiro in 1992 called upon nation-states to provide effective access to judicial proceedings and to enact national laws regarding liability and compensation for the victims of environmental degradation. India's second phase of environmental jurisprudence grew out of response to the commitment made in the Rio Declaration. The government responded by legislating two specialized institutions to alleviate the pressure of the increasing number of environmental petitions and the complexities involved in their adjudication.

In 1995, the government enacted the National Environmental Tribunal (NET) Act to provide effective and expeditious relief, restitution and compensation for damages to human property and the environment arising out of accidents caused from the handling of hazardous substances (Dwivedi, 1997: 101). The Tribunal was to consist of judicial and technical members who would be recommended by a selection committee representing various government ministries. The qualifications of members stipulated in the Act posed serious issues to the Tribunal as it did not emphasize sufficiently the recruitment of experienced judges from the High Court or Supreme Court ranks. In fact, the NET Act provided enough leverage to recruit retired administrative bureaucrats to all positions, including that of chairperson of the Tribunal. The NET's jurisdiction prevailed over civil courts in environmental matters but it faced a challenge in gaining recognition in the judicial ranks due to the underrepresentation of judicial members in the Tribunal. Further, the NET had a very narrow environmental mandate, which focused only on cases involving 'hazardous' chemicals. In spite of some promising features, the NET never became functional and existed merely as a document.

In 1997, the government established the National Environmental Appellate Authority (NEAA) as a mechanism for any aggrieved person to appeal environmental clearances granted to industrial and infrastructure projects by the MoEF. The NEAA was based in Delhi and was to be constituted of a chairperson, vice-chairperson and a maximum of three expert members. The NEAA Act (Article 5) stipulates that only retired or current judges from the Supreme Court or High Courts could qualify for the post of chairperson. A legal background or experience was however not emphasized for vice-chairperson and expert members. The NEAA's jurisdiction was inherently narrow as it could only adjudicate environmental appeals that were linked with the clearance process stipulated under the Environment Protection Act and granted by the MoEF. It had no expertise or jurisdiction to hear cases related to harmful impacts on health, property damage, compensation, and infringement of rights under Article 21 of the Constitution. The NEAA had a fully functional bench from 1997 to 2000 under the chairmanship of Justice (Retired) N. Venkatachala, but it heard and adjudicated few cases (Kohli, 2011). Since the year 2000, no judicial member was appointed to the NEAA (LCI, 2003: 6) due to the lack of recognition of the NEAA within the judicial hierarchy and downgraded remuneration package as compared to the Supreme Court or High Courts (The Access Initiative, 2010). The NEAA failed, in part, because it was predominantly made up of retired bureaucrats who had been earlier involved in granting environmental clearance and who had little experience in law or the environmental impact assessment process.

Both the NET and the NEAA became merely cosmetic institutional structures. The potential success of both of these specialized courts was plagued by a lack of political will for creating independent institutions that could attain the confidence of people and the mainstream judiciary. That citizens lacked confidence in these tribunals was evident from the small number of cases received by the appellate authority during its entire lifespan. The failure of the tribunals increased the influx of environment-related PILs and private cases in mainstream courts. Consequently, in the post-Rio era, the judiciary was left again to find its ways in dealing with the increased volume and complexity of environmental cases.

Realizing the importance of technical expertise and consistency in jurisprudence, the Supreme Court established an informal bench of select judges in 1995 that would be assigned to environmental cases. The bench set aside all Friday afternoons to screen environmental PILs to be heard in the Supreme Court. It was this informal bench that inspired the creation of provincial level green benches. Under the directive issued by the Supreme Court in 1996 as a result of a writ petition filed before the court (Writ Petition No. 385 (W) of 1995), the High Court of West Bengal constituted India's first specialized provincial level green bench to hear all environment-related cases in its jurisdiction with the highest degree of environmental sensitivity and objectivity. Subsequently, eight other green benches were set up in the High Courts of Tamil Nadu, Gujarat, Maharashtra, Punjab and Haryana, Karnataka, Kerala, Madhya Pradesh and Himachal Pradesh. Unlike the Supreme Court green bench, the High Court Green benches were permanent; however, their structure varies a great deal across provinces. In spite of their disparity in structure, context of origin, availability of institutional resources, and provincial environmental policies, the High Court green benches, along with Supreme Court's green bench, contributed tremendously to environmental jurisprudence in India. Many judgments[4] passed by these green benches embraced international principles laid out in the 1992 Rio Declaration, such as the principle of polluter pays, precautionary action, sustainable development and absolute liability (Sahu, 2008). These innovations have brought positive change to the traditional function of courts in interpreting environmental law and resolving litigation and have instilled a sense of societal responsibility on the judiciary. However, the legislative and executive branches expressed displeasure, at times, towards the green benches and sought ways to restrain their power. Because the green benches exist within the mainstream judiciary where the government has very little role in assigning judges to a particular bench, defining jurisdiction and the process of adjudication, limiting power of the green benches was a difficult task for the state. On the other hand, state controlled NET and NEAA proved ineffective in protecting government interests, linked with neo-liberal agenda in post-Rio era, as they utterly failed to enforce their jurisdiction over green benches.

The National Green Tribunal (2010–11): Beginning of a New Era

The Supreme Court of India highlighted the need for an effective environmental court in its several different rulings since the mid-1980s. The NGT owes its inception, at least in part, to declarations made by the Supreme Court in three different cases.[5] In each of these cases, the court clearly advocated for the creation of a specialized environmental court to deal with the complexities in examining environmental issues with multidisciplinary perspectives in a timely and efficient manner. Following these observations and in recognition that the functioning of the existing environmental quasi-judicial bodies was inadequate, the Law Commission of India (LCI) initiated a detailed study on the topic. In its 186th report of 2003, the LCI recommended the establishment of a specialized environmental court with both original and appellate jurisdiction for the purpose of reducing the pressure of environmental cases on both the Supreme Court and High Courts (LCI, 2003). In pursuance to the report, the MoEF presented the National Green Tribunal Bill to the lower house of parliament in July of 2009. The bill was stalled in parliament for an extended period of time because of the competing interests but was passed after incorporating several changes in June 2010. The NGT Act marked the beginning of new era for environmental jurisprudence in India, with a clear mandate to provide effective access to judicial and administrative proceedings as envisioned by world leaders at the Rio Conference in 1992.

With the passing of the NGT Act, India joined a group of 41 nation-states that have created specialized courts or tribunals for adjudicating environmental cases. The first chairperson of the NGT was appointed on October 18, 2010 and the principal bench of the NGT located in Delhi began hearing cases from July 4, 2011. The subsequent appointment of judges and technical experts for four regional benches of the NGT is still in process. Pring and Pring (2009), in their comparative study of environmental courts across countries, have identified best practices in relation to access rights, structure of courts, process of appointing judges, role of technical experts, jurisdiction and case management. Notably, the NGT Act meets several best practices in important areas, including its legislated trial and appellate jurisdiction, open rule of standing and the directed application of the precautionary principle, polluter pays and the principle of sustainable development in any decision, order or award. While it is too early to speculate the future success or failure of the NGT, the following sections examine the potential implications of the NGT Act on environmental jurisprudence and on the poor.

An Overview of the NGT: Structure and Appointment Process

India's NGT resembles with the best models of freestanding specialized environmental courts set up by Australia and New Zealand. The composition of the NGT will consist of a full-time chairperson and no less than 10, but no more than 20, full-time judicial members who have been members of the Supreme Court or High Courts of India. While the appointment process for the chairperson meets international expectations stipulated by Pring and Pring (2009), the NGT Act is vague in who will constitute the selection committee responsible for the remaining appointments. The heavy reliance on the Union Government for appointment of the crucial selection committee raises concerns considering past experience of either inaction or what Nambiar (2010) calls 'post-retirement rehabilitation'. The NGT Act includes equivalent representation of technical experts who can bring expertise in various environment-related fields. The technical expert shall hold minimum master's degree either in physical sciences, life sciences, engineering or technology and should have no less than 15 years of professional experience. The NGT Act makes no provisions for a social scientist, human ecologist, development professional working with small NGOs or civil society groups who have been active in the realm of environmental protection. This could prove to be an important omission given the most recent attitude of the court and the government's drive for large infrastructure and development projects involving the displacement of communities. Having social scientists or development professionals on the NGT bench could impart important perspectives for balancing environmental and socio-economic concerns. Further, technical experts in the NGT must have at least five years of work experience related to environmental issues from a 'reputable' institution. The interpretation of the term *reputable* in the NGT Act and subsequent rules lends a strong bias towards candidates who have worked within the administrative bureaucracy or state-run technical institutions. This would imply that the bureaucratic officers responsible for environmental clearances and/or enforcement can, at some point of time, be responsible for deciding its validity (Nambiar, 2010: 17). Gill (2010) suggests that the appointment of bureaucrats in the NGT could become a system of rewarding inefficiency as the inadequate performance of regulatory institutions run by the same cadre of bureaucrats led to the backlog of cases and the emergence of the NGT.

Access and Jurisdiction of the NGT

The NGT (Article 14: 3) will only entertain grievances filed within six months from the date on which the action for such dispute arose. There are provisions to increase this time limit for a period not to exceed 60 days where the Tribunal finds sufficient cause for extension. The full extent of ecological and human damage caused by any specific activity, however, is unlikely to be realized in six months. The poor need a much longer period to detect the detrimental impacts of a specific pollutant, such as chemical pesticides or asbestos, on their health due to lack of effective public healthcare programmes in the country. Thus, the limit of six to eight months to approach the court for seeking environmental grievances warrants careful reconsideration.

Of serious concern in relation to access for India's rural poor is that the NGT will serve in only five locations throughout the country with the main branch in Delhi and circuit branches in Kolkata, Pune, Bhopal and Chennai. Civil courts, located at each block level, are undoubtedly the first venue of action for many local communities to seek environmental redress, as they are within travelling distance to rural villages. Under the NGT, civil courts will no longer have jurisdiction in matters relating to the environment (Article 29: 1, 2). Further, civil courts conduct their business in local language and lawyer's fees in those local courts are relatively low. Transferring all pending and future environmental cases to circuit branches of the NGT will be disadvantageous for the poor considering cost of travel, language barriers, and higher legal fees of English-speaking environmental lawyers. The supporters of specialized courts may argue that allowing civil courts to adjudicate environmental cases will defeat the purpose of specialized court and may create unnecessary confusion over jurisdiction. Unless there is unswerving support from external agencies like NGOs or individual activists, poor communities are unlikely to approach the NGT. Civil court judges or benches may not have the best expertise in determining causal factors, environmental assessment, and social costs estimation, but they are sufficiently equipped to enforce precautionary principles and oversee compliance of orders issued by the regulatory agencies.

The inclusion of technical experts is a defining feature of the NGT, but this also implies that the bench will expect concerned parties in all cases to present irrefutable evidence generated by scientific methods. The NGT Act is silent on the issue of burden of proof. This implies poor communities or small NGOs supporting public interest petitions may have to pay costs for producing scientific evidence indicating harmful impacts on their health and the environment. The track record of public sector research and development institutions to furnish competent evidence for marginalized communities is dismal in India. While adjudicating some of the public interest litigations, several courts in recent years have made it clear that if a development project is stayed on account of a public interest petition, which is subsequently dismissed, the petitioner could be made liable to pay for the damages occasioned by the delay in the project (Gonsalves and Sahu, 2011: 19). The NGT Act (Article 23: 2) enforces this trend by allowing the court to assign any penalty, if it sees fit, in cases that are found 'not maintainable' by the court. This clause may be justifiable as a stick to deter parties who bring false or malicious public interest petitions to the court. However, most environmental litigations in India are found to be genuine and brought with sincere concerns for the environment (Access Initiative, 2010: 24). The notion that the court, at its discretion, is able to find a claim not maintainable and thus impose some penalty, could cause apprehension about the NGT among the poor and NGOs. These individuals and NGOs may not approach the NGT as the fear of losing a legitimate claim becomes overwhelming due to possibility of attracting a penalty. This issue necessitates serious attention because, as Gauri (2010) observes, the number of PILs filed in support of causes representing the poor is declining.

Compensation under the NGT

Article 15:1 of the NGT Act empowers the Tribunal to order relief or compensation for victims of pollution or persons who are aggrieved by the environmental damage arising from decisions or order made under the Water (Prevention and Control of Pollution) Act (1974), Forest Conservation Act (1980), Air (Prevention and Control Pollution) Act (1981), Environment Protection Act (1986) and Biological Diversity Act (2002). The relief or compensation order may include cost of restitution of damaged property or environmental degradation resulting from the activities under dispute. Compensation may be awarded to any person who has sustained injury, an owner whose property has suffered damage or a legal representative of a diseased person where death has resulted from environmental damage. Many tribal and socially disadvantaged communities living in forests and hilly regions do not have private property rights over land, forest or other natural resources. Their livelihood is primarily dependent on usufructs rights to harvest forest products and farm common property or de facto open access land. This is of a particular concern because a large portion of India's most vulnerable or disfranchised citizens continue their struggle in mainstream courts claiming fair compensation for resources that they historically used and managed under the non-private property rights regimes. Though the NGT Act ambiguously claims to apply the principle of sustainable development, it has not made any explicit provision to recognize the right to livelihood and socio-cultural lifestyle based on usufruct rights over land and other natural resources. Based on the evidence presented, the NGT Act sticks to a conventional theory of justice and does not make any explicit provision for alternative dispute resolution methods such as mediation, conciliation, restorative justice, ombudsman programme, and collaborative decision-making. These alternative methods of conflict resolution create institutional space for embracing the concepts of sustainable development, environmental ethics and indigenous values in adjudication. They also reduce the cost of litigation and expedite the process of adjudication (Pring and Pring, 2009: 72)

The NGT Act has made provisions under Article 26(1) to impose steep financial penalty[6] and imprisonment for any party that fails to comply with any order or award of the Green Tribunal. Though these upper limits are substantial, they fail to reflect even a fraction of the irreparable damage caused to human life for cases such as Bhopal gas leak. Neither does it reflect the scale of profits that Union Carbide, the company responsible for Bhopal tragedy, made for years. In order to deter parties from potential non-compliance of the NGT order or award, the upper limits set for financial penalty and imprisonment term should be left to the court's discretion. In the circumstance of non-compliance, the NGT Act does not clearly assign any power to the court to summon the state, being a regulatory and enforcement authority for the environment, to provide fair compensation to victims and restore the degraded environment on priority.

Challenges Faced by the NGT: Environmentalism of Elites versus Environmentalism of Poor

The establishment of specialized environmental courts is commonly justified by lack of expertise in existing civil courts to infuse environmental sensitivity, technical objectivity, and consistency into the adjudication of inherently complex environmental cases. However, the concern for protecting the environment in developing countries such as India is not merely an issue of scientific and legal expertise. In the post-Rio era, India has become perfect example of Kuznet's inverted-U curve where income inequality and ecological degradation increase as a result of negative externality of high economic growth. The ramifications of ecological degradation are particularly harsh for the poor who are directly exposed to environmentally hazardous living and working conditions. The efficacy of environmental jurisprudence should be measured on how it protects the constitutional rights and the needs of poor and marginalized sections of society. The creation of PIL is undoubtedly a credible indicator of judiciary's intention to address poverty, social exclusion, income inequality, and power imbalance. The courts delivered important verdicts on several PILs until the early 1990s, which were instrumental in bringing to light many issues of government apathy for ecological damage and for the impacts of that damage on the lives and livelihood of the poor. Thus, the judiciary developed its identity as defenders of the environment and the rights of the poor.

This pro-poor reputation of the judiciary has come under question in the post-Rio era. In his recent study examining PILs filed in the Supreme Court, Gauri (2009) found win-rates for PILs seeking the protection of fundamental rights was significantly higher in recent decades when the claimants were from advantaged social groups. This trend indicates social reversal, both from the original objective of PIL and from the relative win-rates of PILs filed by poor claimants in the 1980s. Political ecologists argue that the environment is not a neutral entity; it represents different material and cultural significances for the people, depending on their socio-economic class, ethnicity and gender (Veron, 2006). PIL cases filed by environmental organizations and activists primarily reflect the priorities and values of the urban middle class (Bhan, 2009). For instance, a series of judicial orders by the Supreme Court for closure of small polluting factories and removal of squatter settlements from public spaces in Delhi had profound negative impacts on the livelihoods of more than two million urban poor. Baviskar (2003) labelled such processes of filing PILs and their adjudication by the Supreme Court—dominated by English-speaking, urban middle class activists, journalists and judges—as 'bourgeois environmentalism'. In the context of environmental justice, the poor have become victims of the same legal instruments, in particularly PIL and judiciary activism, which were originally introduced to liberate them from poverty, pollution, and a skewed power structure. Bhushan (2004) cautioned that the judiciary is influenced by the ideology of the neo-liberalism that promotes the privatization of natural resources and social services. The courts are becoming increasingly reluctant to admit public interest petitions against state-led development projects that have potential adverse environmental and social impacts.

Sharma (2008) and several other scholars illustrated examples of court verdicts, such as *Deepak Nitrate Ltd.* v. *State of Gujarat* (6, SSC, 402), *Essar Oil Ltd* v. *Halar Utkarsh Samiti & Others* (2 SCC 392,408) and *Karnataka Industrial Area Development Board* v. *Sri. C. Kenchappa & Others* (6 SCC 371) where courts ignored expert panel's advice, precautionary principles, and the polluter pays principle and delivered patently pro-industry verdicts. Bhushan (2009) argues that whenever environmental protection comes into conflict with private sector interests, interpreted as 'development' in societal interests, courts subordinate the environmental cause and side with the private sector. However, the same courts are reluctant to compromise with environmental causes when they are pitted against socio-economic rights and the livelihood of the poor. For instance, in *Almitra Patel* v. the Union of India (2000 2 SC 341), Justice B.N. Kirpal ruled that slum dwellers are 'encroachers on public space' and rewarding them 'with free alternate site, at the taxpayers cost', is like giving a reward to a 'pickpocket'.

Further, legislative branches in India conveniently seek intervention from the judicial branch to make unpopular or anti-poor decisions that may backfire in the next election. For instance, if slum dwellers had to be removed to build residential apartments for the middle class or commercial property, the government may hesitate in making such a decision in fear of democratic backlash from the poor. The courts, being an authority of law and indirect supporter of the government's neo-liberal values and development agenda, are viewed as the best instrument to reinforce interests of the higher and middle classes. Gauri (2010: 13) attributes the urban middle class bias of courts to class structure, which is ingrained in the Indian judiciary. Judges in higher courts in India almost invariably come from the elite section of the society and have become a self-perpetuating oligarchy (Bhushan, 2009). Defying these trends in the Indian judiciary will be a herculean task for the NGT. Further, the NGT has to remember that the court is not an instrument for denying poor's chance of bargaining, sometimes based on their sheer votes, in the legislature or other democratic institutions where they have reasonable chance to prevail in India. The process of enforcing the rule of law and protecting the environment, under the authority of NGT, should not become an instrument of reinforcing existing socio-economic inequality. This will undermine the principles of participatory democracy, sustainable development and environmental stewardship.

Notes

1. Under Article 352 of the Indian Constitution, a state of Emergency was declared in India from 1975–1977 suspending elections and civil liberties and giving the executive extraordinary power.
2. For example, see *Francis Coralie Mullin* v. *Union Territory of Delhi & Others*, AIR (1981) 746., *Bandhua Mukti Morcha* v. *Union of India*, AIR (1984) 802 and *Olga Tellis & Others* v. *Bombay Municipal Corporation & Others,* AIR (1986) 180.

3. Prior to the court relaxing the rule of standing, as in nearly every other country in the world, petitioners of the court were required to prove they were directly affected by the action involved in the claim.
4. For example, see *Vellore Citizens' Welfare Forum* v. *Union of India,* 1996 (5) SC 647, *Indian Council for Enviro-Legal Action* v. *Union of India,* (1996) 3 SCC 212 and *State of Himachal Pradesh* v. *Ganesh Wood Products,* (1995) SCC 6 363.
5. *M.C. Mehta* v. *Union of India* (1986) 2 SCC 176, *Council for Environmental Legal Action* v. *Union of India,* (1996) 3 SCC 212 and *A.P. Pollution Control Board* v. *M.V. Nayudu,* (1999) 2 SCC 718.
6. The penalty for individuals may extend up to ₹ 100 million. If a company fails to comply, the fine is extended to ₹ 250 million.

References

Baar, C. (1990). Social Action Litigation in India: The Operation and Limitations of the World's Most Active Judiciary. *Policy Studies Journal,* 19(1): 140–50.

Baviskar, A. (2003). Between Violence and Desire: Space, Power, and Identity in the Making of Metropolitan Delhi. *International Social Science Journal,* 55: 89–98.

Bhan, G. (2009). This is No Longer the City I Once New: Evictions, the Urban Poor and the Right to the City in Millennial Delhi. *Environment and Urbanization,* 21 (1): 127–42.

Bhushan, P. (2004). Supreme Court and PIL: Changing Perspectives Under Liberalization. *Economic and Political Weekly,* 39 (18): 1770–74.

——. (2009). Misplaced Priorities and Class Bias of the Judiciary. *Economic and Political Weekly,* 44(14): 32–37.

Dwivedi, O.P. (1997). Green Justice: An Overview of Environmental Laws and Regulations, in *India's Environmental Policies, Programs and Stewardship,* New York: St. Martin's Press, pp.79–110.

Gauri, V. (2009). Public Interest Litigation in India: Overreaching or Underachieving? *Selected Works of Varun Guari.* Available at: http://works.bepress.com/varun_gauri/3

Gill, G.N. (2010). A Green Tribunal for India. *Journal of Environmental Law,* 22:3: 461–74.

Gonsalves, C. and Sahu, G. (2010). Litigating Against Corporations for Human Rights, *Economic and Political Weekly,* 46 (14): 18–21.

Government of India (2010). National Green Tribunal Act, of 2010. *The Gazette of India,* June 2, 2010, New Delhi: The Controller of Publication, pp. 1–18.

Kohli, K. (2011). A Functional Green Tribunal. July 06, 2011. Available at: http://mylawu.net/Article/A_functional_Green_Tribunal/

Law Commission of India (2003). *One Hundred Eighty Sixth Report: Proposal to Constitute Environment Courts,* A Report Submitted to the Government of India on September 23, 2003. New Delhi: Law Commission of India.

Nambiar, S. (2010). Paradigm of "Green" Adjudication: Developing Principles for Indian Environmental Decision-Making in Disputes Involving Scientific Uncertainty. *ILI Law Review*, 1 (1): 1–24.

Pring G. and C. Pring (2009). Greening Justice: Creating and Improving Environmental Courts and Tribunals, Washington: The Access Initiative, World Resource Institute.

Sahu, G. (2008). Implications of Indian Supreme Court's Innovations for Environmental Jurisprudence, *Law, Environment and Development Journal*, 4 (1): 1–19.

Sharma, R. (2008). Green Courts in India: Strengthening Environmental Governance? *Law, Environment and Development Journal*, 4 (1): 50–71.

The Access Initiative-India (2010). *How Green Will be the Green Tribunal? Concerns and Suggestions on the National Green Tribunal Bill, 2009*. New Delhi: Environics Trust.

The World Bank (2011). Data: GDP Growth Rate, India, 2011. Available at http://data.worldbank.org/indicator/NY.GDP.MKTP.KD.ZG

United Nations Development Programme (2011). *The 2011 Global Human Development Report: Inequalities and Environmental Challenges Threaten Progress in Asia, Pacific*. New York: Palgrave Macmillan.

Veron, R. (2006). Remaking Urban Environments: The Political Ecology of Air Pollution in Delhi, *Environment and Planning*, 38: 2093–2109.

11

Environment and Climate Change-Induced Natural Disasters in India

VINOD K. SHARMA AND A.D. KAUSHIK

The environment may be viewed in its totality, which comprises the whole set of natural or biophysical, and man-made or socio-cultural systems in which man and other organisms live and interact. In ecology, environment means all factors, which affect the survival and reproduction of living organisms (Napoleon, 1980). In India, where the population explosion is too high, the problem of environmental pollution is further being aggravated by both poverty and underdevelopment as well as by the negative effects of the very process of development. In other words, malnutrition, lack of sanitation, massive industrialization, mechanization, motorization and chemicalization of agriculture have added new dimensions to the problem of environmental pollution vis-à-vis its protection and control. The two important documents, i.e., the Stockholm Declaration (1972) and the Charter of Economic Rights and Duties of States (1974), show the deep concern of the international community for taking preventive steps to protect the environment. In the Indian context, the Sixth Five-Year Plan (1980–85) also attached a great importance to the protection of environment. In this, it had clearly been emphasized that the environment should form a crucial guiding dimension for planning and development. Environment management has to take note of the impact on the health and integrity of our natural resources like soil, water, forests, wildlife, etc. But, environmental conservation is really the very basis of all development. The establishment of the National Ganga Authority for cleaning the water of the Ganges and the surrounding slums was a step in the right direction. The Environment (Protection) Act, 1986 was enacted to tackle major environmental issues related to atmospheric and water pollution and the increasing concentration of CO_2 in the atmosphere.

The living planet, i.e., earth, is surrounded by a blanket of gases. This blanket of gases acts like the giant glass sphere that traps energy in the atmosphere. This results in an accumulation of energy, and the overall warming of the atmosphere when energy radiated by the earth is prevented from escaping to an outer space. This is termed the 'greenhouse effect'. This problem starts when human activities, i.e., deforestation or depletion of land resources, add much more of these greenhouse gases into the atmosphere.

The atmospheric concentrations of CO_2, O_3, CH_4 and N_2O have increased 31 per cent, 36 per cent, 151 per cent and 17 per cent respectively (Attri, 2003). These together make up less than 1 per cent of the atmosphere. This is enough to produce a natural greenhouse effect that keeps the planet some 300°C warmer than it would otherwise be essential for life, as we know it.

Among the greenhouse gases, carbon dioxide (CO_2) results in over 60 per cent of the 'enhanced' greenhouse effect, which is responsible for climate change. This gas occurs naturally in the atmosphere, but anthropogenic sources such as burning coal, oil and natural gas are releasing the carbon stored in these 'fossil fuels' at an unprecedented rate. Likewise, deforestation releases carbon stored in trees. Current emissions amount to over 7 billion tonnes of carbon, or almost 1 per cent of the total mass of CO_2 in the atmosphere. CO_2 produced by human activities enters the natural carbon cycle. Many billion tonnes of carbon are exchanged naturally each year between the atmosphere, the oceans and land vegetation. In the 200 years since 1800, however, levels have risen by almost 30 per cent. Even with half of humanity's CO_2 emissions being absorbed by the oceans and land vegetation, atmospheric levels continue to rise by over 10 per cent every twenty years.

The greenhouse effect causes an accumulation of heat (or energy) in the earth's atmosphere. The global climate must then adjust to deal with that extra accumulation of energy, and these adjustments result in global warming and climate change. The Inter-Governmental Panel on Climate Change (IPCC) of the United Nations, in its recent report, has again confirmed the global warming trend and projected that the globally averaged temperature of the air above the earth's surface would rise by 1.4–5.8°C over the next 100 years (IPCC, 2001).

Impacts of Climate Change in India

In developing countries like India, climate change could represent an additional stress on ecological and socio-economic systems that are already facing tremendous pressures due to rapid urbanization, industrialization and economic development. With its huge and growing population, 8,000 km-long densely populated and low-lying coastline, and an economy that is closely tied to its natural resource base, India is considerably vulnerable to the different natural disasters induced by climate change. It is observed that there will be an increase in the frequency of heavy rainfall events in South and Southeast Asia due to the doubling in CO_2 concentrations in the atmosphere. Lal et al. (1995) presented a climate change scenario for the Indian subcontinent, taking projected emissions of greenhouse gases and sulphate aerosols into account. It predicts an increase in annual mean maximum and minimum surface air temperatures of 0.7°C and 1.0°C over land in the 2040s with respect to the 1980s. Human society will face new risks and pressures. Some regions are likely to experience food shortages and hunger. Water resources will be affected as precipitation and evaporation patterns change around the world. Economic activities, human settlements and human health will experience many direct and indirect impacts of climate change.

Impact on Cities

The two most relevant to the subject are the progressive rise in sea level and the increased intensity and frequency of climatic episodes leading to natural disasters. Both represent a significant threat to urban areas in developing countries. According to several projections, the sea level is expected to increase anywhere from 8 to 88 centimetres during the twenty-first century, mostly due to thermal expansion and the loss of mass from glaciers and ice caps. The frequency and intensity of natural disasters are also growing rapidly worldwide. A recent analysis of great natural catastrophes since 1960 shows an increase in the 1990s by a factor of three and this seems to be directly correlated with global warming.

The rapid pace of urbanization, compounded with an ever-increasing population burden, has also significantly increased the overall vulnerability of urban areas to natural disasters. The location of many urban areas with large populations and critical economic assets

Recent Floods in India

Recently, the following events of floods occurred in different parts of India were due to heavy precipitation of rainfall most probably under the impact of climate change:

Mumbai Floods 2005: The intensity of rainfall of around 944 mm in 24 hours has been rarely observed in the country over a century and not at all in the region of Mumbai—it is truly a freak rain that concentrated over a small location extending from Dharavi (499 mm), Santacruz (944 mm), Bhandup (815 mm) and Vihar-Powai Lake (1,045 mm). Nearly 600 lives were lost on 26–27 July and more than 150 due to illness post floods.

Barmer Floods 2006: Heavy rain (600 mm against normal annual of 200 mm) in the desert districts of Barmer and some parts of Jaisalmer in the last few days raised flood scare in August 2006, the usually drought-prone Barmer district was hit by flash flood, causing death of 104 people, mainly in the villages of Kawas and Malwa. Kharif crop worth ₹ 1,300 crore was damaged and about 75,194 cattle perished in the flood.

Karnataka and Andhra Pradesh Floods 2009: Floods triggered by heavy rains due to cyclonic winds killed at least 210 people in Andhra Pradesh and Karnataka, and destroyed standing crops and left tens of thousands of people homeless. The floods in the state were described as the worst in 10,000 years.

Leh Floods 2010: Occurred on 6 August 2010 in Leh, the largest town in Ladakh, a region of the northernmost Indian state of Jammu and Kashmir. At least 193 people were reported to have died, 200 people were reported missing and thousands more were rendered homeless after the flooding caused extensive damage to property and infrastructure. The cloudburst occurred leading to flash floods and mud slides over the region. Leh, being in a cold desert, gets an average rainfall for the month of August of 15.4 mm with the highest rainfall ever recorded during a 24-hour period has been 51.3 mm recorded on 22 August, 1933. In contrast, in 2010, in the space of an hour and half, Leh received a large amount of rain, ranging from 12.8 mm to 250 mm.

Delhi Floods 2011: The airport terminal at IGI airport, New Delhi was flooded after a sudden cloudburst in September 2011.The Met department said that this was the highest recorded rainfall in a single hour since 1959. Safdarjung recorded only 35 mm rain between 8.30 am and 5.30 pm against Palam's total of 120 mm.

in high-risk zones contributes to the increased attention given to impacts in urban areas of disasters induced or enhanced by climate change. In the case of cities in developing countries, the size and vulnerability of informal settlements, generally built in unstable areas such as coastal zones, flood-prone planes and ravines, and geologically unstable slopes, greatly increases their vulnerability. The impacts of a rising sea level and more frequent and intense natural disasters in rural areas will likely generate an additional influx of people to cities. Such 'environmental refugees' often become permanent, thus increasing the vulnerability of cities yet again. Developing countries are considered to be particularly vulnerable to climate change as many are in tropical and sub-tropical zones with economies and societies highly dependent upon the climate and heavily impacted by its variations. Many of the largest cities in Africa, Asia and Latin America are port cities, historically linked to a colonial past, and directly subjected to the impacts of a rising sea level. The high cost of land in a central city and around ports has often encouraged major commercial developments on land reclaimed from sea and river estuaries that are especially vulnerable to a rise in the sea level.

Impact on Agriculture

The magnitude of projected changes in temperature, rainfall and CO_2 in the future of different parts of the world, including India, has been compiled by IPCC (Watson et al., 1998). According to this report, by 2010, CO_2 level will increase to 397–416 ppm from the existing level of 368 ppm in the year of 2000. This will further increase to 605–755 ppm by 2070. There is considerable uncertainty in the projected magnitude of change in rainfall and temperature for India (Table 1). The increase in temperature is less in kharif than in rabi crops. The rabi rainfall will, however, have larger uncertainty. Kharif rainfall is likely to increase by as much as 10 per cent.

Table 1

Expected Magnitude of Change in Climatic Factors in South Asia by 2010 and 2070 AD due to Global Warming

Climatic Factors	*Rabi*		*Kharif*	
	2010	*2070*	*2010*	*2070*
Temperature increase (°C)	0.3 to 0.7	1.1 to 4.5	0.1 to 0.3	0.4 to 2.0
CO_2	397 to 416	605 to 755	397 to 416	605 to 755
Rainfall change in southwest monsoon region (%)	0	–10 to 10	0	0 to +10

Source: Inter-Governmental Panel on Climate Change (IPCC) of United Nations Report (Watson et al., 1998)

Such global climatic changes will affect agriculture through their direct and indirect effects on kharif and rabi crops, soils, livestock and pests. An increase in atmospheric CO_2 has a fertilization effect on crops. An increase in temperature can reduce crop duration; an increase crop respiration rates alters photosynthesis and affects the survival and distributions of pest populations, thus developing new equilibrium between crops and pests. This equilibrium decreases fertilizer use efficiencies and increases evapotranspiration. Indirectly, there may be considerable effects on land use due to snowmelt, irrigation, frequency and intensity of inter- and intra-seasonal droughts and floods, soil organic matter transformations, soil erosion decline in arable areas due to submergence of coastal lands, and availability of energy. All these can have a tremendous impact on agricultural production and hence food security of any region. Equally important determinants of food supply are the socio-economic environment including government policies, capital availability, prices and returns, infrastructure, land reforms, and inter- and intra-national trade that might be affected by climate change.

Impact on Forest Ecosystems

The response of forests to climatic changes is both complex and uncertain and involves dynamic interactions between various plant species in an ecosystem. There are risks involved in scaling up the short-term transient responses of individual plant species or trees to long response of entire forest ecosystems.

The impact of climate change on the biodiversity of tropical forests is quite speculative. Plants are stressed and become vulnerable to pest attacks under increased temperature and low soil water availability. This diversity of tropical forests, however, provides some protection against widespread attack of pests and diseases. The intensity and frequency of forest fires in tropical forests is of serious concern under climate change situations. Dry weather would upset the water balance and lead to increased frequency of fires as reported in boreal forests by Acharya (1995). Thus, increased temperature, lower humidity and reduced precipitation increase the risk of forest fires, which ultimately lead to lower plant diversity.

The productivity increases with an increase in ambient temperature, given sufficient availability of moisture and nutrients. However, the process of photosynthesis responds differently to increased temperatures, i.e., it initially increases and then slows down. Respiration is slow initially, but it then increases. This increase continues until equilibrium is reached between photosynthesis and respiration and there is no net carbon assimilation. There is consensus that any positive influence of increased CO_2 concentration on productivity will be small and negligible.

Impact on Water Resources

The climatic changes affect water supply, quality and demand and may have also ramifications for decision-makers. Water demand generally increases with time as population and per capita consumption increases. Climate change may either increase or decrease water availability through precipitation, temperature, cloudiness and humidity, increasing the level of uncertainty, which can result in increased recurrence of hydrologic hazards such as floods and droughts. A number of studies have evaluated the relationship between stream flows and the occurrence of El Nino and La Nina (Chiew et al., 1998).

In India, the major river systems of the Indian subcontinent, namely, Brahmaputra, Ganga and Indus, which originate in the Himalayas, are more vulnerable to climate change because of the substantial contribution from snow and glaciers into these river systems (Singh and Kumar, 1997). Studies have shown that an increase in the temperature by 1.5°C will increase the risk of some floods in the Ganga and Brahmaputra plains (Siedel et al., 2000). A warmer climate would cause a reduction in water availability excepting the flows in summer. It was also concluded that the impact of warmer climate on water availability would be felt more in basins with seasonal than in basins covered with permanent snow and glaciers (Ramasastri, 2003). Mehrotra (2000), while using disaggregated General Circulation Model (GCM) and a conceptual rainfall runoff model for the Damanganga (Gujarat), Sher and Kolar sub-basins in Narmada basin and Hemavati in Cavery basin, studied that monsoon and annual runoff is expected to decrease due to the projected climate changes in Damanganga and to increase in Sher and Kolar sub-basins. Further, it was noted that basins located in the sub-humid and semi-arid and arid regions are more sensitive to climate changes than those in humid regions of the country as reported by Dooge (1989).

Impact on Vulnerability

As climate change is coupled with other global changes, vulnerability needs to be evaluated against a background of dynamic flux of both anthropogenic and biophysical factors. Vulnerability of mountain ecosystems assumes more importance when one realizes that impacts of global change in mountains will have profound effects not only on hill people but also those in the adjoining plains (Maikhuri et al., 2003). Natural disasters or hazards are an important cause of the loss of land in the coastal region of our country. The deltaic regions of West Bengal, Orissa and Andhra Pradesh are especially vulnerable to cyclones and the storm surges associated with them. Global warming is expected to result in the global sea level rise affecting various marine habitats in the low-lying areas.

In coastal areas, the mangrove forest ecosystems are more vulnerable to the climatic changes, as directly influenced by tides. Due to sea level rise, the intertidal and supra littoral zones are likely to be extended farther inland causing destruction of existing mangroves and associated biota. Climate changes, coupled with anthropogenic pressures and poor management practices, may reduce productivity and loss of mangrove dependent biodiversity, adversely impacting ecological and socio-economic benefits. The mangroves being more vulnerable are constantly under threat from increasing anthropogenic pressures, such as indiscriminate cutting, reclamation mainly for agriculture and urbanization, fuel and construction and overgrazing by domestic cattle as well as from sea level rise due to global warming (Ellison and Stoddart, 1991). In the country, 30 per cent of the mangrove area has been reclaimed for different anthropogenic activities during the period of 1975–90 (Jagtap et al., 1993). Rao et al. (1999) studied that the maximum damage to mangrove forests is caused by habitat loss, human interference and trade. By using time series data on a set of forestry parameters, the vulnerability of mangrove forests to the changing climate can be assessed. Unfortunately, such data for the mangroves of India do not exist. Considering the projection of climate change resulting in sea level rise and vulnerability and adaptability of mangrove forests to these changes of climate, it is necessary to develop a national level programme to collect the required data for Indian mangroves.

There is a direct impact of climate change reported on the vulnerability of rice crop yield in Northwest India. It is because the changed climate, along with doubling of CO_2, seems to have enhanced the yield potential of rice, while the irrigated rice yield seems to have decreased as compared to present climate, leading to more yield gap between achievable rice yield and potential rice crop yield in the 2050s climate as compared to gap under existing climate. Reduction in irrigated rice crop yield ranges from about 12 per cent at Saharanpur (Uttar Pradesh) to 25 per cent at Hisar of Haryana (Gosain and Tripathi,

2002). The variability in the irrigated rice crop yield increases by the factors of 1.3 to 1.6 in the 2050s anomalous climate as compared to the present climate at various locations in India. This enhancement in year-to-year variability in rice crop yield raises concerns about food security in India.

Climate-induced natural disasters (CINDs) like droughts, floods and cyclones become serious problems to coastal areas. These are of a regular occurrence particularly in the coastal areas of Orissa and have become the part of normal life. The 1999 tropical cyclone that hit Orissa resulted in a death toll of about 10,000, and demonstrates the extreme significance of coastal vulnerability related to climate variability. A study of Jawaharlal Nehru University in 1993 reveals that in the absence of protection, a one-metre sea level rise on the Indian coastline is likely to affect a total area of 5,763 km^2, and put 7.1 million people at risk as well as indicates that the dominant cost is land loss, which accounts for 83 per cent of all damages (Table 2). The extent of vulnerability, however, depends not only on physical exposure, but also on the level of economic activity in the coastal region.

Table 2

Effect of 1–m Sea-Level Rise on Coastal Area and Population

State/Union Territory	*Coastal Area (million hectares)*			*Population (million)*		
	Total	*Inundated*	*Percentage*	*Total*	*Affected*	*Percentage*
Andhra Pradesh	27.504	0.055	0.19	66.36	0.617	0.93
Goa	0.37	0.016	4.34	1.17	0.085	7.25
Gujarat	19.602	0.181	0.92	41.17	0.441	1.07
Karnataka	19.179	0.029	0.15	44.81	0.25	0.56
Kerala	3.886	0.012	0.3	29.08	0.454	1.56
Maharashtra	30.771	0.041	0.13	78.75	1.376	1.75
Orissa	15.571	0.048	0.31	31.51	0.555	1.76
Tamil Nadu	13.006	0.067	0.52	55.64	1.621	2.91
West Bengal	8.875	0.122	1.38	67.98	1.6	2.35
Andaman and Nicobar Islands	0.825	0.006	0.72		0	0
India	139.594	0.571	0.41	416.74	7.1	1.68

Note: Costal area and population are based on the 1981 and 1991 census.

Source: Jawaharlal Nehru University, 1993.

Climate Change-induced Natural Disasters

Climate change is likely to have a significant impact on the global environment. In general, the faster the climate changes, the greater will be the risk of damage. The mean sea level is expected to cause flooding of low-lying areas and other damage. Climatic zones including agricultural zones could shift towards the poles. Forests, deserts, rangelands, and other unmanaged ecosystems would face new climatic stresses. As a result, many will decline or fragment and individual species will become extinct.

The natural disasters, particularly floods and droughts, even if local phenomena, can be related to large-scale or global climate mechanisms. Through the study of atmospheric teleconnection mechanisms between remote areas of the planet, scientists are now increasingly able to link extreme weather events such as droughts and storms with climate variations and climate change. The common perception of remote areas including rural households of the coastal areas is that the climate has changed for the worse with increased frequency as well as intensity of CIND events in recent years. Although the warning system was also developed and found to be timely and largely accurate, the rainfall forecasting in drought years was misleading. Further, the cyclone warning was ignored by the rural households, which resulted in higher causality than expected (Roy et al., 2002).

There is evidence from climate models and hydrological impact studies that flood frequencies are likely to increase with global warming, which may produce changes in the frequency of intense rainfall (IPCC, 1995). In temperate regions, more floods are caused by changes in the magnitudes of snowmelt and rain on snow. Impacts of climate change are expected to be greater on *Tundra* lands and alpine regions. Deglaciation on temperate mountains would increase sediment loads in alpine rivers and accelerated sedimentation in lakes and artificial reservoirs. Lakes dammed by landslides, moraines and glaciers may drain suddenly and produce floods or debris flows of an order of magnitude larger than normal stream flow.

The records of recent flooding and paleoflooding indicate the high sensitivity of flood occurrence to changing climate for river basins in the USA and Europe. Analyses also indicate that there is no simple proportionality between the scale and frequency of floods and climate variations. However, in general, increases in precipitation lead to proportionally larger increases in runoff. The recent floods cannot also be taken as a proof of climate change as the associated rainfall events still fit in the natural variability of our climate, and floods of comparable magnitude have been observed earlier this century. Some research studies like government research (England) observed that global warming does not necessarily cause all devastating floods.

Less snow and glacier ice will influence the seasonality of river flow by reducing melt water production in the warm season. The expected smoothing of the annual runoff amplitude could be both beneficial, e.g., energy production in winter, reduction of summer flood peaks and adverse, e.g., reduced water supply for summer irrigation in dry areas, more frequent winter floods. The general tendency in high mountains will be an increased vulnerability of people, transport routes and economic infrastructures.

As climatic warming occurs, there will be notable changes in the hydrology of Arctic areas. River ice regime might be altered and substantial effects on the hydrology can be expected that will affect flow, water levels and storage. For cold continental rivers, many hydrologic extremes, such as low flows and floods, are frequently more a function of ice effects than landscape runoff. Projected climates will delay the timing of freeze up and so prolong the autumn low flow period. At break up, the rapid hydraulic storage and release of water by river ice jams often forms the most significant hydrologic event of the year. Of all river ice processes ice jams are the major source of economic damages. Changes in damages from such events depend on how climate change affects the frequency and severity of river ice freeze up and break up events.

Drought has generally received little attention, but it is reasonable to think that there will be an increase in the occurrence and severity of droughts in order to compensate the first extreme and to re-establish the natural energy and water balance.

A deadly cocktail of floods, cyclones and droughts has made Orissa the capital of disasters in India. Of the last 100 years, the state has been disaster affected for 90 years; floods have occurred for 49 years, droughts for 30 and cyclones have hit the state for 11 years. Since 1965, calamities are not only becoming more frequent but striking areas that never had a vulnerability record and climatic variability in Orissa during the last three decades has shown deviations in rainfall of 20 per cent or more every third year (Down to Earth, 2001).

It appears that progress in climatology and in the development of numerical models not only enables scientists to relate extreme weather events such as floods and droughts, with climate variations, but they can provide some insight into the climate change scenarios due to global warming such as sea level rise and changes in frequency, strength and geographical distribution of extreme events. These results should be of great help in taking the right measures and in building up the adapted policies.

Mitigation Policy on Climate Change

Climate change is having an impact on India as well. These changes may include a decrease in crop productivity, water availability, an increase in vector-borne diseases, extreme weather events like floods, cyclones and droughts and changes in perception patterns. In order to advance the preparedness of the country to deal with climate change, at present, the following activities are being undertaken:

- Capacity building at appropriate levels for taking climate change considerations in social, economic and developmental planning.
- Impact assessment including impacts on food and water resources, eco-system and bio-diversity, human settlements and human health.
- Promotion of scientific and technological research and systematic observation with a view to furthering understanding of climate change.
- Education, training and public awareness.
- Enhancement of international cooperation in pursuance of the objectives of the United Nations Framework Convention on Climate Change (UNFCCC).

India figures among the top ten contributors to greenhouse gas emissions. However, current per capita gross emissions in India are only one-sixth of the world's average. India is highly vulnerable to climate change as its economy is heavily reliant on climate-sensitive sectors like agriculture and forestry and its low-lying densely populated coastline is threatened by a potential rise in sea level. The Clean Development Mechanism (CDM), which was created in 1977 under Kyoto Protocol to the UNFCCC, is important for India as it allows developed countries to use Certified Emissions Reduction (CER) credits from project activities in developing countries, and also assists developing countries in achieving their sustainable development objectives.

The Eighth Conference of the Parties (COP-8) of the UNFCCC organized in New Delhi (23rd October–1st November, 2002) will tremendously help in raising the awareness level in the country regarding climate change and would demonstrate to the world the impressive strides made in India in various sectors in conformity with sustainable development. The conference would also provide an opportunity to project what India can offer to the world, particularly the developing countries by way of its Environmental Management Technology (EMT) in various sectors like industry, transport, power, renewable energy, agriculture and forestry. This conference would become quite important, as the chances of the ratification of Kyoto Protocol have brightened as a consequence of agreements arrived at Bonn and expected to take a number of major decisions relating to implementation of the Kyoto Protocol.

Conclusion

The global warming process is already engaged and we cannot stop it in the near future. Indeed, thermal inertia is protecting us now by retarding the effects of trace gas build-up, but this same inertia will ensure continued perturbations for centuries, even after correction becomes efficient. What is most important now is synthesis, the overall appreciation of the problem of global climate change and possibilities for correction, bearing in mind regional constraints and desirable changes. This should be the concern of the nascent international community of person interested in the survival and well-being of the biosphere. Undoubtedly, the CDM created under Kyoto Protocol (1977) to the UNFCCC, is important for India as it allows developed countries to not only use CER credits from project activities in developing countries but also assists developing countries in achieving their sustainable development objectives. India's stand in recent COP-17 at Durban (2011) was appreciated by entire developing world including China.

References

Acharya, A. (1995). Climate Change Endangers the Northern Forests, *World Watch,* January/February: 8.

Attri, S.D. (2003). Status of Climate Change in India. Assessment of Climate Change in India and Mitigation Policies: Proceedings (2003) Produced by *Indira Gandhi Conservation Monitoring Centre, World Wide Fund for Nature-India,* New Delhi.

Chiew, F.H.S., McMohan, T.A., Dracup, J.A. and Piechota, T. (1998). El Nino/Southern Oscillation and Australian Rainfall, Stream Flow and Drought: Links and Potential for Forecasting. *Journal of Hydrology,* Vol. 204, pp. 138–49.

Das, P.K. (2003). Some Aspects of Climate Change Over India. Assessment of Climate Change in India and Mitigation Policies: Proceedings of Indira

Gandhi Conservation Monitoring Centre, World Wide Fund for Nature-India, New Delhi, pp. 26–28.

Dooge, J.C.I. (1989). Effect of CO_2 Increase on Hydrology and Water Resources. In *Carbon Dioxide and other Green House Gases,* edited by R. Fantechi and A. Ghazi. London: Kluwer, pp. 204–13.

Down to Earth (2001). Vol. 10, No. 10, October 15.

Ellison, J.C. and Stoddart, D.R. (1991). Mangrove Ecosystem Collapse During Predicted Sea Level Rise: Holocene Analogues and Implications, *Journal of Coastal Research,* Vol. 7, pp. 151–65.

Gosain, A.K., and Tripathi, C.N. (2002). Global Warming and India's Food Security. Report of 2nd Year Submitted to Rockefeller Foundation, USA.

IPCC, UN (1995). Climate Change: J.T. Houghton, G.J. Jenkins and J.J. Ephruaṇs, (HG) S.2–64, Cambridge University Press.

IPCC, UN (2001). Climate Change 2001: Impacts, Adaptation and Vulnerability. Inter-Governmental Panel on Climate Change. Report of the Working Group II. Cambridge, UK, p. 967.

Jagtap, T.G., Chavan, V. and Untawale, A.G. (1993). Mangrove Ecosystems of India: A Need for Protection, *Ambio,* 22 (4): 252–54.

Jawaharlal Nehru University (1993). Impacts of Greenhouse Inducted Sea-level Rise on the Islands and Coasts of India New Delhi: School of Environmental Sciences, Jawaharlal Nehru University.

Lal, M., Cubasch, U., Voss, R. and Waszkewitz, J. (1995). Effect of Transient Increase in Greenhouse Gases and Sulphate Aerosols on Monsoon Climate, *Current Science,* 69(9): 752–63.

Maikhuri, R.K., K.S. Rao, S. Patnaik, K.G. Saxena and P.S. Ramakrishnan (2003). Assessment of Vulnerability of Forests, Meadows and Mountain Ecosystems due to Climate Change, *ENVIS Bulletin: Himalayan Ecology,* 11(2).

Mehrotra, R. (2000). Hydrologic Sensitivity of Some Indian Basins to Expected Climate Change and Its Effect on Water Availability Using Disaggregated GCM Outputs: *Proceedings of the International Conference on Integrated Water Resources Management for Sustainable Development* New Delhi, 19–21 December 2000, pp. 1029–38.

Napoleon, Wolanski (1980). "Environmental Hazards and the Future of Man," in J.P. Singh and S.C. Tiwari, eds., *Man and His Environment*, pp. 1–3.

Piechota, T.C. and J.A. Dracup (1996). Drought and Regional Hydrologic Variation in the United States: Associations with the El Nino Southern Oscillation, *Water Resources Research*, Vol. 32, pp. 1359–73.

Ramasastri, K.S. (2003). Climate Change and Its Impact on Hydrological Regime: *Proceedings of Indira Gandhi Conservation Monitoring Centre, World Wide Fund for Nature-India*, New Delhi, pp. 161–69.

Rao, T.A., Molur, S. and Walker, S. (1999). Indian Mangrove Ecosystem: Report Summary, 1998, published by Zoo Outreach Organization, pp. 1–50.

Roy, B.C., Mruthyunjaya and S. Selvarajan (2002). Vulnerability to Climate-Induced Natural Disasters with Special Emphasis on Coping Strategies of the Rural Poor in Coastal Orissa, India. Paper for the UNFCC COP8 Conference Organized by the Government of India, United Nations Environment Programmes, and FICCI during October 23-November 1, New Delhi.

Siedel, Klaus, J. Matrinec and M.F. Baumgartner (2000). Modeling Runoff and Impact on Climate Change in Large Himalayas Basins. *Proceedings of the International Conference on Integrated Water Resources Management for Sustainable Development*, New Delhi, 19–21 December, pp. 1045–54.

Singh, P. and Naresh Kumar (1997). Impact of Climate Change on the Hydrological Response of Snow and Glacier Melt Runoff Dominated Himalayan River, *Journal of Hydrology*, Vol. 193, pp. 316–50.

Sixth Five-Year Plan (1980–85). p. 343, in Suresh Jain, ed., *Environmental Laws in India* (1985), p. 592.

Watson, R.T., Zinyowera, M.C. and Moss, R.H. (eds.) (1998). The Regional Impacts of Climate Change: An Assessment of Vulnerability. IPCC II Report. Cambridge University Press, p. 517.

12

Environment-Friendly Industrial Production and Green Product Usage

Indian Scenario

R.K. TRIVEDI

The major objective of this chapter is to familiarize the readers with a few scholarly works in the form of partnership projects which were carried out with initiation and continuous support of Prof. O.P. Dwivedi.

I was involved in two Shastri Indo-Canadian Institute (SICI) and Canadian International Development Agency (CIDA) sponsored partnership research projects undertaken jointly by Harcourt Butler Technological Institute (HBTI), India and the University of Guelph, Canada. As the name implies, one of the basic objectives of the projects is to form long-lasting working partnerships between faculty members and institutions in Canada and India. These projects were meant to have a social policy orientation, were to rely primarily on secondary information sources and serve as much to identify gaps in as to provide answers. The research projects were multidisciplinary collaborative endeavours across institutions and cultures, spanning almost two years. The first project, entitled 'Waste Management for Sustainable Development in Kanpur, was initiated by Dr O.P. Dwivedi, in which Dr Nonita Yap led the team of researchers from the Canadian side, and Dr S.K. Awasthi from Indian side. The project looked at the problem of waste disposal in Kanpur. The treatment of such waste was, typically, to take place at the 'end of the pipeline', albeit at the plant or industry level. From this emerged the belief that environmental degradation might be better avoided by preventing waste entering the pipeline in the first place, and particularly by reducing household usage of harmful products. We then searched for a likely product, and in particular one that was relevant to both India and Canada, as a fundamental objective of the second research project was to facilitate exchanges across institutions. In the second project, entitled 'Managing Environmental Risks: An Analysis of India's Regulatory Policy on the Use of Harmful Household Products: The Case of Household Detergent, the Canadian side was led by Dr Clive Southy and the Indian side by Dr R.K. Trivedi. The research site was largely in India and the product selected is an extensively used harmful household product, specifically detergents. Both the projects resulted in the publication of several research papers and books. This chapter has been written keeping in mind the research outcome of the partnership projects between India and Canada.

Manufacturing firms all over the world are undergoing fundamental changes in the way they address environmental issues. The corporate response to this environmental mandate has gone through three phases, from opposition to reluctant compliance with the adoption of pollution control measures, and finally to a more productive response seeking to redesign products and processes that meet and even surpasses pollution standards. Through the ages, Darwin's theory of 'Survival of the Fittest' has impacted the lives of the human species. Not many thought that the great scientist was prophesying the future of generations to come. Recently, the US President was quoted saying, 'The nation that leads the clean energy economy will be the nation that leads the global economy'.

Now, when our environment fights us back, we are forced to rethink and amend our ways of living to become more eco-friendly. Hence, a new trend was given birth in our endeavour to become eco-friendly, which many define as 'being green'.

'Being green' is becoming a big trend. Invented by our need to become eco-friendly and to survive in harmony with our environment, the trend is fast spreading all across the globe. Nowadays, many, if not all people, have developed a need to redesign their lifestyles and get on the green mode. India has joined this new trend and is striving to achieve the best result possible.

The increased concentrations of key greenhouse gases in the atmosphere are a direct consequence of human activities. Since anthropogenic greenhouse gases accumulate in the atmosphere, they produce net warming by strengthening the natural 'greenhouse effect'. Carbon dioxide (CO_2) concentrations in the atmosphere have been increasing over the past century compared to the rather steady level of the pre-industrial era (about 280 parts per million in volume, or ppmv). In 2005, concentration of CO_2 (379 ppmv) was about 35 per cent higher than in the mid-1800s, with the fastest growth occurring in the last few years (1.9 ppmv/year in the period 1995–2005). Recent data show that global CO_2 emissions increased by 0.4 Gt CO_2 between 2007 and 2008, which represented a growth rate of 1.5 per cent. Significant increases have also occurred in levels of methane (CH_4) and nitrous oxide (N_2O). A growing body of evidence has established the links between climate change and the CO_2 emissions that arise from energy production and consumption. In its *Fourth Assessment Report*, the IPCC concluded: 'Most of the observed increase in global average temperatures since the mid-20th century is *very likely* due to the observed increase in anthropogenic greenhouse gas concentrations'. Energy production and use play an important role because energy represents about 65 per cent of global anthropogenic greenhouse gas emissions. Therefore, reducing emissions must necessarily start with reduced energy consumption and associated emissions from fuel combustion.

Engaging in volunteer initiatives to improve the environmental performance of their products and processes is mainly motivated by:

(i) Changing regulations and standards.
(ii) Environmental awareness among customers.
(iii) Realization that paying attention to environmental responsibility can increase profitability.

Thankfully, the need for design of environment (DFE) and environment-friendly processes and products (EFPPs) has been well recognized. The environment-friendly practices (EFPs)/cleaner production has a big range starting from good housekeeping to physical and chemical transformations.

UNEP (1994) defines cleaner production in the following terms:

(i) It is the continuous application of an integrated preventive environment strategy to processes and products to reduce risks on humans and the environment.
(ii) For production, EFP includes conserving
   - Raw materials and energy
   - Eliminating toxic raw materials
   - Reducing the quantity and toxicity of all emissions and wastes before they leave a process

Energy and emission: Worldwide economic stability and development require energy. The global total primary energy supply doubled between 1971 and 2008, mainly relying on fossil fuels. One of the most important developments in the world economy and energy use is due to increasing economic integration of large non-OECD countries, such as Brazil, Russian Federation, India, China and South Africa and represent over one-fourth of world GDP, up by 18 per cent from 1990. In 2008, these five countries represented 31 per cent of global energy use and 35 per cent of CO_2 emissions from fuel combustion. These shares are likely to rise further in coming years due to strong economic performance currently occurring in most of these countries.

(iii) For products, the strategy focuses on reducing impacts along the entire life cycle of the product, from raw material extraction to ultimate disposal of the product.

Viewed from a life cycle perspective, a product is a part of a larger system, namely, the value added chain from raw materials to end users. EFP can introduce design changes that makes this overall system more efficient in terms of resource usage or waste generation. Those changes may have an associated link with a particular product feature, the industry structure and economic benefits.

Examples: Trade-off decision in selection of materials for durable goods.

Selection of metals in automobiles:

Metals	*Plastics*
Easier in recycling but more energy demands	Different from a life cycle environment perspective
Within metals: steel and aluminium • steel has strength but heavy • aluminium light but more energy in extraction and processing	

(iv) Consumer preference look and feel.

(v) *Emergence of Sustainable Product Development:* It deals with elementary demands:

- Essential products functions, the system in which product functions, the nature, availability and selection of resources, and distribution of those resources among nations and generations. It goes beyond the environment-friendly product design.

(vi) In lowering the level of overall material used and hence reducing the adverse effect of waste and pollutants, the quality of the environment would benefit tremendously.

(vii) Save resources

- Establish that the type of material should be based on the future destination, in process and product.

A sound raw material policy would favour:

(viii) Renewable resources over non-renewable ones.

(ix) Abundant resources over those that are scarce.

(x) Less polluting over heavily polluting resources.

(xi) Product development deals with these issues:

- Actual needs and wants
- Life cycle design, product durability
- Long-term resource availability and product compatibility.

Integrated Product Development

A process whereby all functional groups (e.g., engineering, manufacturing, marketing, etc.) that are involved in a product life cycle participate as a team in the early understanding and resolution of key product development issues, including quality, manufacturability, reliability, maintainability, environmental safety, etc.

Eco-efficiency

This is the link between resource efficiency (which leads to productivity and profitability) and environmental responsibility. Eco-efficiency makes business sense. Through eliminating waste and using resources more wisely, eco-efficient companies can reduce costs and become more competitive.

Cleaner Process (CP)

Pollution Prevention (PP)

The pollution prevention movement represents the first significant step along the road to sustainability. The best known corporate pollution prevention programmes done on a voluntary basis are the Pollution Prevention Pays (3P) programme of 3M Corporation, SMART (Save Money And Reduce Toxics) of Chevorn, WRAP of Dow Chemicals, etc.

There are four major categories of PP:

1. Good housekeeping practices to ensure that resources are utilized efficiently and that preventable material losses are not occurring through leakage of excessive use.

2. Material substitution to reduce or eliminate the presence of undesirable substances such as heavy metals, carcinogens, CFCs.
3. Production process modification to optimize reactions and raw materials use or introduce closed loop recycling.
4. Recycling and reuse to capture waste materials and reuse them either as an input to other manufacturing process or for secondary application.

They represent a shift in thinking from 'end of pipe' waste treatment to 'in the pipe' material management. They break through the traditional conflict between profitability and environmental protection.

For Best Results of PP

Pollution prevention thinking should be shifted back into the design cycle before the products are specified and plants are constructed.

Elements of Pollution Prevention Design

For an effective integration of important elements of the pollution prevention concept in product and process development, the key elements required are:

- Eco-efficiency metrics, driven by fundamental customer needs or corporate goals to support environmental performance measurement.
- Eco-efficient design practices, based on an in-depth understanding of relevant technologies and supported by engineering guidelines.
- Eco-efficiency analysis methods, to assess proposed designs with respect to the above metrics and analyse costs and quality trade-offs.

Metrics: A variety of performance measures are used in various industries, reflecting industry-specific environmental issues:

- Adopted by eco-labelling programmes.

Examples:

- Toxic use measures (total kilograms of solvents purchased per unit of production);
- Resource utilization measures (total energy consumed during the life cycle);
- Environmental emission measures (greenhouse gases and ozone-depleting substances released per unit of production); and
- Waste minimization measures (per cent of product materials recovered at end of life).

Design Practices

Complete product system is considered upstream and downstream process components:

- Material substitution
- Waste source reduction
- Substance use reduction
- Energy use reduction
- Life extension
- Design for separability and disassembly
- Design for recyclability
- Design for disposability (non-recyclables)
- Design for reusability
- Design for re-manufacture
- Design for energy recovery

Indian Scenario

India's National Waste Management Council (NWMC) reported in 1990 that due to the prevailing use of outdated technology and the unsystematic ways of handling hazardous industrial waste management, India has been experiencing 'serious environmental degradation'. The business corporate environment policies still continue to be driven by compliance, rather than a genuine interest in minimizing the environmental impacts of plant operations. India possesses a comprehensive policy agenda favouring the use of LWTs (Green Technologies) but because of inadequacies or dysfunction in terms of human resources, rules or organizations (institutional impediments) effective industrial waste management is not being achieved.

The World Bank (1994) has estimated that municipal sources generate three-fourths of the volume of waste water whereas the industrial waste water constitutes one-half of the pollution load in India. India emits nearly 5 per cent of the global CO_2 emissions, and it continues to grow. CO_2 emissions have more than doubled between 1990 and 2008 and it is projected to increase by more than 2.5 times by 2030. A large share of these emissions is produced by the electricity and heat sector, which represented 56 per cent of CO_2 in 2008, up by 42 per cent from 1990.

A basic misconception in developing countries like India is that environmental protection is a cost-incurring activity, which cannot be sustained without continuous support. This has led to weak implementation of environmental strategies and a lack of commitment among implementing authorities. Now, there is growing awareness that pollution prevention/cleaner production/ eco-efficiency not only helps to reduce pollution discharge by as much as 40–60 per cent, but can also be a profit boosting activity.

There are several agencies and organizations which are supporting the environment-friendly processes and products. The Government of India's Ministry of Environment has established a cell which deals with the cleaner production and waste minimization approaches. The creation of environmental tribunals is another very positive step in this direction. In 1992, the Government of India introduced a requirement for industries to annually undertake and submit an audit statement in which the details of raw material consumption and emission per unit of product are stated. The National Environment Engineering Research Institute (NEERI) maintains a database on cleaner technologies applicable in different industrial sectors. The UNIDO has supported a demonstration project 'DISIRE' (Demonstrating in Small Industries for Reducing Waste) with collaboration of the NPC (National Productivity Council). Practical demonstration of cleaner/eco-efficient technologies in selected small-scale industries, such as agro-based paper and pulp and textile dyeing, has been able to give confidence among all the stakeholders. Out of 450 waste minimization opportunities 300 were implemented with savings of ₹ 35.8 million.

The national CSIR laboratories such as the Central Leather Research Institute (CLRI), Indian Institute of Chemical Technology (IICT) and National Chemical Laboratory (NCL) are actively involved in the design and development of environment-friendly technologies and products. The Confederation of Indian Industries (CII), with 3,000 member-companies, has an environment management division which is regularly providing assistance and flow of information on EFPP. The World Bank has founded an industrial pollution prevention project for establishing clean technology centres across the country. A grant from the Japanese government has also been used by the Government of India for the design of a waste minimization database (1994).

Indo-India has demonstrated the feasibility of the EFPP approach in the waste management project undertaken jointly by HBTI, India and the University of Guelph, Canada during the 1994–96 time period.

The role of environmental NGOs has been steadily growing and is also recognized by the Government of India and donor agencies. It is proposed that a locus standi may be given to have better mobilization in support of EFPP. In 1994, the Government of India, through the Bureau of Indian Standards, started an 'Eco Mark' label scheme for products, manufactured by environment-friendly firms.

India already has many ongoing initiatives to talk about in the context of 'being green'. No doubt, 'the early bird catches the worm', and so do initiatives that drive the green lifestyle. For instance, the Tata Group has taken the lead in setting its goal to reduce CO_2 emissions at its manufacturing plant, setting up an eco-friendly showroom with natural building material for its flooring and energy-efficient lights. It has also declared that 25 per cent of the total power it would generate in the next 10 years would be from renewable energy sources.

Agreeing to follow the trend of being green, several other companies are also in the process of implementing clean development mechanism (CDM) projects. The Delhi government has, for example, introduced the Energy Conservation Building Code (ECDC) to give clear instructions on construction of new government buildings. This code is already in use in various commonwealth projects in the state. Its successful implementation will save 30 to 40 per cent energy.

Brands in India are now focusing more on policies that will help them tap consumers' choice for green products and promotion of eco-friendly mechanism in their respective markets. The trend has even swept across the country's fashion industry. Many designers now work on environment-friendly clothing and showcase their support for the 'green' cause during many fashion weeks. Natural fabrics like hand-woven wool, natural silks, recycled junk jewellery, organic knits, etc., are being widely used.

Another trend of being green for publicity has also been reported among many celebrities who support various green causes. Besides celebrities, many Indian citizens are coming up with different ways of being green. A good example of that is Mawlynnong, the cleanest village in Asia. The village is situated 90 km away from the state capital of Meghalaya. It has over 80 houses and the villagers are the green ambassadors who have worked hard to attain such green prestige. They kept their surroundings clean by doing simple voluntary services like sweeping the roads and lanes, watering the plants and cleaning the drains.

The many non-profit organizations that strive to safeguard the eco-realm work very hard to keep the trend going and to create more awareness. Not only do they advocate being green but also set out to implement eco-friendly initiatives to ensure the survival of all creatures in harmony. Renewable energy, environmental regulation, clean energy, energy independence, green jobs, eco-tourism, etc., are some of the areas of concern they work on.

Different reasons might have prompted different people to adopt this new trend of being green but it surely has proved popular. The real success can only be measured in terms of the change witnessed by people in their lifestyle towards being more eco-friendly and adhering to sustainable ways of protecting the environment that will eventually stop global climate change threats.

Problems and Barriers

The institutional impediments include the barriers at the level of the industry, i.e., organization and the government. As in other low consumption countries, in India there is also a big gap between the demands of the law and the technical and financial resources required to implement them. Reliance on a command and control approach is more prevalent than market-based instruments, i.e., self-assessment and voluntary initiation for EFPPs. In course of evolving and implementing EFPPs several barriers are encountered, which can be classified and described as follows:

Organizational Barriers

For making any programme implementation successful, the structure of the management staff and employees, both technical and managerial, and their total involvement with the programme, are of paramount importance. If the organizational functioning suffers from a lack of recognition by the staff/employees and if it is devoid of decision-making power at appropriate level, the desired results could never be achieved. The organization is also expected to lay the 'right emphasis' on all the activities it performs. Finally, if management is able to induce and motivate the employees to make it their own programme, and if it could overcome one of the major barriers, i.e., the bureaucrat dysfunction and high turnover of technical staff, it can ensure successful implementation of the programme.

Systematic Barriers

For achieving good results in adopting Green Technology over End of the Pipe (EoP) Technology, the whole system has to be geared up considering human resource management, the work culture, production activity and the potential of people serving the organization. The management system has to be made effective and inadequacies therein have to be removed. The hierarchy of the decision-making, communication, authority and responsibility, etc., should be reviewed to make the system effective. The management of the organization has to make sure that the organization does not suffer from the handicap of financial and technical inability of people to innovate. Capable and competent people should be employed and encouraged in the organization.

Many times it has been observed that the confidentiality concerns of an organization become a major barrier in imparting technical consultation for affecting low waste technology. This needs to evolve and a strategy to overcome confidentiality concerns becoming a hurdle in the way of adopting Green Technology must be adopted. Further, the reporting system and recordkeeping of the organization should be improved by way of modification or changes. If recordkeeping is not perfect, any information required for purposes like an energy audit, environmental audit, environmental statement, etc., would not be retractable, then the whole system would become a mess and ultimately collapse. Proper classification needs to be done and information recorded accordingly. For implementing Green Technology effectively, one of the approaches which helps most is fragmentation of the production activity of the organization. For minimizing waste, sources of waste generation have to be identified. Hence, after breaking the production process into several parts, the source of waste generation is clearer and then by applying the the appropriate method like reuse, recycle or recovery, the waste generated can be reduced.

Technical/Technological Barriers

Green Technology implementation needs to overcome both technical and technological barriers. If certain changes in the design of a piece of equipment are to be made, i.e., if some of the features are to be modified, this is considered technical, but if in the process there is a change in the raw material or the process line, this would be deemed to be technological because with a change in raw material there may be a change in the processing route itself.

The adoption of Green Technology is possible only by the proper initiative in an industrial organization. Such an initiative can be taken when the source of technical information is accessible with ease. Often, it is seen that the source of information being not known and, having limited access to the technical information, these industries end up using EoP technology only. This could be attributed to the complete absence of a pro-active information dissemination mechanism. Information, if not disseminated to the right and genuine user, will not fructify and give expected results. For the dissemination of information, a mechanism has to evolve and a strategy worked out to make the information flow to the user. To arrive at the best decision for the application of the appropriate technology, all alternatives should be looked into and their effects assessed. The effort should always be made to apply the 'Best Applicable Technology' (BAT) to get the best results.

Financial/Economic Barriers

Financial constraints have often been seen as a major stumbling block in the way of affecting a major technology transfer programme. It is basically the resource crunch, especially financial, which has hit the industrial organizations. Other factors like inadequate investment planning and resource pricing and its availability are too vital to marginalize the limitations effecting a positive change. At times, while carrying out economic analysis, the environmental cost gets overlooked and is not given due consideration. Its exclusion from economic analysis has often been seen to jeopardize the success of the programme.

Attitudinal Barriers

It has been observed that any organizational change not only meets with lot of resistance from within but also takes quite some time to have the intended effect. It may be due to job insecurity or the fear of failure which inhibits the personnel to adopt to the new changed environment. Sometimes the lack of leadership and effective supervision also serves as a barrier in implementing low waste technology in place of conventional 'EoP technology'. This makes it difficult to realize the goals of implementing simple improvements like good housekeeping, which without any investment promises more than a 20 per cent improvement in the existing states of the plants.

Regulatory/Governmental Barriers

In India, one of the major barriers in the promotion of LWT (Green Technology) is a short and rigid compliance period. It may be the enforcing agencies like CPCB and SPCBS on their own or due to the enforcement of court orders following public interest litigation asking the industries to combat pollution in a short duration. In such a situation, the easy and sure solution is putting up a treatment plant with the application of EoP technology, and the application of LWT takes a back seat. The common misconception related to LWT is its high implementation cost. These erroneous conceptions are often due to misdirected incentives. In fact, various policy pronouncements on LWT are merely statements of intent. As such, there exists no clear-cut directive from the government on incentives, subsidies, soft loans, etc., for the adoption of LWT by industries. Further, there is no mandatory provision in regulatory terms for the adoption of LWT for the industries which in turn can be a big disincentive as compared to adoption of EoP.

Community or consumer pressure is an important precursor to the industrial units making a change for the adoption of LWT. In India, the potential for this pressure is there: several examples exist in which the community was organized on several environmental issues. Public consultation mechanisms are almost non-existent in the case of decisions concerning industrial development and the related environmental issues.

Conclusion: Lack of Public and Consumer Pressure

We must make a dramatic shift in the way we consume our resources and produce, distribute, consume and dispose our goods. We must work to speed up the adoption of EFPPs utilization.

The potential for EFPPs will only be effectively and independently pursued by the industries if the true environmental costs are reflected in the pricing policy and information on environment-friendly technologies are shared and made available with the support of government agencies and R&D institutions.

What we have to aim at is to contribute to a new partnership between technical assistance organizations, governments, industries, and financing institutions for environmentally sound and economically healthy industry and green product usage.

References

Asian and Pacific Centre for Transfer of Technology. Asia Pacific Tech Monitor: Your Technology Window to Asia and Pacific, March-April, 1994 (Special Feature on Clean Technologies).

CO_2 Emissions from Fuel Combustion (IEA STATISTICS, 2010 Edition), International Energy Agency, 9 rue de la Fédération, 75739 Paris Cedex 15, France.

Dwivedi, O.P., Jain, R.B and Vajpeyi, D.K. (1998). "Stewardship of Governance: Ethics and Values of the Public Service" in *Governing India: Issues Concerning Public Policy, Institutions and Administration*, Delhi: B.R. Publications.

Energy Efficient Technologies and CO_2 Reduction Potentials in the Pulp and Paper Industry: A Workshop in the Framework of the G8 Dialogue on

Climate Change, Clean Energy and Sustainable Development in collaboration with WBCSD—Final version 24 October 2006.

Estimating Greenhouse Gas Emissions from Pulp and Paper Mills (Version 1.1), July 8, 2005: A Project of the Climate Change Working Group of The International Council of Forest and Paper Associations (ICFPA) Prepared by: National Council for Air and Stream Improvement, Inc. (NCASI) Research Triangle Park, NC, USA.

IPCC Expert Meeting on Detection and Attribution Related to Anthropogenic Climate Change, The World Meteorological Organization, Geneva, Switzerland, 14–16 September 2009, Meeting Report (Edited by: Thomas Stocker, Christopher Field, Qin Dahe, Vicente Barros, Gian-Kasper Plattner, Melinda Tignor, Pauline Midgley, Kristie Ebi).

IPCC WGII Fourth Assessment Report, Summary for Policymakers April 6th, 2007, Climate Change Impacts, Adaptation and Vulnerability Summary for Policymakers Implications of proposed CO_2 emissions limitations. IPPC Technical Paper 4. www.IPPC.org

Josep, G. et al. (2007). Contributions to Accelerating Atmospheric CO_2 Growth from Economic Activity, Carbon Intensity, and Efficiency of Natural Sinks (www.pnas.org).

Trivedi, R.K., "Environmental Friendly Industrial Production Product Usage: Indian Scenario". Paper Presented in Learned Societies Congress of Canadian Asian Studies Association Conference, June 29–31, 1996, Brock University, ONT, Canada.

United Nations Environment Programme (UNEP). *Industry and Environment*, (10)2: April/May/June 1987.

Yap, Nonita and Awasthi, S.K. (1995). *Waste Management for Sustainable Development in India: Policy Planning and Administrative Dimensions with Case Studies from Kanpur*, New Delhi: Tata McGraw-Hill.

13

Global Sustainability in Indian Traditions

Hinduism, Gandhi's Successors and Sikhism

CHRISTOPHER KEY CHAPPLE

We are in conflict with our environment due to the denial of the unsustainability of the global consumerist economic model. The Hindu traditions of India suggest that personal and social ethics, also referred to as *dharma,* can help deal with the ongoing clash between human greed and the carrying capacity of the planet. In the practice of yoga within the Hindu traditions, all actions must be viewed in light of the core teaching of *ahimsa* or non-violence. At its best, peace and frugality characterize this important faith, values needed for global sustainability. Gandhi interpreted the *Bhagavad Gita* as calling for an inner change, a mastery over one's lower urges in service of the welfare of all. Gandhi has inspired generations of activists who seek in different ways to implement his vision. In the Sikh tradition, the *Guru Granth Sahib* calls for a recognition of God in all things, resulting in a deep appreciation for creation. These religions and thinkers recognize the need for responsible human behaviour within the world and suggest that each individual must strive for inner balance in order to create enduring calm and economic sanity.

The dharma traditions of India offer a path through which humans might connect individual human works with the planet in a manner that is mutually enhancing, salubrious for both self and community. To begin, humans need to acknowledge that we live in a state of constant relationship with our external circumstances. A shift in emphasis must take place away from selfish individual consumerism toward a concern for the common good. The earth community faces great personal and environmental challenges. Hopefully, growing awareness of these challenges will prompt a move toward a sustainable lifestyle that leads to human flourishing and freedom.

Sustainability and Spirituality

The move toward sustainability requires a shift in discourse. Technological, industrial and economic growth no longer define the core benchmark for human well-being. As we grapple with various human-caused environmental dilemmas, and as our scope of knowledge has changed our very relationship with the cosmos, we stand poised at a great crossroads. In ancient times, humans were not immune from planetary disturbances, droughts, floods and disease. Religions developed belief systems and rituals not only to appease what some considered to be the angry gods, but also to bring solace to survivors. Modern science, for the most part, has made the coping systems provided by religious institutions largely obsolete. Particularly in Europe, but throughout the developed world, the role of religion in giving meaning to human life has been dramatically diminished. Because the old model of religion placed ultimate meaning beyond the grasp or ken of the human realm, it has lost its relevance, at least in terms of cosmological certitude. However, the enduring lessons of the world's religions can help inform our move forward. This chapter will explore messages from Hinduism, Gandhi's legacy, and Sikhism that can help provide alternative inspirations for redressing the problems of ecological degradation.

Hindu Spirituality and Sustainability

In Hinduism, the correlation of the cosmic person and the sacrificial horse to the broader forces of the universe and the ritual dismemberment of a goat in the contemporary sacrifice to the goddess Durga provide a different sacrificial mode. Rather than placing an emphasis on loss, this approach to sacrificial ritual emphasized connectivity. These rituals do not provoke recollections of a broken past or advocate social change or tweak an individual's conscience. The exuberant rituals of India proclaim that humans stand in solidarity with and in celebration of the great forces that drive the universe. By seeing the changing nature of the human mind in the phases of the moon, by seeing the warmth of the heart reflected in the household heart, sacrifice and ritual bring an individual to a place of identification with and empathy for the natural order.

The foundations of the Hindu faith can be traced to the *RgVeda*. Composed more than 3,500 years ago, this collection of more than 1,000 chants gives praise to the powers of the universe, from the heat of fire to the glorious power of human speech, from the magnificence of the sunrise to the flowing of India's great rivers. In addition to including primal, archetypal myths such as the battle between the god Indra and the drought-bringing dragon Vrtra, the Vedas also praise the pinnacle of human accomplishment, referred to as *rta*, the attainment of artistry and ritual and fulfilment within life itself.

One of the best-known hymns, the *Purusa Sukta* (X:190), contains a message that holds a model for thinking about the human-cosmos relationship. The hymn correlates the human body with the far-flung regions of the universe:

> The moon was born of his mind; of his eyes, the sun was born;
> From his mouth, Indra and fire; from his breath, wind was born;
> From his navel there was the atmosphere;
> From his head, heaven was rolled together;
> From his feet, the earth; from his ears the directions.

By identifying body parts with heavenly bodies, the heavens and the earth, and the elements of fire and wind, sanctity is given to both self and cosmos. Like the moon, our mind reflects and changes. Without the light of the sun, we cannot see. Our mouth proclaims our intentions and desires, and like the God of war, Indra, allows us to stake our claim in the world. Each breath we take generates and relies on the circulation of air. Our head pulls upward; our belly gathers us toward the centre and allows us to expand; our feet anchor us to the earth. Our ears stabilize us within the space of the four directions. Through this sacrificial vision, each human being finds a place of importance within the cosmos. This sacrifice signals a continuity between humans and their place in society and within nature.

A later Vedic passage, the *Prthivi Sukta*, from the *Atharva Veda*, gives praise to human reliance upon Mother Earth for sustenance:

> O Mother Earth! You are the world for us and we are your children. Empower us to speak in one accord, steer us to live in peace and harmony, and guide us in our behaviour so that we have cordial and gracious relationships with all other people. (16)

The earth provides the context for human flourishing. The Vedic peoples recognized her importance and called for acknowledgement of her beneficence:

> We venerate Mother Earth, the sustainer and preserver of forests, vegetation, and all things that are held together firmly. She is the source of a stable environment. (27)

The text also calls upon humans to protect and preserve nature's resources:

O Mother Earth!
May our bodies enjoy only water that is clean.
May you keep away from us all that is polluted.
May we always do only good deeds. (30)

The composers of the text see a reciprocal relationship between human kind and the earth; if humans care for the earth, the text hints, a covenantal agreement might be formed wherein Mother Earth will extend her protection:

The Earth is adorned with many hills, plains, and slopes.
She bears plants with medicinal properties.
May no person oppress her and may she spread prosperity for us all around. (2)

Whereas the *Purusa Sukta* in the *RgVeda* emphasizes the interconnectivity between humans and the five great elements, the posture taken in the *Prthivi Sukta* evokes feelings of humility and awe at the power of Mother Earth. By recognizing and enhancing qualities of 'truth, strength, artistry, ferocity, dedication, fervour, effulgence, and sacrifice (1)' that sustain the earth, humans can hope to become worthy of her blessings.

Another genre of Hindu spiritual literature, the epic, spins tales of war and conquest. However, the teaching of non-violence (*ahimsa*) has been declared in the great Indian epic, the *Mahabharata*, to be highest religious teaching (*dharma*): *Ahimsa Paramo Dharmah.* Several chapters of the eighteenth book are dedicated to non-violence, suggesting that the highest human achievement lies in being able to see others as oneself and oneself as others. Such a person is said to surpass even the accomplishment of the gods and goddesses in heaven, who still live in a dualistic state:

Even the gods are bewildered at the path
of the one who seeks the abode of no abode,
who sees all beings as oneself,
as not different from oneself. (*Mahabharata* XIII: 14.8)

By moving one's identity to a place of virtual homelessness, and by not attaching primary importance to the ego, the practitioner of non-violence attains great peace, leading to the highest dharma:

When one strides among others seeing them as oneself,
others also fall in step and see the self as well.

This is to be followed indeed in the world of living beings;
by this all dharma is taught. (*Mahabharata* XIII: 14.10)

Similarly, *Yoga Sutra* (II:35) states: 'When in the presence of one established in non-violence, there is the abandonment of hostility'. By adopting an attitude of similitude with others, a sense of calm and peace can prevail. This feeling of sameness, however, must not be predicated upon externals such as possessions or national identity or even a presumption of like-mindedness. Rather, in order to move toward a deep level of sustainability, it must arise from a shared sense of quiet, of a space beyond quantifiable things into a sense of shared humanity or fellowship. The Hindu concept of sacrifice (*yajna*) suggests the cultivation of a vision of self that sees action as moving toward a goal beyond selfishness. The self extends to include the other, facilitated rituals that develop a sense of interconnectivity. Each of the elements listed above—the five great elements of earth, water, fire, air and space—become part of a recognition of the essentials required for human flourishing. The icons and exemplars as set forth in the array of Hinduism's gods and goddesses provide encouragement and direction for developing and maintaining stability and happiness.

One example of Hindu respect for nature can be found in the abundant literature that extols the beauties of rivers. For instance, Panditaraja Jagannatha's Ganga Lahari praises the Ganges river in the following words:

Your water is bliss incarnate.
Your water is forever pure.
The glory of your waves, Mother,
is unequalled anywhere in the world.
(Jagannatha, in Cort, 42)

In a similar vein, Rupa Gosvamin's *Yamunashatakam* offers praise for the Yamuna river:

She beautifies the spacious forests with her flow of alluring water;
She dances with the birds and bees flying around her lotus fields;
She completely destroys all disease, sickness, and sin
For those who desire to bathe in her;
May the Daughter of the Sun always purify me.
(Gosvamin in Haberman, 197–98)

Sadly, we know that both rivers carry dangerously high levels of pollution and 'Action Plans' have been developed for each to help improve their current degraded state. By recalling and reviving traditions of river veneration, it is hoped that corrective actions may prevail. An ethic of sustainability can arise from feelings of connection with the natural world. By understanding our place in nature, we can develop feelings of appreciation that will result in a natural desire to praise and protect the wonders of the world. Engaging one's body and senses in, for instance, the elegance of a free flowing river, one cannot help but develop feels of love.

With the advent of global consumer economies, and the co-opting of human happiness by market forces and the thrills and skills of marketing, Hindu spirituality, which emphasizes contentment with the bare essentials, is in danger of being eclipsed. Yoga, one aspect of Hindu spirituality, has itself entered the global marketplace of ideas and spiritualities and, if approached prudently, might help worldwide remembrance that happiness cannot be found through the accumulation of things, but through appreciation and cultivation of simplicity. Beyond the ritual traditions of India, yoga offers a pan-Asian modality for reflecting on the human condition that offers various entry points into sustainable values. This tradition was codified by Patañjali, a scholar, who most likely lived around 300 C.E. Yoga begins with a series of ethical values (*yama)* adhered to by Buddhists and Jainas as well as Hindus: non-violence, truthfulness, not stealing, sexual restraint and non-possession. In light of sustainability, non-violence might be employed to help slow the pace of habitat destruction and the decimation of species around the planet. Truthfulness might encourage the better dissemination of knowledge about the harmful effects of resource exploitation such as the destruction of forests, monoculture and global warming. Through recognition of how cutting the forests and the pumping of oil and the wastage of water robs the bounty of the earth, persons might refrain from such rampant and rapacious activities. By controlling sexual impulses, the rate of population growth might be slowed. Through the minimization of possessions, people might grow accustomed to living on the bare necessities of life, a requisite step toward sustainability.

The other stages of yoga might also be helpful in developing a spirituality of sustainability. The cultivation of positive observances (*niyama*) can help reground the self within modes of self-reliance and serve as an antidote to the all-pervasive consumer message that true happiness lies in shopping. These observances include searching for and developing purity, contentment, austerity, self-reflection, and an attitude of grateful devotion. By purposefully engaging the body in movement (*asana*) and purposeful breathing exercises (*pranayama*), a centering and inwardness (*pratyahara*) can emerge. As described in Patanjali's *Yoga Sutra* one can then develop great powers of concentration, meditation and *samadhi*, allowing a restructuring of one's being away from familial and cultural constructions toward a point of total freedom (*kaivalyam*) and an automatic positioning of one's actions in accordance with the needs of the universe (*dharma megha samadhi*). Newly interpreted in light of environmental distress, the yoga practice can help inspire a life of sustainability characterized by healthy habits, meagre consumption of resources and overall sense of cheerfulness.

The Gandhian Legacy

Mahatma Gandhi (1869–1948) took the yogic values of non-violence (*ahimsa*) and holding to truth (*satyagraha*) onto the world stage. He forever changed the course of world history by throwing off the shackles of European colonialism non-violently, a process that spread infectiously throughout the rest of Asia and Africa. His methods have been used with success in the Philippines, the countries of the former Soviet Union, and most recently in the Middle East and Africa. His analysis of social woes and his corrective methods hold great lessons to be learned as the world confronts the ravages climate changes and species decimation. His work may be summarized as the encouragement, through self-discipline and mastery of the self, to do with less so that others may thrive. The austerity of Gandhi's methods, combined with technological ingenuity, may pave a path from uncertainty to sustainability. Emerging Gandhian modes of spirituality, such as those espoused in the Occupy Movement of the 2010s, can help provide meaning and hope, giving purpose to the quest for a sustainable planet. Drawing from an underlying ethic of non-violence, this spirituality will offer new definitions of human well-being, body-based forms of spiritual practice, and the transformation of food production and patterns of food consumption toward a more sustainable model.

Gandhi suggested that by returning to the bare necessities of life, India could disentangle itself from the ravages of the British colonial system. He spun his own thread and wove his own clothing. He led salt marches that helped spare people from taxation and reliance on imported goods. India's response to the difficulties of an enmeshed global economy was well-served by the Gandhian creed and adage: 'There is enough in this world for every person's need, but not enough for every person's greed'.

Narayan Desai

Narayan Desai serves as Chancellor of Gujarat Vidyápeeth, the university that Mahatma Gandhi established in Ahmedabad, India. Desai, following the footsteps of his father, served as Gandhi's personal secretary. Desai continues to set forth Gandhi's core message: holding to truth in a spirit of non-violence. He states that we need overcome our all-too-human greed and fear with love and cooperation. Greed and fear plague the US and can be found throughout the world today. Debts, individual and governmental, have been poorly managed with dire consequences. Signs of greed can be found throughout the world in obesity and other food-related crises, and in lumbering, energy-guzzling cars, trucks, and overbuilt houses. Likewise, fear can be seen in a deepening split between political parties, between religions that ironically all preach peace and love, between rich and poor. All these tensions can lead to mistrust and the potential for violence. No political figure today will dare suggest that citizens should alter their lifestyle and reduce their consumption willingly for the sake of the common good. Desai offers a radical personal solution to the world's ills: live within your means, occupy your hands with creative work, and be open to the ideas and views of others. Even when engaged in world travel, Desai, following the model of Gandhi, spins tuffs of cotton into thread, adding to his spool each day. After several weeks or months, he weaves his thread into homespun cloth and wears only self-crafted clothes. All the students and faculty at his university do the same, engaging head, heart, and hands. This simple act helped India cast off its colonial oppressors. Gandhians today continue to espouse the ideals and realities of self-control, moving toward self-sufficiency and self-respect.

Vandana Shiva

Gandhi-inspired activist Vandana Shiva has become the world's most outspoken critic of globalization and has provided a trenchant critique of 'patenting' of traditional ways of knowledge for economic gain by corporations. Her activism in the realm of seeds serves as a paradigm for exposing the excesses of the human attempt to manipulate nature. She takes a broad historical view in developing her analysis of 'enclosure' or the marketing off what once held in common, to be commoditized and controlled by industrial and commercial forces.

Shiva's advocacy of sustenance economy would require a shift from a corporate model to one in balance in nature, valuing relationships over and above commodities. She has taken up food production as her primary arena for activism. Shiva writes:

> … I launched a national program to save seed diversity in farmers' fields. We call it Navdanya, which literally means nine seeds …. The farmers [had] become mere consumers of corporate seed. This excludes the farmer from the critical role of conserver of genetic diversity and development of seed. It robs farmers of their rights to their biological and intellectual heritage …. Navdanya wanted to build a program in which farmers and scientists relate horizontally rather than vertically, in which biodiversity and production of food go hand in hand, and in which farmers' knowledge is strengthened, not robbed. (2005: 92)

The corporatization of agriculture, including the patenting of seeds and the mass marketing of herbicides, pesticides and petroleum-based fertilizers, has created a horrific situation, turning farmers away from organic practices and into debtors. Shiva, citing government statistics, notes: 'According to India's National Crime Bureau, 16,000 farmers in India committed suicide during 2004. During one six-month span in 2004, there were 1,860 suicides by farmers in the State of Andhra Pradesh alone' (ibid.: 120). During the first decade of the 21st century, 250,000 farmers committed suicide in India (Shiva, Loyola Marymount University, November 1, 2011). This great tragedy has received scant attention from the international press. Shiva advocates for individual farmers and their families, and has helped urge legislation to help India's rural poor.

As a solution to the globalized, corporate model, Shiva advocates 'living economies' such as Mumbai's magnificent lunch distribution system, by the Mumbai Tiffin Box Suppliers Association, which delivers 175,000 lunches each day. 'With no documentation, no order, no bosses' this group makes only one mistake every 16 million deliveries (Shiva, 2005: 70). This organization has been studied by the Harvard Business School as a model for human and social ingenuity (*Economist,* July 12–18, 2008: 73). For Shiva, this exemplifies the sort of people-based economy required for sustainability, joining self-determination with interdependence.

M.C. Mehta

In 1996, the Supreme Court lawyer M.C. Mehta won the Goldman prize for his advocacy on behalf of protecting the Taj Mahal. For years, the industrial grime generated by the city of Agra had degraded the once-gleaming marble of the famous building. Through his efforts, several industries relocated and a stringent programme for reducing air pollution was enacted, including a ban on non-electric vehicles within several hundred yards of the Mughal masterpiece.

On April 1, 2001, Mehta achieved another landmark victory. On that day, all public transport vehicles in the Delhi capital region converted from gasoline, diesel, and kerosene fuels to compressed natural gas. The air quality improved overnight. The new buses, taxis, and auto-rikshaws are brightly painted in yellow and green, celebrating the light of the sun and the bounty of the earth.

M.C. Mehta, with support from the Ford Foundation, has developed a training camp to equip lawyers from throughout South Asia to face the challenges presented by environmental conditions. While visiting this camp, Eco-Ashram, near Rishikesh in 2006, I witnessed a dozen young brilliant lawyers from Nepal, India, Bangladesh, Bhutan, Sri Lanka and Pakistan being taught by Mehta as part of a six-week residential course. Everyone lived in straw huts, shared simple food and attempted to keep warm, even when pelted by Himalayan hail. The lectures on industrial pollution included heartbreaking tales of miscarriages, birth defects, and early deaths. Mehta states that religion played an important role in his formation as a child noting that:

> When I was a child my father was a very learned person in the sense that he knew the Quran and he knew all about the Hindu religion and used to read Gita everyday. I think this was what influenced me and all the children. I used to go to temple, but I had the feeling that we didn't mind going anywhere to learn. In the village, the Muslims were there, the Hindus were there, and my father was protective of the minorities. My father said that we are all human beings; we should all live happily, and should not discourage each other.

One of Mehta's first environmental cases included the protection of children working in 'electro plating, chemical industries, mining, so many different industries'. If he succeeds in his legal efforts, 40 million children will be removed from these work places and be able to begin an education.

Mehta became involved with the rehabilitation of the Ganges river in 1986. He said:

> I fought this case when I came to know that Ganga caught fire. I came over and investigated and fought that case first against two industries. Now more than 150,000 industries in 300 towns are all affected by this case; 600 tanneries were closed down in Calcutta. And now, similarly the court has directed other industries to use air pollution control and water pollution control. The monitoring process is going on.

The rivers of India not only suffer from pollution but from canalization and siphoning for irrigation. Mehta said:

> I am fighting for the rights of the rivers. The rights of the rivers mean that the river has a right to live, to exist. One should not touch the river bed because there are too many species that live in the river or near the river bed, like birds, that live along the riverbed. Now you only see the river when there is a monsoon. The river is channelled through the canals so it goes everywhere.

Mehta also notes that Americans who come to India to study yoga in ashrams mistreat the river. He called a meeting of religious leaders urging them to develop adequate sanitation.

> That is really important. A few years back I organized a meeting at Haridwar, where I invited all [religious leaders and pilgrims] it was very interesting what they did not know. They did not know where all their waste was going. So I was very hard with them and asked them if they had ever seen it, thousands of people go to the Ashram to defecate everyday and have you ever noticed where it goes? I told them, "You are committing sin, you are doing something wrong, and it is your duty to tell them to not do it or either you put up a system so that it will treat the problem." If all these Ashrams started treating this problem (and they have the money to do it because they are quite rich), then it will help the cleaning process all along the Ganga. It is mandatory to put up a treatment plant in for the industry. Similarly, it should be so for the Ashram, which has thousands of people going there. They should do the same thing, it is their responsibility.

Mehta claims that

> Gandhi was a true environmentalist. He said, "we should not live in debt, we should help others to grow". I like Gandhi for his spiritual values, and for his cultural values, and for his vision about India. He said, "don't put up all the big industries, there is no need, we should try to give a job to each hand". In India we are lucky that way, we have more than two billion hands. It was Mahatma Gandhi's vision to give jobs to the people. India is unique because of its magnetic power and vibrations that go deep into our mind and soul. Each country, each continent has its own uniqueness, so in my view we should respect that.

Mehta spoke of three primary concerns:

> Health, the environment, and education, these three things are important. A push should be given so that people feel more secure. Apart from the unemployment, I am worried about the food security, because the way housing projects are going in the country. The

industries are taking over the land, and the land is limited, it cannot be expanded. So if India has a limited land, then we should see how in the best way we should give the maximum amount for the growth of food only, and that is agriculture, and that is what 70 per cent of India should be. So in India we need organically made foods. People can export it, it can improve the economy. And the youth should be involved in so many areas, like instead of cutting the trees; I always tell the states that they should be put in forestation programs. Don't cut the trees, make more trees, all medicinal plants, all that are here in the Himalayas, grow them and see that the economy will grow. So there are many ways where the youth can be put up for this, to do constructive work.

In 1989, Mehta initiated annual Green Marches. He said:

Every year we cover about 300 miles. It takes place for about a month. We have a group of 30–35 engineers, doctors, lawyers, agricultural experts, economists, whoever wants to join. We make a group and then make a core group and we start walking. If a good environmentalist is with us he will go into a school, organize a program, give in advance information for that program of when we will be arriving on such and such date here and these will be the different activities. So then the school will go and organize a competition or a talk on environment. So the children will take part. The doctor will go to the village if the people are sick or there are some other problems and he will attend to them. If there are veterinarians, they will go attend sick animals. If there is an agricultural expert, he will give a talk to the villagers. It is an educational project. Then we will go on and on and on and on, so this way it goes on. In the evening we sit in one place and have a meeting and then we choose a group of up to ten people for the monitoring, so that the next day we do not forget where to go or what we've done, to ensure that some activities go on in those areas. Sometimes the people come in thousands, sometimes in hundreds they come and they meet us, and in those 25 days we meet maybe more than 1 million, 2 million people. So that is what we do. It gives me a lot of education also about what is happening in those areas. I learn about the air pollution or water pollution and other problems in that area like insect problems.

Mehta expressed deep concern for children who do not have a direct experience of the outdoors. He comments:

The city children have not been exposed to the wild life, to nature. They don't know where milk comes from. When they come over here

> first they are terrified of the forests and then they become ok. It is fascinating for them when they see the birds around and we tell them, 'how many varieties of birds are over there?' When I came over here there were just two to three varieties, now there are 30 types of birds, because I planted all sorts of trees, different sorts of trees. They are attracted to this and start taking pictures, and then we tell them the plants affect the birds and the wildlife. They feel so happy and when they go back they really feel passionate.
>
> I will give you an example. One day, a child's father called me and said, "what have you done to my son?" I said, "what, I don't know". He said, "in the morning when he was going to school he refused to sit in the car," I said, "why?" he said, "because from the tailpipe the smoke was coming out" and he said, "I don't want to sit in this car, this car is polluting!" I said, "well then what did you do?" he said, "then I will not got to school so then I sent the car to the garage".

Global warming worries Mehta, who had a direct encounter with the collapse of a glacier while hiking in the Himalayas:

> I think only if we sensitize the people all over the world, then only we can reduce green house gas emissions and we can bring back the climate. Otherwise it is too late. The glaciers are melting on the Himalayas, yet no body is bothered. I saw it myself when I went 14,000 feet high there. It was so sad that the glaciers are melting so fast. In the morning I went this way and by the evening the people said don't go this way. I asked what happened and the people said that the water in the glaciers had already caused a huge area to collapse. We have to be sensitive.

Mehta shared that his next project will be to initiate and support legislation within India that will help slow climate change.

Mehta has acknowledged that India's traditional environmental wisdom can provide a valuable resource for moving the public will into supporting the steps necessary to improve air quality, deal with water pollution and take the necessary steps to slow global warming. He commented:

> The elements of nature such as air and water are being overtaken by greed. Greed has overtaken us, leaving us under the cloak of greed. For people wearing the cloak of greed, it is very hard to come out and see real life. With correct understanding they will be in a position to respect law, and enforce it. Then we have sustainable elements. (Mehta, 2006)

For India, the sacrificial model calls for a reconnection with the elements that have been celebrated since the Vedic period, and acknowledgement of the real connection between the human order and the cosmic order.

Sikhism and Sustainability

Sikh theology, as established by Guru Nanak (1469–1539), combines a committed monotheism with a progressive notion of spiritual attainment that includes teachings of yoga and takes into account the Hindu, Jaina and Buddhist beliefs in reincarnation. The fifth Guru, Arjan (1563–1606), compiled a collection of texts sacred to the Sikhs known as the *Adi Granth*. The tenth and last Guru, Guru Gobind Singh (1666–1708), added hymns by subsequent Gurus and established the expanded *Guru Granth Sahib* as the abiding teacher of the tradition, a status it still holds today. Consequently, Sikh theology relies upon this scripture as providing authority and guidance for individuals and society at large.

In alignment with the practice of constructive theology, Mary Evelyn Tucker and John Grim have suggested a method to be employed when asking religious traditions to respond to the issues of environmental ethics. This includes '*critical understanding* of the complexity, contexts, and frameworks in which these religions articulate such views ... *empathetic appreciation* for the traditions ... and *creative revisioning* of mutually enhancing human-earth relations' (Tucker and Grim, 2000: xxii). With the Sikh tradition, two notable scholars, Surjit Jolly and Amarjit Singh, have employed this method to rethink the Sikh tradition and its scripture in terms of ecological sustainability. As seen in their writing, they see great value in revisiting the Sikh concept of God in such a way as to encourage increased human responsibility for pollution and other forms of ecological degradation. They also praise the greatness of creation, not only as an expression of God's goodness, but also to assert that human beings carry an innate affection for and understanding of the animal realm in particular because of experiences as various species in past lives.

Surjit Jolly writes that 'God did not confer absolute power on man to control and dominate nature. The human race is not an alien species foisted upon this planet to dominate and exploit it, but rather as an integral part of nature itself liked to the rest of creation by indissoluble bonds' (1989: 282). The human is subsidiary to God, and hence to nature herself. Jolly further comments that 'Guru Nanak calls God the Karta Purukh, the creating power of the universe. He perceives him as the inner self of all living beings' (ibid.: 283). In this perception, God is to be found in all beings, all aspects of creation. He quotes the *Guru Granth Sahib:*

> Thou: the Primal Being
> All pervasive beyond extent
> Creator
> Unknowable thy limit
> Thou are immanent too
> Pervading all
> Merging in one.
> (*Adi Sri Guru Granth Sahib*, 448)

The text goes on to offer praise to creation in its various forms, specifically the elements of air, water and fire:

> Marvellous the multiplicity of creation
> Wonderful; their distinctions
> Marvellous creation's form
> Wonderful its variety
> Marvelous the motion of air
> Wonderful its water
> Marvelous its fire.
> (*Adi Sri Guru Granth Sahib*, 463)

Surjit Jolly then continues his analysis, quoting scripture on the special powers of these three elements:

> Air is the vital force
> Water the progenitor
> The vast earth the mother of all.
> (*Adi Sri Guru Granth Sahib*, 8)

Many passages in the *Guru Granth Sahib* similarly praise plants and vegetation, described both as plants-as-plants and plants as metaphor and allegory. For instance:

> The mind is the ploughman
> The practice its husbandry
> The effort its water
> The body its field
> Sow the name
> Fertilize contentment
> Keep the garb of humility
> With karmas of love
> The crop will grow.
> (*Adi Sri Guru Granth Sahib*, 595)

Jolly chooses another metaphor that combines immanence and transcendence:

> Purusha is like the
> Beautifully coloured earth
> Studded with gems of grass.
> (*Adi Sri Guru Granth Sahib*, 322)

Animals also provide metaphors for the good life. The *Guru Granth Sahib* notes that 'birds carry no gold' (p.144) and that humans need to 'love the Lord like the fish loves water' (p. 60). According to Jolly, wisdom can be found in the ways of nature. Nature provides instruction and an example for living a life mindful of God. Just as birds depend on nature for their survival it can be inferred that in order for human beings to thrive they must rely on the bounty of nature.

Amarjit Singh, in a book published by Guru Jambheshwar University in Hisar, builds on a statement by Avtar Singh: 'The Gurus were ... sensitive to ... socio-natural environments' (2002: 196). He correlates the flaring forth or big bang that started the universe with the *Guru Granth Sahib* account of the origin of the universe through God's will. In the style of Pierre Teilhard de Chardin and Thomas Berry, he celebrates the evolution of life as an unfolding expression of this creation moment. Amarjit Singh finds amazement that 'organisms survive over a wide range of environments—from the sub-zero temperatures of the arctic to the sizzling heat of the tropics, from the bottom of the sea to the middle of the desert' (ibid.: 2002). He goes on to remark 'about organisms, ... their fitness of design: how well-suited their shapes, sizes, structures and habits are to their ways of living. The thick white fur of the arctic animals, the bright colours for attracting pollinators, the streamlined bodies of fishes, the perfectly designed wings of birds, the night vision of owls are a few examples' (ibid.).

Quoting Gauri Cheti Mahlal, Amarjit Singh sees a continuity of God and soul in all creations, alluding to the presence of God in each form of life: 'We saw (assumed) the forms of numerous trees and plants, and many a time we were born as beasts. Many times we entered the family of serpents and many times we were flown as birds' (ibid.). Amarjit Singh sees a connection between the reincarnation or 'recycling' of life forms and evolution of the biosphere as articulated by Vernadsky, the famed geochemist who articulated the earth as a self-generating, self-regulating system. For Amarjit Singh, the complexity and magnificence of the process is God. Homeostasis, the emergence of perfectly niched, self-supporting, and yet interdependent ecosystems as well as biodiversity constitute one way of communicating the profound mystery of life. Guru Arjan Dev praises the many forms of life as follows:

> For several births you became
> A worm and a moth
> In several births you became an
> Elephant, a fish, and a deer.
> For several births you became
> A bird and a snake.
> In several births you were yoked
> As a horse and an ox.
> Meet the Lord of the universe.
> This is the time to meet.
> After a long time this human body is gloriously fashioned.
> (for citation and translation details, see Amarjit Singh, 2002: 207)

In the Sikh tradition, God pervades all things; all things are considered to be sacred. Life, grounded in the elements, takes many forms, culminating in human birth, the state of existence in which the universe becomes aware of itself. Amarjit Singh refers to Darwin, Lamarck, and Osborn as developing, through their articulation of and amazement at the diversity of animal and plant life, confirmation of the wonders of the universe. He creatively links scientific theories of biogeochemical cycles with Indian teachings on interdependence and reincarnation.

Conclusion

The great thinkers cited in this chapter suggest that human beings need to re-train their affect, their feeling-tone, in relation to the nature. Rather than seeing animals, trees, rivers and mountains as inert, traditional world views in India celebrate their life-giving qualities, and the qualities of life that each expresses in its own manner. This connection with nature can lead to, in the words of Tucker and Grim, a 'creative revisioning' of ancient traditions to respond to our difficult contemporary environmental situation.

Mahatma Gandhi utilized khadi—homespun and home-woven cloth—as an icon against colonial oppression. It carried both a powerful economic and psychological message, both symbolic and real. What is the khadi for the 21st century? In order to find an answer, we must identify the tyrannical forces that afflict our affect and endanger our relationship with the material world. What commodities prevent us from being in touch with our bodies, the elements, one another?

Various new technologies have colonized our bodies and minds. Due to industrialized farming, our foods have become largely estranged from our direct experience. Additionally, contemporary societies worldwide have developed to new addictions: an addiction to transportation and an addiction to information. Just as Gandhi's seminal book, *Hind Swaraj*, warned against railroads, pharmaceuticals, and lawsuits one hundred years ago, we need to be wary of negativities that arise from automotive pollution, an ever-intrusive medical establishment, and overly litigious inclinations.

Each of the traditions we have considered above, whether the Hindu tradition or the wisdom of the post-Gandhians or the spiritual insights of the Sikhs, would agree that modern peoples need to slow down. Emerging transition movements encourage local gardening and food production that relies on organic processes and minimal transportation needs. Alternative technologies are now available that use less imported fuels: hybrid and electric automobiles as well as electric solar panels hold great promise the decades to come. Furthermore, the abundance of data now available can perhaps be used to share important information and enable a growing sense of community through connectivity. Information can be used to retrieve and recover traditional life ways. Religion and spirituality can become tools for affective and mindful living. Each of us needs to ask the question: How much is enough? How much food? How much entertainment? How large a car? How large a house? From a Gandhian perspective, these questions must be posed repeatedly, relentlessly.

Human abilities to manipulate nature have brought things to a crisis point. The technical skills that have enabled stunning increases in food production and ease of transportation in the short term now imperil the long-term prospects for human flourishing. Climate change and species loss have come to define our current age. The global consumer-based economic system threatens to deplete the earth's resources. The dharma traditions of India suggest that we can and must learn to live within limits, that we must seek inner peace, not outward acquisition. By appreciating the glories of nature as celebrated in the *Prthivi Sukta* of the Hindus and the *Guru Granth Sahib* of the Sikhs, appreciation for the earth, appreciation for the simple gifts of life might be rekindled. By heeding the examples of simple living advocated by Narayan Desai, by increased mindfulness in regard to food production suggested by Vandana Shiva, and by supporting the sorts of judicial initiatives championed by M.C. Mehta, we might learn to cultivate a lifestyle that not only sustains but also allows for human flourishing, in reciprocity with the earth.

References

Adi Sri Guru Granth Sahib Ji (1987). Translated by Gurbachan Singh Talib. Patiala: Punjabi University.

Chapple, Christopher Key (1993). *Nonviolence to Animals, Earth, and Self in Asian Traditions.* Albany: State University of New York Press.

——. (2008). *Yoga and the Luminous: Patanjali's Spiritual Path to Freedom.* Albany: State University of New York Press.

Cort, John E. (tr. 2007). Panditaraja Jagannatha. *The Saving Waves of the Milk-White Ganga.* Calcutta: Writers Workshop.

Desai, Narayan (2008). *Lecture.* Loyola Marymount University. October 9.

Dwivedi, O.P. and Christopher Key Chapple (2011). *In Praise of Mother Earth: The Prthivi Sukta of the Atharva Veda.* Los Angeles: Marymount Institute Press.

Haberman, David L. (2006). *River of Love in an Age of Pollution: The Yamuna River of Northern India.* Berkeley: University of California Press.

Jolly, Surjit (1989). "Sikhism and the Environment". In O.P. Dwivedi (ed.), *World Religions and the Environment.* New Delhi: Gitanjali.

Mehta, M.C. (2006). *Interview.* Eco Ashram. Dehra Dun, India. December 12.

Shiva, Vandana (2005). *Earth Democracy: Justice, Sustainability, and Peace.* Cambridge, Massachusetts: South End Press.

Singh, Amarjit (2002). "The Glimpses of Environmental and Evolutionary Biology in Sri Guru Granth Sahib". *Religion and Environment.* Volume II. In Kishna Ram Bishnoi and Narsi Ram Bishnoi (eds.), Hisar, India: Guru Jambheshwar University Publication, pp. 194–212.

Tucker, Mary Evelyn and John Grim (2000). "Series Foreword". In Dieter T. Hessel and Rosemary Radford Ruether (eds.), *Christianity and Ecology: Seeking the Well-Being of Earth and Humans.* Cambridge, Massachusetts: Center for the Study of World Religions. Distributed by Harvard University Press.

—— (2011). *Lecture,* Loyola Marymount University, November 1.

14

Sarve Bhavantu Sukhinah: May All Beings be Free from Affliction

A Foundation for Environmental Sustainability

B.N. TIWARI AND NEELAM TRIVEDI

Earth is the only planet which supports all known forms of life. It did so for millennia by maintaining a natural balance between all biotic and abiotic organisms, which sustained each other and released energy which formed a cycle of regeneration and reproduction. Various agents—the 'producers', the 'consumers' and the 'decomposers'—performed their task in unison and complete harmony. The ecosystem used the matter of earth and solar energy to produce living substance and also to continuously cycle matter to support it. However, when human beings appeared on earth, the biosphere started to be influenced by their presence. For three million years or more, they lived in a reasonable balance with the organisms around them while considering the entire creation to be a divine 'adventure'. According to *Taittariya Upanishad*, creation, then, became an offspring of Supreme Power (*Parmatman*) because it is he who created the entire universe, and entered into it. So long as human beings had this concept in mind, there had been no problem of environmental conservation and preservation of natural wealth. Slowly, they utilized plants and animals, but they exercised great care and respect since their need was small; thus, the natural balance was maintained. However, with the acquisition of 'intellect' and the introduction of science and technology, humans have attempted to exercise mastery over nature. In return, we have created ecological imbalance, environmental degradation, fast-vanishing flora and fauna, and fast-deteriorating human health. Humanity faces these and many other associated environmental problems today.

The continuing and accelerating deterioration of our planet's ecological base has posed a major threat to the viability of our world. We, the people inhabiting this planet, are collectively destroying natural resources; and yet we also know that without sustainable development, we shall be unable to meet the basic needs of a growing population. Thus, both sustainable development and environmental protection are two sides of the same coin. However, in order to reduce further stress on the environment and yet to have sustainable development, we have to set in motion the changes needed to protect the environment. Those changes require a restructuring of the existing institutional arrangements and legal mechanisms. This restructuring also requires a major change in the policy perspective of a government so that environmental considerations become an intrinsic part of national policy-making and are not merely added afterwards. It is this policy stand which may engender the necessary interconnection and coordination between various policy sectors in that government, such as fulfilling basic needs and conserving the natural resources base.

Nowhere is the need for such restructuring of public policy concerning population, resources, economic development, and environmental protection and conservation more important than in developing nations. The environmental crisis in these countries is mainly the result of poverty and population growth, which has led to the massive destruction of natural resources, and been further aggravated by efforts to industrialize fast. India is a prime example of a country that has tried to implement such policy changes, create institutional mechanisms, and establish a set of robust legislation, programmes and judicial conventions for environmental protection. The real challenge before India is how to preserve its environment—about which so much was glorified in its sacred literature—meet the basic needs of its growing population on an overburdened landmass, fulfil domestic and industrial energy requirements, and yet leave a legacy for future generations so that they may also enjoy some of the bounty of nature, which the present generation is so recklessly exploiting. This is a colossal challenge.

The main environmental problems faced by India may be summarized as follows: (a) a continuous degradation of productive land in varying degrees (due to increased salinity and alkalinity, desertification, waterlogging, deforestation, etc.); (b) shortage of fuelwood and fodder for rural needs, which adds to pressure on forests; (c) depletion of forest cover, threatening the survival of indigenous bio-diversity and affecting habitat for the wildlife; (d) excess and unwise use of pesticides and fertilizers, and ill-advised agricultural practices (including monoculture) adding further stress to the fragile environment; and (e) poorly monitored and inadequately enforced environmental regulations for various natural resource extraction activities (such as mining, metallurgy, aggregate production, and other manufacturing industries). In addition to the above issues, which are creating an alarming situation, India faces challenges from the side effects of industrial development and human settlements.

In India, ever since the programme of industrial development was ushered by the first Prime Minister Jawaharlal Nehru, there has been a question of the viability and sustainability of the process and pace of industrialization. The Gandhian view of human progress has been not to emphasize materialism-without-limit, but to bank on the moral progress and spiritual attainment of each and every human being; this he called *Sarvodaya*. His view drew from India's rich cultural and spiritual legacy, which emphasizes the concept of *Vasudhaiva Kutumbakam* (all the people and creatures living on earth are members of the extended family of humans). Sustainable development, from this perspective, ought to include the upliftment (both spiritual and material) of all without the exploitation and destruction of others. The philosophy of *Sarvodaya* is intimately linked with the concept of *Loka Sangrahamevapi* (to secure welfare of all by one's deeds). How to secure a development, which brings welfare of all without harming others and destroying the environment, is the challenge before India. That challenge will have to be based on a socially just and culturally acceptable sustainable development. Can this challenge be met when the nation is confronting two major crises: population growth and the continuation of poverty?

Vasudhaiv Kutumbakam: The Family of Mother Earth

In *Atharva Veda*, an entire chapter consisting of 63 verses has been devoted in praise of the Mother Earth. These verses integrate much of the thoughts of Hindu seers concerning the concept of nature, dependence of human beings on earth, and the resultant respect required. These verses are addressed to Devi Vasundhara, the Mother Earth. Mother Earth is seen as an abode of a large and extended family (the *Kutumba* of *Vasudha*) of all beings (humans and others alike). *Vasudha* means this earth while *Kutumba* means extended family, including human beings, animals and all living beings. Every entity and organism is a part of one large extended family system, which is presided over by the eternal Mother Earth. It is she who supports us from her abundant endowments and riches; it is she who nourishes us; it is she who provides us with a sustainable environment; and it is she who when angered by the misdeeds of her children punishes them with disasters. As the verse 11 tells us: 'O Mother Earth! Sacred are thy hills, snowy mountains, and deep forests. Be kind to us and bestow upon us happiness. May you be fertile, arable, and nourisher of all. May you continue supporting people of all races and nations. May you protect us from your anger (natural disasters). And may no one exploit and subjugate your children' (*Atharva Veda*, XII, hymn I, verse 11).

The Atharva Rishi (who composed this hymn) envisions the Mother Earth at its pristine nature, and not denuded of her natural cover. The *Prithivi Sukta* also exemplifies the relevance of environmental sustenance, agriculture and biodiversity to human beings. All the three main segments of our physical environment, that is, water, air and soil, are highlighted and their usefulness is detailed. The various water resources such as seas, rivers and waterfalls flow on earth (*Atharva Veda*, 12, verse 3). The verse 2 in this hymn depicts the majesty of mountains, rivers, and beauty of small springs, and the invaluable tiny medicinal plants which save lives of humans. But all these elements are treated equal by the Mother Earth who does not discriminate between the high and mighty (*Uddhatah*) such as mountains and oceans or the low (*Prayatah*). For the Mother Earth, all species are of equal value; thus, she has not accorded anyone a special authority over other species. Thus, humans do not have the authority to destroy the environment at the cost of others including their own species in nature.

The *Prithivi Sukta* maintains that attributes of earth (such as its firmness, purity and fertility) are for everyone, and that no one group or nation has special authority over it. That is why the welfare of all and hatred towards none is the core value which people on this planet ought to strive.

The *Prithivi Sukta* enunciates the unity of all races and among all beliefs; further, the concept of religious, linguistic and cultural harmony has been urged with a prayer, which says that the Mother Earth bestows upon all the people living in any part of the world the same prosperity that has been pleaded by the Rishi Atharva in verse 45 in the following manner: 'The Mother Earth where people belonging to different races, following separate faiths and religions, and speaking numerous languages cares for them in many ways. May that Mother Earth, like a Cosmic Cow, give us the thousand-fold prosperity without any hesitation without being outraged by our destructive actions' (*Atharva Veda*, XII, hymn I, verse 45).

In the last verse of this hymn, a prayer is offered to the Mother Earth and her blessings are sought for all: 'O our Mother Earth! May we possess the intellect and wisdom which enable us to speak in concord with heavenly beings, may we continue to enjoy your blessing of hidden riches, glory, and realization of material and spiritual well-beings' (*Atharva Veda*, XII, hymn I, verse 63).

In summary, it can be said that the *Prithivi Sukta*, whose entire set of 63 verses has been dedicated to the Mother Earth, is the foremost ancient spiritual text which enjoins all human beings to protect, preserve and care for the environment. This is beautifully illustrated in verse 16, which says that it is up to us, the progeny of Mother Earth, to live in peace and harmony with all others: 'O Mother Earth! you are the world for us and we are your children; let us speak in one accord, let us come together so that we live in peace and harmony, and let us be cordial and gracious in our relationship with other human beings'.

These sentiments denote the deep bond between earth and human beings, and exemplify the true relationship between the earth and all living beings, as well as between humans and other forms of life. Such a comprehensive exposition depicting a theory of eco-spirituality is not found in any other religious tradition and beliefs as portrayed by this hymn to the Mother Earth. The *Prithvi Sukta* provides us a guide to behave in an appropriate manner towards nature and our duty towards the environment.

Duty towards the Welfare of All Beings: *Sarva Bhuta Hitey Ratah*

Duty towards humanity and God's creation is an integral part of Hindu ecology and *dharma*. While all other species conduct themselves as per the dharma of their kind, only a human being because of free will thinks that he or she is very powerful and can act in an *adharmic* or irreligious or unrighteously manner. Such acts must be avoided as declared in *Mahabharata* by Rishi Markandeya during a conversation with Pandavas: 'O King, all creatures act according to the laws of their specific species as laid down by the Creator. Therefore, none should act unrighteously (*adharmic* way), thinking that it is they who are most powerful' (*Mahabharata*, Vanparva, Chapter 25, verse 16).

Dharma requires that one consider the entire universe as his/her extended family with all living beings as the members of the same household. This concept, known as *Vasudhaiv Kutumbakam*, has been discussed earlier. Only by considering the entire universe as a part of one's extended family, one can develop the necessary maturity and respect for all other living beings. The welfare and caring of all would be realized through the golden thread of spiritual understanding and cooperation, which is based on *dharma* and *karma* of individuals and institutions.

Dharma is one of the most intractable and unyielding terms in Hindu, Buddhist and Jain religions and philosophy. Here, instead of discussing the root and theological or philosophical definition of the term, we will come directly to the common usage of the term. Ordinarily, the term *'dharma'* is translated as a religious code—as righteousness, as a system of morality and as duty. It denotes not only righteousness, but also the essential nature of any object, without which its entire existence and being cannot make any sense. For example, it is the true nature of a lion to hunt other animals *when hungry*; it is the *dharma* of fire to burn; similarly, it is the true nature of a person to act in a *dharmic* way although he/she may be capable of both the good and evil tendencies. This is what the Shanti Parva of *Mahabharata* states: 'Dharma exists for the general welfare (*abhyudaya*) of all living beings; hence by which the welfare of all living creatures *is* sustained, that for sure is Dharma' (*Mahabharata*, Shanti Parva, Chapter 109, verse 10).

Dharma consists of two major attributes: first, it enables us to express ourselves in acts of service and impels us to avoid exploiting other human beings as well as other living organisms. In so doing, we have two-fold duties: one to the self, whereby we seek inner strength through spiritual action, and the other to the community-at-large (i.e., global *dharma*), whereby we work for the social good. Secondly, it provides for *abhyudaya* (attainment and sustenance of universe). As such, *dharma* regulates human conduct and moulds individuals into the right character by inculcating in them spiritual, social and moral virtues. As such, *dharma* can be considered as an ethos that holds the social and moral fabric together, by maintaining order in society, building individual and group character, and giving rise to harmony and understanding in our relationships with all of God's creation. It is also true that *dharma* may lead to mastery over our base characteristics such as greed, exploitation, abuse, mistreatment and defilement of nature. Before we can hope to change the exploitative tendencies of society, it is absolutely essential that we discipline our inner thoughts. This is where the role of *dharma* comes into play. It is important to appreciate that the concept of *dharma* (although the term has become synonymous with the practices and rituals of Hinduism, Buddhism and Jainism) can be used in any culture. *Dharma* is the mechanism which creates respect for nature since it is devoid of institutional structures, bureaucratic impediments, and rituals associated with organized religions; it enables people to centre their values upon the notion that there is a cosmic ordinance and a natural or divine law, which must be maintained, if only everyone could agree with this concept! *Dharma* thereby provides a code of conduct as well as a vision. It serves both as a model and operative strategy for the transformation of human character. And, if the goal of transformation is to achieve an environmentally conscious and sustainable world, then *dharma's* precept that reward after death can be attained through actions in this world, can provide the incentive for humanity to seek peace with nature (Dwivedi, 1994). The manifestation of *dharma* necessitates the acceptance of the concept of *karma*.

The term *'karma'* comes from the root *kri* which means 'to do', and thus has a general connotation of 'action', but in its broadest sense it applies also to the effects of such actions. People often confuse the *law of karma* with the *law of destiny*. This misunderstanding needs to be rectified because an appropriate understanding is essential to appreciate the use of this precept in Hindu and Buddhist ways of life. A brief definition of the *law of karma* is that each act, wilfully performed, leaves a consequence in its wake. These consequences, also called *karma-phala* (fruits or effects of action) will always be with us, although their impact may not be felt immediately. The law related to *karma* tells us that every action performed creates its own chain of reactions and events, some of which are immediately visible, while others take time to surface. Environmental pollution is but one example of the *karma* of those people who thought that they could continue polluting the environment without realizing the consequences of their actions for future generations. Every action creates its own reaction. What is important to know is that a right action, that is a *dharmic* action, generates beneficial results, while an *adharmic* action results in harmful effects. Of course, it is not easy to foresee the consequences of one's actions, but one should be ready either to overcome obstacles that arise or suffer the repercussions of one's actions.

A story from Hindu scriptures illustrates this point. Once, due to a curse of Maharshi Durbasha, the *Devas* (demigods) were deprived of their divine vigour and strength. Soon, they were defeated by the *Asuras* (demons) and dislodged from their heavenly abode. So they went to pray to Lord Vishnu and seek his intervention. Lord Vishnu suggested that the only course open to them lay in securing the nectar of immortality (*amrit*), which would make them invincible. But, in order to obtain this nectar, they had to put all herbs in the cosmic sea of milk and churn it by using Mandarachal mountain as a pestle and the snake king, Vasuki, as the noose. But they needed the assistance of the demons to hold one side of the rope. The demons agreed to assist on the condition that the nectar received from this churning would be shared equally. Through this churning, the most sought after nectar was obtained along with many precious stones, wealth and worldly riches. But along with these priceless and rare items, a most venomous poison was produced. If that poison was not immediately disposed of, *sarvanash* (total annihilation) of the entire universe could result; however, no one—god or demon—was willing to touch this most fatal toxic waste created due to churning. Finally, all went to Lord Shiva for help to stop the eventual obliteration of the universe. He agreed to take care of the toxic waste by drinking it, and thus the impending disaster was averted. Later, with the assistance of Lord Vishnu, the demigods were able to trick the demons out of their share of the nectar, so that only the gods became immortal. This story instructs us that the consequences of an activity could be both beneficial and disastrous. Both nectar and poison are the effects of the same cause; and in the same way, prosperity and pollution are the two sides of the same cause—the *karma* of humanity. Both effects must be accepted, and as we crave for the nectar of riches, we must also be ready to face the side effects (i.e., poison) of technology and industrialization.

Once the *karma* has started, it continues without a break; and although the person may be dead, yet his/her *karma* survives in the form of a memory on to the next life of a departed soul, as stated in *Mahabharata*: 'A karma: an action which has been committed by a human-being in the present life, follows him again and again (whether he wishes it or not' (*Mahabharata*, Shanti Parva, Chapter 232, verse 16).

Sometimes the *karmic* justice appears indecipherable to individuals when his/her family and later descendants are forced to pay for the past crimes and mistakes of that person. This aspect is further explained by Bhisma to King Yudhisthira in Mahabharata: 'O King, although a particular person or society may not be seen suffering the results of his evil actions, yet his children and grand children as well as great grand children will have to suffer them' (*Mahabharata,* Shanti Parva, Chapter 139, verse 22).

Such a suffering may continue to visit humanity unless we realize that the destruction we are inflicting on our natural surroundings will result in dire consequences for the present and succeeding generations. If we recognize and act on this philosophy of life, then and only will people start paying due respect to nature as well as taking a stake in the care for the environment. This appreciation is the key to the point being made here, and it draws on the concept that people living in any part of the world are our brothers and sisters. All of our actions are interrelated with and interconnected to what eventually happens in this world. Although we may not face the consequences individually, nevertheless, someone else is going to be burdened with or benefit from our actions. It is in this context that the concepts of *dharma* and *karma* become meaningful.

Once our *dharma* and *karma* to the environment are appropriately understood, their precepts recognized, and their relevance in environmental protection and conservation accepted, then a common strategy for eco-spirituality and stewardship can be developed. Such a strategy will depend much upon how different people together (a) perceive a common future for society; (b) act both individually and as a group towards that end; and (c) realize that each individual has a moral obligation to support their society's goal since their acts will have repercussions on the future of the society and their own destiny.

Concluding Observations

In the past we have witnessed the overexploitation of nature and its resources to the point where human intervention in natural ecosystems has caused genetic mutations, the emission of heat and noxious gases into the atmosphere, the destruction of forests and many other effects that are heading not only towards irreversible global damage but also to the annihilation of the natural world. These interventions are so drastic in scale and impact that our life support systems, both locally and globally, are being threatened. Consequently, at a minimum, our activities should be such that they do not endanger the natural systems that support life of all. Until limits are set on our prevailing ethic of acquisitive materialism, unending growth, and demands for resource use, continued global ecological damage is unavoidable. The manifestation of a global community oriented towards environmental stewardship can provide the means by which local, regional and international commons or ecosystems can be maintained.

While the divinity was driven out of nature when the Graeco-Roman was converted to Christianity, and was concentrated in one unique transcendent God, Hindu religion kept it because the Godhood is considered to be diffused throughout the universe and nature. Divinity, according to Hindu religion, has been and is present all over including mountains, in rivers and forests, in plants and grains, in animals and beasts, in stars and planets, and in earthquakes and in lightning and thunder. Thus, the Hindu divinity has never been singular or a unique almighty Superbeing. Man has always been made conscious of his obligations and duties towards nature, its creatures and the universe. But, presently, in modern India, a good many Hindu would not hesitate to tamper with nature in order to satisfy their own greed.

The words of Arnold J. Toynbee are especially relevant to modern Indian situation: 'technology is the magic that grinds out wealth and power; and human beings rush to buy wealth and power at almost any price'. Technology 'at almost any price' is surely going to affect nature. Yet it seems to be highly improbable that the process of technological advance could be deliberately arrested. It is a worldwide phenomenon. Indians too are eager to join the world race for technological progress; not only that, even various events point out that in nearly every aspect of technology, India has mastered it. Soon, if the process continues, India too would be a beneficiary of technology in the same manner that the West has been; but at the same time, evils of technology would also be with us. It is therefore essential that a balance be struck between technology and conservation. If enough and adequate care is not taken, then further degradation of the environment will be a signal for the slow spiritual and cultural death of India.

This need not happen. The nation should immediately re-dedicate itself towards the conservation and preservation of the environment. There is a need to strike a balance between the material aspirations and spiritual survival. Among the cultures of the world, it is much easier for India to strike such a balance. It is relatively less difficult to bring a revival of moral dedication in India, which has had a rich tradition of respect for nature. Learning from the lessons of environmental degradation in the West, and drawing upon the teachings and preaching of the ancient scriptures, would not cause any damage to the secularism as practised in India now. We believe that environmental protection is in the interest of all religions. Writings have amply demonstrated that inherently no religion preaches disrespect to the nature. Thus, religion has a special place and value in protecting the environment.

In order to raise the human spirit and create a worldwide family or community of an ecologically sound and sustainable order, a universal code of conduct for environmental conservation based on the concept of *dharma* and *abhyudaya* should be designed. This could be an instrument through which a new common conscience can be created to transform that human purpose which unites material realities and spiritual imperatives. It is that conscience which could restore and nourish a harmonized world through trusteeship, stewardship and accountability for present and future generations. Global action is required to enhance and nurture the spirit of this code in all strata of society and to sow the seeds of responsibility for environmental protection and conservation. This global action is not only *Swadharma* and *Sarvadharma;* it is also the global *dharma* of all the people.

If environmental problems are to be solved, then a change in the way individuals think about and interact with their environment must occur. It is for this reason that the cultural and spiritual underpinnings of stewardship, which is the primary virtue in eastern cultural and religious traditions, can be of benefit to all humanity. Our spiritual heritage can provide new ways of valuing, thinking and acting that are necessary if respect for nature is to be achieved and future ecological disasters are to be averted. Furthermore, if the ecological crisis that we face today is largely due to our attitudes toward nature, and if it can be solved for the most part by changing values and beliefs about the environment as well as changing our lifestyle, then motivations for environmentally unacceptable acts will have to be understood. At this time we can begin to change our attitudes towards nature, and in so doing understand the benefit environmental stewardship can bring in helping us evade a global ecological catastrophe.

References

Atharva Veda (1982). Translated by Devi Chand. New Delhi: Munshiram Manoharlal Publishers.

Bhagavadgita (1996). Gorakhpur, Gita Press.

Dwivedi, O.P. (1994). "Our Karma and Dharma to the Environment", in Mary Ann Beavis (ed.), *Environmental Stewardship: History, Theory and Practice,* Institute of Urban Studies, University of Winnipeg, Winnipeg, Canada, pp. 59–74.

——. (1997). "Vedic Heritage for Environmental Stewardship", *Worldviews: Environment, Culture and Religion,* 1 (1), April: 25–36.

——. (1997). *India's Environmental Policies, Programmes and Stewardship.* London: Macmillan Press.

——. (1998). *Vasudhaiv Kutumbakam: A Commentary on Atharvediya Prithivi Sukta.* Institute for Research and Advanced Studies, Jaipur, 2nd edition (1st edition published in 1995).

——. (2000). "Dharmic Ecology", in Christopher K. Chapple and Mary E. Tucker (eds.), *Hinduism and Ecology: The Interaction of Earth, Sky and Water*, Cambridge, Mass., Harvard University Press, pp. 4–22.

Dwivedi, O.P. and Tiwari, B.N. (1987). *Environmental Crisis and Hindu Religion*, New Delhi: Gitanjali Publishing House.

Dwivedi, O.P., Tiwari B.N. and Tripathi, R.N. (1984). "Hindu Concept of Ecology and the Environmental Crisis", *Indian Journal of Public Administration*, 30:1, pp. 33–67.

Mahabharata (1988). Translated by M.N. Dutta, Delhi: Parimal Publications, See also, *Mahabharata* (1994) (Gita Press, Gorakhpur, India) in Sanskrit with Hindi translation.

Satvalekar, Pandit Shripad Damodar (1958). *Prithivi-Sukta: Atharvaveda*. Book 12. Swadhyay Mandal, Surat.

Srimad Bhagavata Mahapurana (1982). Translated by C.L. Goswami and M.A. Shastri, Gorakhpur: Gita Press.

15

Introducing Tulsi in Canada

Opportunities and Challenges

MUKUND R. SHUKLA AND PRAVEEN K. SAXENA

Tulsi (*Ocimum sanctum* L.), also known as holy basil or sacred basil, is renowned as one of the holiest and most cherished plants of India for its religious and spiritual sanctity. The name 'Tulsi' is a Sanskrit word for 'the incomparable or matchless one'. Tulsi is also known as the 'Queen of Herbs' and 'Mother Medicine of Nature' and has a peerless importance in Indian culture, traditions and health care. Tulsi plants, often placed in special pots, symbolize the purity and sacredness of a Hindu home. In large dwellings, many Tulsi plants are grown in the garden as a miniature holy forest. Tulsi is considered a symbol of utmost purity and is believed to ward off the evil. The significance of this plant can be seen in many of the rituals practised in India for centuries. Thus, it is not surprising that Tulsi has been a permanent fixture in Hindu homes (Figure 1A), temples and sacred shrines.

The widespread tradition of worshipping Tulsi has its origin in numerous mythological tales described in ancient Indian literature. These beliefs define and reflect on the significance of this legendary plant used since time immemorial and are summarized below:

- Tulsi originated as one of the 14 'ratnas' (gems or treasures) from the ocean as the ultimate sacred plant to remove the diseases and enhance health. Thus, it is believed that caring of Tulsi plant with devotion, respect and reverence removes the effect of sins and drinking the water in which Tulsi leaves have been soaked can cure diseases.
- Tulsi represents home of Hindu gods and goddesses who reside in various parts of the plants. The Trinity—Brahma, Vishnu and Mahesh—reside in top, middle and leaf stalks of the plant,

Figure 1

A: Tulsi in a Canadian home temple, B: Necklace or mala made from Tulsi stem, C: 'Krishna' Tulsi with inflorescence, D: Tulsi plant growing under In vitro condition, E: Dr Mukund Shukla with an in vitro propagated Tulsi plant growing under controlled environment green house conditions.

respectively, whereas the goddesses like Lakshmi, Saraswati, Parvati and others reside in branches, leaves and flowers. It is believed that worshippers of Tulsi will be blessed with health, wealth and a long life.

- Hindus believe that Tulsi plants keep the home pure, prosperous and peaceful. The entrance of homes and businesses are decorated with branches of the plant to gain protection from supernatural causes and leaves are consumed with food and water to reduce the influences of eclipses.
- Prayers offered to the Lord Vishnu with Tulsi leaves can render the soul ultimate peace and cease the cycle of birth and death. It is a common practice to place a Tulsi leaf in the mouth of the dying person to ensure an easy journey of the soul beyond the body. Abundance of Tulsi plants in places used for meditation and seeking divine inspiration has been described in several religious texts.
- Tulsi is also worshipped as the wife of the Lord Vishnu, ceremonially married to him annually, and the day marks the beginning of marriage season in India. Young women pray to the Goddess Tulsi for marriage with suitable grooms. Tulsi is also worshipped by Hindu women to gain blessings for their husbands and sons.

- Necklaces made from Tulsi stems or roots are considered auspicious and worn by the devotees around the neck or wrist as a symbol of continuous surrender to divinity (Figure 1B).

Tulsi: The Plant

Tulsi (*Ocimum sanctum* L.) belongs to the plant genus *Ocimum* in the Lamiaceae/Labiatae family and is closely related to sweet basil (*Ocimum basilicum*), a commonly-used herb in Europe and North America. Tulsi has also been described as *Ocimum tenuiflorum* (basil with small flowers) or *Ocimum gratissimum* (very grateful basil). Species of *Ocimum* as well as their commercial cultivars vary in growth habit, colour and aromatic composition and are commonly named on the basis of such characteristics, e.g., sweet, Greek, purple and scented basil. Some varieties of Tulsi are highly aromatic and may contain flavours of spices such as mint and cloves along with other unique scents. Three distinct forms of Tulsi are commonly distributed throughout the Indian subcontinent: (1) Sri or Rama Tulsi with green leaves; (2) Krishna Tulsi with dark green to purple leaves (Figure 1C); and (3) Van Tulsi with green leaves but the plant grows in wild. Of these, the Rama and Krishna are the most commonly grown forms in homes and widely used in Ayurvedic preparations.

Tulsi is an upright plant with many branches and can grow up to 100 cm. Its leaves are small, of green and purple colour, and the flowers appear as purple racemes (Figure 1C). Tulsi grows wild but is now cultivated in many parts of India due to an increased demand for it in teas and other medicinal products. The plant grows well under long days and high temperatures, preferably in full sun, but can tolerate partial shade. Removal of the inflorescence enhances vegetative growth and results in a flush of new leaves throughout the growing season. In tropical climates, the first Tulsi crop can be harvested in about three months and under optimized growth conditions as many as three to four harvests are easily possible.

The chemical composition of Tulsi is highly complex, containing many nutrients, essential oils and other biologically active terpenoids and phenolic derivatives such as hydroxycinnamic acid derivatives, benzoic acid derivatives, flavonoids and their glycosides, and eugenol and eugenol glycosides (Gupta et al., 2007). Specific examples of these medicinally important metabolites include flavonoids (luteolin, orientin and vicenin); triterpenoids (ursolic acid); oils (palmitic, stearic, oleic, linoleic, linolenic, eugenol, camphor, carvacrol, caryophyllene, decylaldehyde, cirsilineol, cirsimartin, isothymusin, isothymosin and tannins. However, the amount of phytochemicals varies with cultivars and is also significantly affected by growing, harvesting, processing and storage conditions and the flavour and taste of the extracts are strongly influenced by weather. Leaves, inflorescenced and stem are the main sources of essential oils with much smaller amounts accumulated in the roots or seeds. Tulsi leaves are rich in minerals such as calcium, zinc, phosphorus, iron and also contain vitamin A and C. The nutritional and pharmacological properties of medicinal plants are a result of synergistic interactions of many different phytochemicals. This inherent biochemical complexity makes it necessary to standardize the overall chemical profiles of the tissues used in medicinal preparations to achieve optimum effect.

Tulsi: The Medicine

Apart from its religious significance, Tulsi has a long history of medicinal use and is mentioned in ancient Ayurvedic texts such as *Charak Samhita*. Ayurveda, the science of life, is a system of traditional medicine native to India and is also practised in other parts of the world as a form of alternative medicine. In Ayurvedic tradition, the emphasis is on disease prevention and maintenance of health through healthy food, lifestyle, yoga and meditation, exercise, and herbal nutrition for cleansing of toxins and rejuvenation of health. Among Ayurvedic practitioners, Tulsi is considered a premier adaptogen capable of sustaining a balance of physiological and psychological functions of the body and the mind through enhanced endurance against the physical, emotional and environmental stresses. Ayurvedic practitioners recommended Tulsi as tea, powders and food additives to treat a range of disorders including nausea, vomiting, cramping, chronic fever, malaria, viral infections, bronchitis, bronchial asthma, diarrhoea, dysentery, skin diseases, arthritis, eye diseases, ulcer and oral infections. Tulsi extract of fresh leaves and stems have high antioxidant activity, which has been implicated in enhanced digestion and the absorption of food nutrients, the purification of blood, as well as reduced blood glucose, cholesterol and urinary uric acid. The leaves may serve as a nerve tonic due to the presence of neurotransmitters, improve cognitive functions and alleviate pain. Essential oil extracted from Tulsi is also used in herbal cosmetics and for the improvement of the shelf life of food products. Tulsi is traditionally consumed as cold and hot tea made with fresh or dried leaves, leaf juice and alcohol tinctures. Formulations are also prepared from Tulsi seeds and other parts of the plant extracted in various oils and *ghee* (clarified butter). Recently, scientific evidence of the therapeutic effect of Tulsi has started to emerge in mainstream medical journals mostly from studies using in vitro bioassays. Current scientific evidence shows the regular use of Tulsi may reduce stress and inflammation, boosts the immune system, protects against radiation damage and lessens ageing factors in addition to its antibiotic, antiviral and antifungal properties. Thus, various compounds of Tulsi have been described as anti-inflammatory, anti-tumorigenesis, anti-convulsant, anthelmintic, anti-bacterial, anti-giardial, anti-stress, anti-ulcer, anti-diabetic, anti-hypercholesterolaemic, antitussive, hepato-protective, immuno-modulatory, chemo-protective, nootropic and wound healing (Prakash and Gupta, 2005; Sing et al., 2011). It is not surprising that the medicinal benefits of Tulsi have been summed up as 'one complete pharmacy' for preventing disease, promoting health and prolonging life.

Plants and Medicines

All life in our biosphere depends on plants for the energy required to sustain biological functions. Plants have evolved in a highly interactive environment and ecosystems where they face numerous challenges. Such interactions are mediated by myriad chemical metabolites referred to as 'secondary metabolites'. The secondary metabolites are produced in addition to the biomolecules plants synthesize for basic structural and functional aspects of their life. Since plants are immobile and are exposed to consistently changing environment, the number of secondary metabolites synthesized by plants to accommodate environmental stresses is very large. More than 500,000 plant species are believed to be present in this planet representing the enormous diversity developed during several billion years of evolution. Presently, about 250,000 taxonomically different plant species have been described. Every year some 4,000 new metabolites are reported in the scientific literature. The chemodiversity found in plants, although evolved as a part of plant defence and adaptation mechanisms, is a rich source for the development of new economically important compounds and products, e.g., flavours, fragrances, insecticides, dyes and, more importantly, medicines. In fact, plants have been for centuries, and still are, used for the treatment of bacterial, fungal, viral and many other diseases. However, consumers are frequently unaware of the plant-origin of pharmaceuticals. Further, the use of a wide variety of terms to describe plant-based medicines, including herbals, botanicals, medicinal plants, phytomedicinals, phytopharmaceuticals, and over-the-counter (OTC) drugs, has also added to the confusion.

Natural Health Products: Canadian Context

The World Health Organization (WHO) has estimated that 65–80 per cent of the world population's primary health care needs are met through plant-based traditional medicines. In recent years, the quest for longevity and an improved quality of life has ventured into the realm of natural therapeutics, resulting in a wider acceptance of plant-based medicine in the western world. The market for herbal remedies has risen by 4–10 per cent per year for the past decade in North America and Europe, and is now in excess of billions of dollars (Saxena et al., 2007). Health Canada surveys indicate that 71 per cent of Canadians regularly take vitamins and minerals, herbal products, homeopathic medicines and other products commonly referred to as Natural Health Products (NHPs; Health Canada 2003) with Canadian sales exceeding $1.5 billion annually. The marketplace for NHPs is rapidly changing in response to a number of reported problems with product safety and ongoing issues with inconsistent results of major clinical trials of plant-based medicines. The Government of Canada created the Natural Health Products Directorate (NHPD) within Health Canada to develop a new legislation to govern the manufacture and marketing of NHPs in order to address the issues of safety, quality and efficacy of NHPs. The goal of NHPD regulations is to ensure a regulatory framework for the manufacture and distribution of high quality NHPs in the Canadian health food sector. Under these regulations, all products are expected to have specific labels describing medicinal and non-medicinal ingredients, their quantity, source and shelf-life, among many other requirements. Under the legislation, it will be permissible to make a medical claim on whole plant preparations and therapeutic alternatives, but the onus will be on manufacturers and producers to provide products free from contamination and with standardized medicinal activity. These products will be required to originate from transparent sources with processing in compliance with General Manufacturing Product (GMP) standard operating protocols. Regulations also prohibit health product advertising which is false, misleading or deceptive, or is likely to create an erroneous impression regarding its character, value, quantity, composition, merit or safety. The labels of all products must have a phone number for consumers to report any problems with the preparations.

Introducing Tulsi Products in Canada: Opportunities and Challenges

Canada is a multicultural society and is ranked as one of the major immigrant-receiving countries in the world, receiving approximately

250,000 permanent residents and over 200,000 temporary foreign workers and international students on an annual basis. Nearly 12 per cent of the total immigrants in Canada arrive from South Asia including India, Sri Lanka and Nepal contributing about 5 per cent of the total Canadian population. Currently, South Asians are the second largest, and one of the fastest growing groups in Canada. A vast majority of the immigrant families maintain ties with relatives in their birth country, place a high value on their cultural and religious traditions, and strive to pass on their linguistic heritage to the next generation. The immigrant community from India with knowledge and experience of traditional medical practices is likely to prefer Ayurvedic medicinal plant products for better health. Strong social networks already exist among the community members through various religious organizations, local radio and television stations, and Ayurvedic practitioners who regularly promote the value of traditional NHPs. There are more than 110 temples in Canada, many of which invite Ayurvedic consultants for advice on traditional medicine and extensively promote the use of NHPs. Additionally, many Indian families are living in Canada for more than two generations and elderly parents who live in predominantly family-oriented households educate the next generation about the benefits of Ayurveda. Thus, the demand and potential for the Tulsi plant and NHPs in Canada is huge. However, increasing interest in natural remedies has also brought about the great challenge of maintaining a balance between the demand of expanding markets for plant-based medicines and the quality of the products. Ayurvedic practice involves the use of medications that typically contain herbs, metals, minerals or other materials.

Recent studies of Ayurvedic products in the USA raised safety concerns related to toxicity of formulations, drug interactions and lack of scientific evidence. A study funded by the National Centre for Complementary and Alternative Medicine (NCCAM) (Anonymous, 2009) found that of the 70 Ayurvedic remedies purchased over-the-counter (all manufactured in South Asia), 14 contained lead, mercury, and/or arsenic at levels that could be harmful to human health. In 2004, the Centre for Disease Control and Prevention reported 12 cases of lead poisoning linked to the use of Ayurvedic medications (Anonymous, 2009). Health Canada also has issued warning against the use of certain Ayurvedic medicinal products because they contain high levels of heavy metals such as lead, mercury and/or arsenic. Other concerns of Ayurvedic medicines include adulteration with poor substitute plants and wide variation in bioactive compounds. Very few Ayurvedic plants have been thoroughly studied in either western or Indian research community. A range of Ayurvedic products is commonly consumed by South Asian immigrants, but these imported products are often not approved by NHPD due to safety concerns. Health Canada is taking action to remove these products from the market and to prevent further importation into Canada.

Controlled Environment Cultivation of Medicinal Plants

The quality of medicinal plants is affected by conditions of cultivation, storage, manufacturing, marketing and distribution. The factors that affect biochemical profiles and medicinal metabolite production in plants include physiology, genetics and environmental conditions (photoperiod, climate, soil conditions, nutrient availability and moisture). Field cultivation of medicinal plants has many challenges such as contamination with heavy metals, soil and soil-borne organisms, diseases, herbicides and pesticides, as well as weeds and other plant materials. Field cultivation also takes long periods for crop production and is especially difficult in cold climate zones such as Canada. As stated above, regulatory agencies in North America, Europe and many other countries have adopted more restrictive regulations on herbal medicines. The manufacturers and producers are required to provide evidence of the safety, quality and efficacy of all NHPs. The use of controlled environment systems offers a unique resolution for meeting both market demands as well as governmental regulations with regards to medicinal plant production. In controlled environments such as tissue culture and greenhouses, growth environments can be routinely adjusted to ensure homogeneous and high quality crop production. Producers can also implement good manufacturing practices to ensure the quality of medicinal plant products to meet the highest production standards.

In vitro plant production by tissue culture entails the growth of whole plants or their organs in a highly controlled sterile environment. In vitro propagation of plant relies on the fact that virtually any living plant cell contains a complete copy of the genetic code of the organism. By providing cells and tissues with a suitable environment and the correct combination of growth regulators it is possible to cause them to redirect their developmental pathway. Depending on the environmental conditions and combination of growth regulators employed it is possible to re-direct the development of cells from plant parts such as leaves, roots, or stems to form new plants. Thus, in vitro plant propagation offers a technique by which large numbers of genetically and physiologically similar plants can be produced in a short time frame and small amount of space. In vitro production is geographically and seasonally independent allowing year-round production in all climates and also reduces the pressure on increasingly valuable agricultural land. The sterile environment eliminates contamination with microbes, heavy metals, mycotoxins and foreign plant material. Genetic and physiological uniformity also ensures that plants exhibit a consistent chemical profile. In addition to increasing the uniformity of the plant population, it is possible to propagate individual plants that possess superior agronomic traits. Such plants with superior phenotypes enable the production of consistently high quality plant material. Therapeutic properties of medicinal plants are attributed to multiple compounds acting synergistically. Thus, the use of whole plant preparations from chemically consistent crops is essential. The technology of controlled environment growing systems combining in vitro propagation and continued growth in environmentally controlled greenhouse is a unique new concept in medicinal plant production. The advantages of controlled environment production of medicinal plants for basic research and the development of commercial products have been discussed in several earlier publications from our laboratory (Murch et al., 2000a; 2000b; Saxena, 2001; Murch and Saxena, 2006).

The combination of in vitro technology with controlled environment production systems would avoid many of the problems associated with field production of Tulsi. Also, Tulsi is a temperature-sensitive plant and thus hard to grow in Canadian field conditions throughout the year. As shown in Figure 1 the tissue culture raised plantlets (Figure 1D) can be grown in the greenhouse at a rapid rate and with a high degree of survival following proper acclimatization (Figure 1E). Controlled cultivation of medicinal plants is very likely to change the way plant-based medicines will be harvested and processed in Canada in the near future. Tulsi is one of the best models to introduce traditional Ayurvedic medicinal plants to Canadian agriculture using modern production technologies due to its proven safety, popularity and health benefits. In vitro technologies and greenhouse production of Tulsi plants is relatively new to plant-based medicines, but the technology is likely to play a significant role in the production of high quality, chemically-consistent plant material as shown for many other medicinal plants researched in our laboratory (Murch et al., 2002; Zheng et al., 2006). The controlled environment technology is also potentially useful for other Ayurvedic medicinal plant products for the Canadian market and can facilitate the introduction of novel, cost-effective ethnic products produced by local growers.

References

Anonymous (2009). "Ayurvedic Medicine: An Introduction". The National Center for Complementary and Alternative Medicine (NCCAM), US Department of Health and Human Services. July: 1–8 (nccam.nih.gov/health/ayurveda/introduction.htm).

Gupta, P., Yadav, D.K., Siripurapu, K.B., Palit, G. and Maurya, R. (2007). Constituents of *Ocimum sanctum* with Antistress Activity. *J. Natural Products*, 70: 1410–16.

Murch, S.J., Krishna Raj, S. and Saxena, P.K. (2000a). Phytopharmaceuticals: Problems, Limitations, and Solutions. *Scientific Reviews Alternate Medicine,* 4:33–38.

——. (2000b). Phytopharmaceuticals: Mass Production, Standardization, and Conservation. *Scientific Reviews Alternate Medicine,* 4:39–43.

Murch, S.J., Rupasinghe, H.P.V. and Saxena, P.K. (2002). An in Vitro and Hydroponic Growing System for Hypericin, Pseudohypericin, and Hyperforin Production of St John's Wort (*Hypericum Perforatum* LCV New Stem). *Planta Medica,* 68:1–5.

Murch, S.J. and Saxena, P.K. (2006). St John's Wort (*Hypericum Perforatum* L.): Challenges and Strategies for Production of Chemically-Consistent Plants. *Canadian Journal Plant Science*, 86:765–71.

Prakash, P. and Gupta, N. (2005). Therapeutic Uses of *Ocimum Sanctum* Linn (Tulsi) with a Note on Eugenol and its Pharmacological Actions: A Short Review. *Indian Journal Physiology and Pharmacology,* 49:125–31.

Saxena, P.K., Ian, Col and Murch, S.J. (2007). Approaches to Quality Plant Based Medicine: Significance of Chemical Profiling. In Verpoorte et al. (eds.), *Applications of Plant Metabolic Engineering,* Springer, pp. 311–30.

Saxena, P.K. (2001). *Development of Plant-Based Medicines: Conservation, Efficacy and Safety*: MA, USA Kluwer Academic Publishers.

Sing, V., Birendra, V.K. and Suvagiya, V. (2011). A Review on Ethnomedical Uses of Ocimum Sanctum (Tulsi). *International Research Journal of Pharmacy,* 2:1–3.

Zheng, Y., Dixon, M.A. and Saxena, P.K. (2006). Growing Environment and Nutrient Availability Affect the Content of Some Phenolic Compounds in *Echinacea Purpurea* and *Echinacea Angustifolia*. *Planta Medica,* 72: 1407–14.

16

Grassroots Innovations for Poverty Alleviation

An Entrepreneurial Approach

ANIL K. GUPTA

Economic meltdown has affected almost everybody to a varying extent around the world. It has brought to fore the need for questioning certain paradigms of thinking, feeling and acting. Some people, unaffected by the non-inclusive economic growth and absent from the developmental radar of state, markets and even civil society, developed a body of knowledge that can provide solutions to the contemporary problems. These people could not wait for their problems to be solved by outsiders. They did not also adjust or adapt with, or assimilate the constraints. They tried to overcome these. Over more than two decades, Honey Bee Network has learnt a great deal of lessons from the experience of such people, whom we call, grassroots innovators. If they could do so much without outside help, how much more they could do with the help of the institutions and knowledge networks keen to engage with them.

For every one person who overcomes the constraints, there are thousands who somehow try to cope with them. There is obviously a need to share the insights from the innovative experiences with others. But who will have a vested interest in such dissemination? Creating common goods is not something that public policies in most countries care a great deal about. Knowledge networks of people themselves can be helpful provided they can be facilitated to acquire, process and

Presented at the Annual Conference on Rural Innovations and Technologies, Loyola University Medical Center, Maywood, Illinois, Chicago, organized by India Development Centre and Loyola University, 3–4 April 2009.

disseminate stories of innovations in different languages. This is what Honey Bee Network has been doing with limited success. In the next part of this chapter, I will share some of the recent lessons from grassroots innovations. I will then identify various initiatives that are called for, to replicate the model in a transparent and trustful manner. Finally, I will share some challenges, which remain to be addressed both by academics as well as by practitioners.

Lessons from Grassroots Innovations

Honey Bee Network (Gupta, 2006: 49–66) has dealt with innovations in primary education, natural resource management, technological change and various other related areas of survival of common people at the community level (SRISTI). We have not achieved equal success in each of these domains. While the initiatives in technological (contemporary as well as traditional knowledge-based innovations) have moved farthest and an impact has been made on the lives of people, initiatives in innovations by primary school teachers and creativity in the common property institutions have not made as much impact as yet. But, education, technology, institutions and cultural innovations have to synergise for any long-term sustainable change at the community level. The education provides tools and perspectives for imagination, aspiration and practical pursuits of one's livelihood options. If at an early stage, the possibilities of imagination are nipped in the bud, no amount of institutional support may generally be able to trigger it. At the same time, education is not what one gets in schools. Life experiences teach one a great deal more than what one gets in schools. If such was not the case, we would not have formed such a large proportion of grassroots innovators having dropped out of the schools or colleges. That says something about the education but it also says a great deal about the spirit of these people.

Technological innovations also are contingent on the access to tools, techniques and the knowledge systems produced by individuals and groups locally as well as outside. Those who have been denied these tools often suffer drudgery and are unable to overcome many of these constraints despite having imagination and aspiration. In Asian societies, women were not allowed to access blacksmithy or carpentry tools. The cultural norms were evolved to justify such exclusions. It is not surprising that this cultural project has been extremely successful. Women-based innovations requiring mechanical changes have been very few and far in between. It is not because they are less innovative (we will see examples of their innovations later), but they lack tools and also culturally have been ingrained with the desire to adapt and adjust rather than overcome many of these constraints. Autumn Stanley (1993), in her extraordinary research-based book drawing upon 13 year-long investigation of the 200–year history of patents in USA, found many reasons why the share of women inventors was hardly 2 per cent until the late 70s rising to about 8 per cent later in the 80s. If women have been so disadvantaged in one of the most liberal societies, then their fate in other parts of the world can well be imagined. It is true, however, that in the domain in which they control resources, tools and/or decision-making power, they demonstrate themselves to be extremely creative.

Lessons from Educational Innovations

Fifteen years ago, a senior official in Gujarat government asked me to help in preparing a management plan for primary education. I had not done any research in the field before. However, on their insistence, I asked the concerned secretary whether he could help in bringing together 15–20 teachers who had achieved the goals of primary education without any help from the government or NGOs. It was not easy to make such a list. We then requested the Teachers' Federation in the state having more than 1.4 lakh members at that stage to help. Accordingly, a meeting was held in the Federation office to learn from such teachers. Prof. Vijaya Sherry Chand (2007) at IIMA took this initiative forward and gave it a tremendous push all over the country by documenting hundreds of such examples from different states. Each of these examples illustrates how much can be done by empowering the already inspired teachers themselves. We have tried many models and many with good results, may be this idea also deserves a chance.

Let me illustrate: Bhanumati Upadhyaya had been teaching in primary school for more than 30 years. She was among the few lady teachers invited in that meeting. She was finding it very difficult to get girls in the school. She tried many approaches but none seemed to work effectively. Finally, she thought of an idea. She bought thread normally tied on sacred occasions for about five rupees. She invited all the men of the village to her school on Raksha Bandhan day. This is a day when girls in India tie a 'rakhi' (a sacred thread) around the wrist of their brothers so that brothers would take care of them. Once she tied the thread, the menfolk offered to give some gift to the school. They offered to have a water cooler, fans or some other amenity in the school. Bhanumati Ben kept on refusing each offer. She said, she did not want anything. But when men insisted, she provoked them by saying that they would not be able to give what she wanted. This obviously infuriated the men. Now, they would not relent and insisted on asking her wish. She said, 'Please give me your daughters for the school'. How could they say no. In five rupees, she solved a persistent problem which our planners have still not been able to solve after spending millions of rupees. Another teacher Thakarshi Kunbar found that many of both boys and girls would either not enrol or drop out from the school. He tried to persuade the parents but in vain. He collected the details of the birth dates of all the children in the last five years from the birth and death register maintained by the village attendant. Then he took thirty rupees from his pocket, bought 300 postcards (at that time, one card cost ten paise). He then started sending birthday greetings to all the children. Parents of many of these children were baffled and brought the card to the teacher to ask what was it for. He would look at the card and say, 'Oh, I am waiting for your child after two years, or three years or six months'. Parents were intrigued as to why was he reminding them so much in advance. He replied innocently but effectively, didn't they forget to send their children to school. In thirty rupees, he solved a problem which otherwise had remained poorly addressed. A few others, Rajesh Parmar among them, developed the concept of 'shala bina tala', i.e., a school without locks. They asked the local community members who had actually contributed in building the school as to who should they protect the school from. If the school belonged to them, then shouldn't it be their common property for which they would be responsible. For mobilizing resources, another teacher Ajitsinh Solanki would invite the non-resident visitors belonging to the village and honour them in the school. Invariably, they would offer some support. Like this, there were teachers like Motibhai Naik who used puppets to teach various subjects, and Ramanlal Soni who wrote few hundred songs to communicate different concepts of science. For instance, to explain how the pump helped in filling the air in the tube in a cycle or kerosene stove, he will explain it through a song. While there are many workbooks on the environment, there are few that help children not only learn about the environment but also its social implications. Bavabhai Sondarva asked the children to collect thorns of different kinds. Invariably, the children had to go to the margins of the village, the places seldom visited or where there was not much activity. Only in such places, the thorny plants would generally be allowed to grow. Being less productive, the people who live in and around those places are likely to suffer from more disadvantage compared to others. Children would see the relationship between space and social relationships. SRISTI is proposing to build a database of all these experiences in different languages. The Honey Bee Network members worked with Vijaya to discover such teachers in different parts of the country in addition to various teachers' federations.

Paradoxically, the World Bank's programme, which spent millions of dollars in every district, did not achieve more than a few per cent improvement in most of the parameters. One of the teachers, who was very good in teaching science and maths, offered to go to different schools and build the capacity of the teachers through on-the-job training and demonstration. However, he could not be provided a bus pass to facilitate his travel. That apart, the fact remains that each of these teachers have achieved an extraordinary benchmark in the area of creativity, commitment and cooperation with others to share their ideas. Can this approach of learning from inspired teachers become a model of improving educational quality and its accessibility, affordability and effectiveness, for the children world over? The irony is that many of these teachers could not submit their claims for the President Award because various documentation requirements costed about ₹ 10,000. Undoubtedly, they got a lot of respect from the children and their parents. The challenge is to encourage such teachers to build their own platform for mobilizing innovations from each other and replicate these to the relevant schools. The teachers training institutions should also use such material to inspire teachers. Multimedia, multi-language databases of such innovations should reach every district training school and block level centres. If even one per cent of teachers get inspired and start their own experiments or replicate the others, a great transformation would set in.

Lessons from Institutional and Behavioural Innovations

Common property resource institutions play an important role in the survival of poor people, particularly those who have no other similar private resource to rely upon to meet their needs. Indigenous institutions have evolved all over the country to conserve and manage water, land, animal breeds, forests, etc., and yet there is no major database of such institutions and their variable norms and rules in the country. SRISTI has a small CPR institution database (www.sristi.org/cpri.html) with examples of indigenous/local unaided solutions from 24 countries. Innovations in these institutions were tried at five different levels: (a) boundary rules, i.e., who is in and who is out, how to ensure fairness in admitting new members to a collective institution or on what ground to exclude somebody; (b) resource allocation rules, i.e., who gets what, when, where and why/how. The share of different members was determined by these norms and depending upon various criteria, one could factor different contingencies. In some institutions, share of non-human sentient beings such as wildlife was also planned while developing norms; (c) maintenance and governance rules; and (d) conflict resolution, i.e., ways of sanctioning behaviour, which may lead to modification in boundary, resource allocation or governance rules. There are many creative ways in which conflicts are resolved in these institutions so that the person punished for an offence does not lose the spirit of reform. There is a strong realization that role of decentralized, self-designed and self-governed institutions is going to increase in future due to increasing ecological heterogeneity and environmental fluctuations. But are we really preparing for such diversified, location-specific solutions to emerge at the local level. This is an area where more and more innovations will be required in future so that people can learn from each other, build upon respective ideas, evolve dynamic rules which can adapt to the fluctuating conditions.

Lessons from Technological Innovations

The less material resources people have, the greater is the compulsion for knowledge input in various activities. By this logic the lives of the poorest people should be the most knowledge intensive for mere survival. Is that how the assumptions about human behaviour are made in the public policy arena at various levels ranging from local to national and international level? How else one would explain a massive national rural employment guarantee programme not drawing upon the mental capabilities but only providing opportunities for menial work. Our former President, Dr Kalam's vision for India to become a knowledge society could not be achieved if the bias against knowledge-intensive opportunities for employment continues to be so strong. In an accompanying note, I have explained various strategies by which we can engage 250 million people below the poverty line in various creative and knowledge-based activities.

The idea is that India should aim for an entrepreneurial revolution in the coming decade so that there would not be any need for the state to provide employment thereafter. The role of the state, market and civil society would then be to provide a support system for innovation-based entrepreneurship to flourish in an ethical and transparent manner.

I may add that most grassroots innovators and traditional knowledge holders are not able to convert their innovations or traditional knowledge into enterprises. This may happen for many reasons, such as the persistent desire to improvise ideas and innovations; motivations to solve problems and then move on rather than extract commercial profit out of it; share it widely with others by creating a common or public good; by providing services with or without charges but not scale up the activity; lack access to scale up even if desire exists; lack of access to resources which are necessary for converting innovation into enterprise; and high transaction costs of linking with entrepreneurs and/or investors.

Many times policy makers and even academics tend to underplay the importance of localized solutions. Anything which does not scale up is not considered worthy of attention. The implication is that only a few people should develop innovations and the rest should become passive consumers. We are not yet realizing the potential of large-scale location-specific innovations, which may use local resources or may blend basic building blocks from outside with local resources. If this was not a real possibility, we would not have witnessed so many innovations around exotic technologies like cell phones, antenna for the television, recently introduced plant species, etc. Let me illustrate.

Cell phones were introduced around a decade and half ago and they became a mass consumption good in the last decade. Not only did people develop a language of missed calls but also a lot of other applications. Young innovator Prem Singh developed a remote switch by which farmers could switch on and off their pumpsets, power lines could be tripped or monitored for load, one could get a message whether the milk has boiled or not sitting in a separate room, lock a car if it was stolen, amplify a heart beat and communicate it to the doctor. It is a pity that not many of his ideas could go to the market and become a mass consumption product. But just the range of applications should indicate the way Indian and trained mind can create numerous possibilities. Many other innovators developed a security system so that an image as well as the message would be sent to pre-defined addresses in case an unauthorized person tries to tamper with the lock or open the door. Cell phones can also be used to intimate the water status in the field so that farmers can track the need for irrigation. All these innovations have been evolved by the people who have not even gone to college much less get any technical training. Companies like Nokia never shared the technique of extracting emergency power in a battery which had run down and could not power the cell phone. The young boys in the villages figured out ways of getting that reserve energy from the battery to make an SOS call or SMS. Anurag Rathod, a class nine student, thought of converting the gait of a person into a mobile password system. The moment a phone is used by an unauthorized person, it would stop working until the original user unlocks it. This is an original thought with amazing potential. Every such idea deserves a fair trial and opportunity for value addition and benefit sharing.

When high-tech products are modified by grassroots people or school kids for new applications, not engaging with such minds becomes very difficult to understand. In December 2007, on the last day of Shodh Yatra in Jharkhand and West Bengal in the districts of Patamda, Purulia and Bankura, we were in Basudha village. In an idea competition organized among the rural youth, a school boy, Bappi Roy, asked a question which most of us, though aware of the problem, have never asked. He saw us presenting the innovations on one side of the pandal (enclosure) with a screen. Everybody viewing this presentation with the help of a projector had to face towards the screen. Nobody could see each other's face and thus gauge various reactions. Bappi Roy suggested a four-sided television so that people could sit around it, look at the same content and also watch the reactions on the faces. If they wished, they could communicate with each other alongside the programme on the television and enrich their experience. A vertical arrangement could become circular. A cultural practice may be enabled by the technology rather than changing the same to suit technological requirement. No big company manufacturing televisions realized the tragedy of vertical space in households and communities. They did not see the advantage which Bappi Roy could see. A patent has been filed, and fabrication support is being provided to a technical team to convert his vision into reality.

Every six months the Society for Research and Initiatives for Sustainable Technologies and Institutions (SRISTI) organizes a Shodh Yatra in the summer and winter in different parts of the country. Physically speaking, we have walked more than five-and-half thousand kilometres in different parts of the country, interacted with thousands of knowledge-rich, economically-poor people and learnt from their creativity and generous spirit. The last few walks have been in the regions where either Naxilite or insurgent movement is very strong. Every time we have been struck by the diversity of ideas, innovations and traditional knowledge the country has. And yet building bridges between formal and informal science, technology and structures of governance has not been easy. The National Innovation Foundation set up in February 2000 with the experience of SRISTI and GIAN has mobilized more than hundred thousand ideas, innovations and traditional knowledge practices from over 540 districts (not all unique, not all distinctive). More than two dozen licensing experiences with technologies have provided numerous insights about the ethics of entrepreneurs, sharing of benefits with not only innovators, their communities and nature besides other stakeholder, the acknowledgement of the knowledge rights of common people and many other aspects.

During the last Shodh Yatra in Champaran where Gandhiji was christened as Mahatma and also gave the call for freedom, we came across numerous innovations. Most of the sugar factories were closed. There was hardly any industrial development but an interesting pollution control technology evolved in Motihari. We met Virendra Kumar Sinha who had a school right opposite his workshop where he made steel doors, fencing and other materials. These required lot of energy for which a diesel engine of 15 HP was the only alternative since electricity supply was very erratic. The problem was that the engine made lot of noise and released considerable smoke adding to the pollution. Children were disturbed by sound and smoke. Neither could school be moved away nor the workshop. Virendra realized the difficulty of the children and did what most users of diesel engine in the country have not done. He invented a silencer-cum-pollution control device. In about six to eight months, it collects 12 to 14 kg of carbon which can be easily taken out by beating the cylinder from outside. The smoke, which comes out, is very clean and leaves no trace of carbon on the leaves of the tree growing nearby or in the atmosphere. The sound was considerably reduced. Both the workshop and school could co-exist. The court judgment against him in response to the protest by neighbour had also pushed him to develop an innovation. Now, this innovation is all set to change the emission standards for engines.

Large number of workshop mechanics use such engines which create both noise and air pollution and yet there are not too many examples of such devices. Akasi from Sivakasi, Tamil Nadu had developed one such device way back in 2000 and was awarded in the first annual grassroots innovation award function of NIF in 2001. It was an excellent example of how *samvedana* (ability to feel others' pain as one's own) triggered *srijansheekalata* (creativity and innovation). What was even more interesting was the response of a senior officer of State Bank of India (SBI). He read about this device in the newspaper as a curtain raiser for the Shodh Yatra and asked his team to visit him, and get information about us. Soon after visually verifying the technological claims, SBI wrote to us offering support to the innovator. Shodh Yatra had begun to have an impact even before starting the formal walks. Mr Ansari from Motihari had helped in identifying Virendra and few others like Mohammed Rozadin.

Several Shodh Yatris went for tea or coffee in the nearby market and observed a very ingenious coffee-making machine. A pressure cooker had been modified by attaching a switch, and a copper pipe with a safety valve after making a separate hole in the cover of the cooker. One could release the steam in cooker to make coffee. Unlike the big coffee-making machine, which required electricity for powering it, this one could work on stove or any source of fire with a few hundred rupees, one could enjoy espresso coffee.

There are 100,000 ideas, innovations, and traditional knowledge practices scouted from over 545 districts by the National Innovation Foundation with the help of Honey Bee Network, not all unique, not all different. The majority are herbal practices, and understandably so, to provide health security of whatever quality. After all, it has kept people alive in large parts of the country; it could not be all-ineffective.

Implications for Future

The Indian experiment of harnessing innovations at the grassroots level needs to be replicated in different parts of the world. China has already established CHIN (China Innovation Network) in collaboration with the Honey Bee Network. More than five hundred grassroots innovations have been scouted in China. Likewise, Brazil, Malaysia, Indonesia, Philippines, Sri Lanka, Vietnam, etc., have also shown interest besides South Africa and many other African countries (see sristi.org). Isn't it strange that despite world-wide recognition of the need for innovations at the community level, there is so little content on the internet about unaided, self-managed innovations by common people without any professional degree, training or experience. How do we explain the global silence on this subject? Whether it is the fear of the power of local solutions that threaten the global institutions with power and influence such that the national elite in different countries have acquiesced in this silence.

Grassroots to Global (G^2G) is another possibility ahead, which is not only expanding space for grassroots knowledge, innovations and practices in global markets, but also helping disadvantaged people in other developing countries learn from Indian innovators and vice versa.

Expanding the knowledge network, including NRIs and other concerned professionals, so as to promote lateral learning among people, including experts, might result in the emergence of some partnerships.

When Rama Tiwari Devi makes an outstanding sculpture on a grain bin in Chamaparn, or Bhabi Mahato paints the whole wall of her hut, or an anonymous lady makes an abstract art on cow dung heap in western UP, they are making a statement: 'Give us a space, or else where we have, we will demonstrate our creativity'.

How will we expand the space for grassroots creative and innovative people is a challenge that Honey Bee invites every thinking person tired of his/her inertia to embrace!

References

Society for Research and Initiatives for Sustainable Technologies and Institutions (SRISTI, www.sirsti.org).

Stanley, Autumn (1993). *Mothers and Daughters of Invention: Notes for a Revised History of Technology*. Metuchen, NJ: Scarecrow.

Vijaya Sherry Chand with others (eds.) (2007). *"Open a School; Close a Few Jails": Primary School Teachers' Innovations, Third Yearbook*. Indian Institute of Management, Ravi J. Matthai Centre for Educational Innovation.; Vijaya Sherry Chand, Geeta Amin-Choudhury and Jeya Inbaraj (eds.)(2006). *"Aren't Four Grades Enough?": Primary School Teachers Innovations, Second Yearbook*. Ahmedabad: Indian Institute of Management, Ravi J. Matthai Centre for Educational Innovation; Vijaya Sherry Chand, Geeta Amin-Choudhury and Samir Joshi (eds.)(2005). *Universalisation has to be from the Village Upwards: Primary School Teachers' Innovations, First Yearbook*. Ahmedabad: Indian Institute of Management, Ravi J. Matthai Centre for Educational Innovation; Vijaya Sherry Chand and S.R. Shukla(1998). *Teachers as Transformers: Learning from Outstanding Primary School Teachers*. UNICEF: Gandhinagar.

www.dsir.gov.in/a_report/english/2006–07E/Chapter-II-E.pdf
www.sristi.org/anilg/apctt
www.sristi.org/cms/china_apctt/apctt_report.pdf
www.sristi.org/globalgian/?q=aastiik

17

A Thousand Small Windows

Pondering the Role of Global IT Communication Towards Adult Education for Sustainability

JANE DOUGAN

On 19 October 2000 Carnegie Mellon University hosted a day-long symposium forecasting 'A Good World in 2050: Will Computers Help or Hinder?' One presenter was Carnegie Professor and 1978 Nobel Laureate in Economics Herbert A. Simon. Simon researched cognitive science (particularly bounded rationality) and the impact of computer technology. At the seminar, he proposed that:

> We must look ahead at today's radical changes in technology, not just as forecasters but as actors charged with designing and bringing about a sustainable and acceptable world. New knowledge gives us power for change: for good or ill, for knowledge is neutral. The problems we face go well beyond technology: problems of living in harmony with nature, and most important, living in harmony with each other. Information technology, so closely tied to the properties of the human mind, can give us, if we ask the right questions, the special insights we need to advance these goals. (http://www.cs.cmu.edu/~earthware/SimonAbstract.html)

A decade later, how much closer are we to asking 'the right questions' about the use of IT to share knowledge, and in so doing build a more equitable, harmonious and sustainable world? Two years later, Kofi Annan (2002) challenged those in a position to do so to energetically promote the use of IT as a powerful force for global peace

I have been privileged to witness the many ways in which that ethics based on spirituality has been a tacit and constant foundation to Dr Dwivedi's educational approach, and success, throughout his distinguished career.

and development. Over the intervening decade, Simon's proposal also was echoed by others who suggested that the increasingly global reach of information technology (IT) could help to foster more equitable communication across cultural, geographic and political borders (World Commission on the Social Dimensions of Globalization, 2004; Friedman, 2005). A major tenet of the United Nations Decade of Education for Sustainable Development was the educational use of IT to help develop students' abilities to understand and take action on related global and local issues (Combes, 2005).

My interest in such questions stems from my work developing and teaching environmental and sustainability-related distance courses to undergraduate and graduate students in Canada and the USA since the mid-1980s. As such, I am a small piece in an interconnected, dynamic and evolving mosaic or web that is global online learning. My introduction to distance learning as a tool in education for sustainability came when I was involved with the preparation of a sustainability-focused distance education course through the University of Guelph's (Ontario, Canada) Office of Open Learning. The course was somewhat unusual in that its impetus came from outside the university. Dr Alexander King, co-founder and then Chair of the Club of Rome (COR), along with members of the Canadian COR, had approached university faculty to help to foster students' awareness and discussion of the 'problematique', i.e., the intertwined complex of local and global socio-environmental and economic challenges that lay on the threshold (King and Schneider, 1993).

The resulting course was prescient in content, reach (available to students across disciplinary boundaries) and method of delivery (distance education). It embraced online delivery and discussion in the early 1990s, as IT became generally available to students at the university. In King's written introduction to the course, he emphasized that resolving the problematique would come about only through the actions of a well-informed public. He went on to paraphrase Harrison Brown's observation of the need for humankind 'to be willing to take a thousand small, wise decisions' (King and Schneider, 1993: 63); perhaps one approach to resolving Simon's concern about asking the right questions.

My involvement in the development and subsequent teaching of the course was also my introduction to an esteemed University of Guelph faculty member, Dr O.P. Dwivedi. Dwivedi got on board right away by enthusiastically supporting the project, and contributed a major section that focused on the role of religion in achieving sustainability. The inclusion of spiritual perspectives alongside economic and scientific considerations within an undergraduate course at a North American university was innovative and unconventional then and, arguably, remains so today. Then, as now, Dr Dwivedi was more than ready to embrace new approaches towards the goal of a more just and sustainable world, and to inspire students and colleagues through his enthusiasm and quiet dedication.

Young adults who are able to attend university are arguably a global elite. Anyone in his or her mid-twenties was born as the concept of sustainable development first emerged on the international stage (Brundtland, 1987). Even if they have not heard of the term, they are aware of scenarios that led to its development; environmental threats such as pollution, climate change, loss of biodiversity, and resulting social disruptions. Implicitly, the vision behind the 1986 blueprint for a more just and sustainable world will flourish or wither according to the decisions and actions of the youth of today and tomorrow.

Educational systems are starting to respond to these present and anticipated challenges. Sustainable development is inherently transdisciplinary, equitable, participatory and future-centred. The concept is contentious, but it has influenced a widening range of philosophy and research in the natural and social sciences. Sustainability is emerging as an academic discipline in its own right, and universities are seen in part as laboratories for ensuring a sustainable future (Calder and Dautremont-Smith, 2009). Education for Sustainable Development (ESD) is an increasingly credible and essential driver within formal and informal education. This encompasses kindergarten to high school, post-secondary and lifelong learning. The overarching goal of sustainable development is now integral within the pedagogical approaches of many newly established and traditional universities.

Research with regard to IT and knowledge for sustainable development initially focused upon ensuring more equitable access, i.e., bridging what has been termed the 'digital divide'. This targeted economically developing countries, although it is recognized that such inequities may occur within any nation's borders (Chen and Wellman, 2004). Documenting and understanding the form and impact of international IT-based learning upon students' relationships with distant colleagues is still in its early stage of evolution (International Development Research Centre, 2006). The main emphasis has been on international exchanges between countries within either the more economically developed or developing world, rather than on how communication and learning is happening across the divide (McFarlane, 2006), or on openness towards new regional conceptualizations, such as what Spivak (2003) has termed 'planetarity'.

Local-to-global environmental literacy, cultural sensitivity and community-based learning are all defining characteristics within environmental education (North American Association for Environmental Education, 2010). Web-based education can potentially foster the global sharing of local knowledge and perceptions. One of the oft-quoted educational and social affordances of web-based learning is that the physical distance between learners and instructors becomes blurred or 'relatively unimportant' (Dabbagh and Reo, 2011). In the context of environmental education, however, the disparate location of learners within different bioregional and social ecologies is not incidental but pedagogically powerful, and active reference to this can become a critical and complex part of the learning process. Each learner's comparative spatial distance (in terms of bioregion) and social proximity (in terms of web-based communication) are equally valued.

Over the intervening years, my work changed from a base at the University of Guelph to creating online courses, master's programmes, and certificates for graduate students at Nova Southeastern University's Oceanographic Center in Florida, USA. The Oceanographic Centre (OC) offers environmental courses and programmes to students studying a broad range of issues related to the marine and coastal environment. Throughout, my contact with Dr Dwivedi remained a source of strength and support towards achieving equitable, innovative student learning. Within the Oceanographic Centre's online MS in Coastal Zone Management, we developed and taught a graduate course that introduced students to the cross-cultural dialogue regarding water management that is occurring between scientific, interfaith and policy communities, both within the USA and internationally. To many students, this seemed initially to be a challenging and somewhat disparate combination.

In one of the courses, we began by asking students to post their individual bioregional portraits about a water place that had particular meaning to them. The majority of postings were from students within the USA, but one particularly memorable posting came from a participant based in Gujarat ... the state with the longest coastline in peninsular India!' She continued:

> Thank you for taking me on a fascinating trip around your 'water worlds'. I virtually enjoyed the serene calmness of your backyard

> ponds with their birds and beasts and the excitement of deep-sea diving. Yet I couldn't help wondering at just how amazingly different my reactions are to the mention of this vital natural resource called the elixir of life.
>
> I can truthfully say: 'My life revolves around water!' Every morning I wake up to the noise of water gushing out of the taps. Bleary-eyed, I ensure that the water filter is ready for action, the geyser switched on and the buckets and water storage drums washed and ready for filling. We must all rush through if we want to finish bathing: cooking, washing and cleaning in running tap water—a luxury that will last only another hour or so. Else I must wait till the next instalment later in the day ... I am talking about a lifestyle that is routine for most of us living in this urban, progressive, elite pocket of one of the major cities of India .... Was this always so? No! We too have been through times when we took water for granted!
>
> ... Water to me means many things. I appreciate its value for all forms of life. I marvel at its capacity to support diverse life forms ... I am also proud of our marine wealth, our wetlands, which are the winter home to thousands of migratory Siberian cranes and our shores where thousands of Olive Ridley Turtles lay their eggs. Yet, to me water is a more mundane everyday matter. Water for drinking, water for basic cleanliness, hygiene and sanitation, water for the fields. Between neighbours, as at international conferences, water is the major topic of discussion. Water is what people fight over—be it a village common tap, or transboundary sharing. Water is a gender and equity issue .... Providing equitable access to water is perhaps one of our gravest challenges.

Even years later, students in the course have told me that post, and the ensuing online discussion, was a transitional learning moment for them in terms of international understanding.

A central tenet of sustainable development is to respect and foster cultural diversity, while at the same time strengthening cross-cultural collaboration towards commonly-held principles and goals. As with biological diversity, cultural diversity helps to ensure flexibility and resilience in responding to changing circumstances (Levin, 1992; Tomlinson, 2010). A diversity of cultural traditions by default includes a diversity of knowledge forms. Advances in sustainability science and technology require the study of specific people interacting within a distinctive environment, over multiple regions (Kates, 2010). This must recognize and explore the value of incorporating forms of scientific and extra-scientific knowledge, such as local and tradition-based ways of knowing (Gallopin and Vessuri, 2006). As an aspiration, learning towards sustainability is global; as an ongoing practical activity, it is local (Mabogunje and Kates, 2004). Researchers in the sciences and technology are paying increased attention to broader knowledge systems and local/cultural context.

At the same time, recalling Simon's concern for the need to live in harmony with nature, an ongoing body of research proposes that technology does not simply mediate human experience of the natural world; it has begun to change it (Kahn, 2009). Kahn heads the Human Interaction with Nature and Technological Systems (HINTS) Laboratory at the University of Washington. Kahn (2011) maintained that human existence worldwide is being reshaped by at least two overriding forces. One is technological development, unprecedented in its reach and in its sophistication. Another is the degeneration of the natural environment. Academic interest in ESD has risen largely out of a sense of concern for the latter, and now embraces a somewhat guarded sense of opportunity regarding the former (Tomlinson, 2010). This is a subtle evolution within ESD since its inception in the 1980s, and distinguishes it from 1960s environmentalism that veered towards a technophobic sensibility (Davison, 2009).

In such considerations, there is an implicit disconnect in that an organic physical reality is communicated by text and sterile, virtual representations. To acknowledge and counter this, students might be asked to think of their individual computers as 'islands', accessible by means of a 'raft' (the mouse, finger or keyboard), navigating and connecting from on to the other within an overall web-based 'ecosystem'. On each of their computer 'islands', students are submitting virtual interpretations of their tangible place-based realities, gradually forming a particular, interconnected, virtual archipelago. This metaphor takes its cue from Tomlinson's (2006) paper.

Another wide-ranging ESD-related body of enquiry recognizes the value and challenge of incorporating scientific, local, tradition-based and other extra-scientific forms of knowledge from across the world within an epistemological framework (Gallopin and Vessuri, 2006). All this has relevance to the form and outcome of emerging approaches to communication, collaboration and leadership in a digital world. Mathematical ecologist Levin observed succinctly that 'the world looks very different, depending on the size of the window you are looking through' (Heise, 2008). Levin was referring primarily to his work modelling ecological scales, but the observation also holds true for the various philosophical, transparent and digital 'windows' or world views through which each person gazes.

Fostering equitable interactive learning across disparate locations may be no less than an ethical imperative (McFarlane, 2006). Argyriades and Dwivedi proposed that:

> Ethical education based on spirituality depends upon three fundamentals. The first is how a group envisions a shared future—a teleology—and hope for the world. The second has to do with the proper relationship between means and ends. The third is a strong sense of individual responsibility and a moral obligation to promote the public interest. ... Both nationally and globally, good governance is possible only when public officials perceive themselves as agents of this greater common good. (2009: 87)

The aforementioned focus is on education towards governance, but the statement could be equally applied towards education for sustainability.

References

Annan, K. (2002). Kofi Annan's IT Challenge to Silicon Valley. *CNet news.com* (online), 5 November 2002. Retrieved February 25, 2008 from http://www.news.com/Kofi-Annans-IT-challenge-to-Silicon-Valley/2010–1069_3–964507.html?tag=item

Argyriades, D. and O.P. Dwivedi (2009). Chapter IV. Beyond Efficiency and Effectiveness: The Significance of Ethics and Spiritual Dimension of Service. pp. 64–90. p. 87 In: I.P. Pagaza and D. Argyriades (eds.) *Winning the Needed Changes: Saving Our Planet Earth.* IOS Press.

Brundtland, G.H. (1987). *Our Common Future: The World Commission on Environment and Development.* NY: Oxford University Press.

Calder, W. and Dautremont-Smith, J. (2009). Higher Education: More and More Laboratories for Inventing a Sustainable Future. In J.C. Dernbach (ed.), *Agenda for a Sustainable America* (pp. 93–107). Environmental Law Institute. Island Press.

Chen, W. and Wellman, B. (2004). The Global Digital Divide: Within and Between Countries. *IT & Society,* 1(7):39–45.

Combes, B.P.Y. (2005). The United Nations Decade of Education for Sustainable Development (2005–2014): Learning to Live Together Sustainably. *Applied Environmental Education and Conservation,* 4: 215–19.

Dabbagh, N. and Reo, R. (2011). Back to the Future: Tracing the Roots and Learning Affordances of Social Software. In M.J.W. Lee and C. McLoughlin. (Eds.), *Web 2.0 Based E-Learning: Applying Social Informatics for Tertiary Teaching.* (pp. 1–20) IGI Global. Retrieved 18 August 2010, from the IGI Global website: http://igi-global.com/Bookstore/TitleDetails.aspx?Titleid=40272

Davison, A. (2009). Living Between Nature and Technology: The Suburban Constitution of Environmentalism in Australia. In D.F. White and C. Wilbert (eds.), *Technonatures: Environments, Technologies, Spaces, and Places in the Twenty-First Century.* Waterloo, Ontario, Canada: Wilfrid Laurier University Press, pp. 167–89.

Friedman, T.L. (2005) *The World is Flat: A Brief History of the Twenty-first Century.* New York: Farrar, Straus and Giroux.

Gallopin, G. and Vessuri, H. (2006). Science for Sustainable Development: Articulating Knowledges. In A. Pereira Guimaraes, S. Vaz Guedes and S. Tognetti (eds.), *Interfaces Between Science and Society.* Sheffield: Greenleaf Publishing, pp. 35–52.

Heise, U.K. (2008). *Sense of Place and Sense of Planet: The Environmental Imagination of the Global.* New York: Oxford University Press.

International Development Research Centre (2006). *Research on Knowledge Systems: Background and Objectives.* Retrieved March 29, 2006 from http://www.idrc.ca/en/ev-10380–201–1–DO_TOPIC.html

Kahn, P.H. (2011). *Technological Nature: Adaptation and the Future of Human Life.* Cambridge, Mass.: MIT Press.

Kahn, P.H., Jr., Severson, R.L. and Ruckert, J.H. (2009). The Human Relation with Nature and Technological Nature. *Current Directions in Psychological Science,* 18: 37–42.

Kates, R.W. (2010). *Readings in Sustainability Science and Technology* (CIT Working Paper No. 213). Cambridge, MA: Harvard University, Center for International Development.

King, A. and Schneider, B. (1991). *The First Global Revolution.* New York: Pantheon Books.

Levin, S.A. (1992). The Problem of Pattern and Scale in Ecology. The Robert H. MacArthur Award Lecture. *Ecology,* 73: 1943–67.

Mabogunje, A.L. and Kates, R.W. (2004). *Sustainable Development in Ijebu-Ode, Nigeria: The Role of Social Capital, Participation, and Science and Technology* (CIT Working Paper No. 102). Cambridge, MA: Harvard University, Center for International Development.

McFarlane, C. (2006). Crossing Borders: Development, Learning and the North-South Divide. *Third World Quarterly,* 27(8): 1413–37.

North American Association for Environmental Education (2010). *NAAEE Adopts Diversity Policy.* Retrieved December 16, 2007 from http://www.naaee.org/programs-and-initiatives/diversity/naaee-adopts-diversity-policy/ (UPDATE)

Spivak, G.C. (2003). *Death of a Discipline*. New York: Columbia University Press.

Tomlinson, B. (2010). *Greening Through IT: Information Technology for Environmental Sustainability*. Cambridge, MA: MIT Press.

Tomlinson, B., Baumer, E. and Yau, M.L. (2006). *The Island Metaphor*. Poster Session presented at the 33rd International Conference and Exhibitions on Computer Graphics and Interactive Techniques, Special Interest Group on Graphics and Interactive Techniques (SIGGRAPH), Boston, Mass. Retrieved July 23, 2011 from http://www.ics.uci.edu/%7Ewmt/pubs/siggraph06TomlinsonEtAl.pdf

Professor Onkar Prasad Dwivedi

A Short Biographical Sketch

Born on 20 January 1937, in a small village, Nibavar, about 8 km from the town of Bindki, district Fatehpur, United Provinces (now Uttar Pradesh), Professor O.P. Dwivedi is the eldest of nine brothers and sisters. His father was serving as the forest officer in the Central Provinces of British India. His grandfather was the patriarch of the Dube clan with 63 members. He was educated in Bindki, Kanpur, Allahabad and Bilaspur; and to finance his post-graduate education after receiving a B.Sc. degree, he taught as a science teacher in a higher secondary school. After receiving his M.A. in Political Science, he was appointed lecturer in a degree college in Mungeli and Bilaspur. In 1963, he was selected for a scholarship to study for an M.A. in Public Administration at Carleton University, Ottawa; thereafter he went to Queen's University, Kingston to do his doctorate in Political Science.

He was appointed Assistant Professor of Political Science, University of Guelph, Canada in 1967, where he became Full Professor in 1976. After completing 35 years of service in 2002, he retired, and on his retirement in May 2002, he was appointed as University Professor Emeritus. He has also held various academic/administrative positions such as Chair of the Department, Chair of several University Senate Committees, and other related university bodies. As a researcher, Professor Dwivedi is known for his work in the field of comparative and development administration, as well as on environmental policy and institutions. Among his scholarly publications, there are 37 books (authored, edited and co-edited) and notables among them are: *Provincial Governments as Employers* (Montreal, 1974); *Public Service Ethics* (Brussels, 1978, also published in French, Spanish and Arabic); *Administrative State in Canada* (Toronto, 1982);

Ethics in the Public Service (Brussels, 1983, also translated into Arabic); *India's Administrative State* (New Delhi, 1985); *Environmental Crisis and Hindu Religion* (New Delhi, 1987); *World Religions and the Environment* (New Delhi, 1989); *Public Service Accountability* (West Hartford, 1988); *Public Administration in World Perspective* (Ames, 1990; *Managing the Environment: an East European Perspective* (Toronto, 1995); *India's Environmental Policies Programmes and Stewardship* (London, 1997); *Governing India* (New Delhi, 1998); *Bureaucracy and the Alternatives in World Perspective* (London, 1999); *Sustainable Development and Canada: National and International Perspectives* (Canada, 2001); *Where Corruption Lives* (2001); *Administrative Culture in a Global Context* (Toronto, 2005); *Managing Development in a Global Context* (London, 2007); *Global Environmental Challenges* (Canada, 2008); *The Evolving Physiology of Governance: Canadian Public Administration in Transition* (Ottawa, 2009); *Public Administration in a Global Context* (Brussels, 2011); and *In Praise of Mother Earth: The Prithivi Sukta of Atharva Veda* (Los Angeles, 2011). In addition, he has published about 150 chapters/articles in professional journals and scholarly books; 14 conference proceedings in book form; and 23 technical and consultancy mission reports for Canada and various international organizations.

Among his international consultancy missions, the notable assignments are: for two years (1990 and 1991), Professor Dwivedi was the Chief Environmental Policy, Law and Management Adviser to the Government of Mauritius, appointed by the World Bank, where he helped to establish a new Department of the Environment, recruiting officers, writing the national environmental policy paper for the government, assisting the government in preparing and the passage of its environmental protection bill through the national parliament, and managing a team of 35 local officers to prepare a sustainable development strategy for Mauritius. From 1985 to 1989, he acted as Public Service Training Adviser to the Government of Papua New Guinea, and conducted a special management training programme for public service officers. During this period, at the request of the PNG government, he published three books for use in public service training on topics such as managing the public service, public service ethics, and public service accountability. Also during 1984–85, Professor Dwivedi worked in New Delhi as a World Health Organization senior adviser to the Government of India and its Ministry of the Environment and Forests by assisting in the preparation of the Environmental Protection Act, 1985.

Professor Dwivedi has received several honours, some of which are listed below: (1) Order of Canada, 2005 (CM), which is the highest civilian honour bestowed by the Government of Canada. The citation reads: 'His contributions span continents and cultures.... Onkar Dwivedi is a renowned scholar and expert in public administration and the environment. Known for his overarching emphasis on ethics, he has advised Canadian and foreign governments as well as the United Nations'. (2) Fellow of the Royal Society of Canada (FRSC), 1999, which is the highest scholarly honour for a Canadian academic. The citation states: 'Dwivedi's scholarly and research contributions have focused on two interrelated fields of comparative/development administration, and environmental policy and management, for which he is recognized as an enabler for other scholars as well as prolific contributor in his own right, [having] attained national distinction and international recognition'. (3) Two honorary degrees by Canadian universities: Doctor of Law (LL.D.), by University of Lethbridge, Canada, in 1988, and Doctor of Environmental Studies (D.Env.S.) by University of Waterloo, Canada in 2008 (in recognition of Dwivedi's world-wide prominence in the field of environmental ethics, and policy management). (4) An International Award for Excellence in Public Administration, established in the name of O.P. Dwivedi by the International Association of Schools and Institutes of Administration (Brussels, Belgium), in 2008 in recognition of decades of Dwivedi's scholarly contributions in the field of comparative public administration and administrative sciences. Recipients of this award in the past include: President of Brazil, a UNO senior official, and others from Australia, Malaysia, and senior minister of South Africa and now UNDP official.

During his career, Professor Dwivedi was invited by various universities as a visiting professor. Some of these institutions are: University of Wilfrid Laurier (Waterloo), Brock University (St. Catharines), McMaster University (Hamilton), Loyola Marymount University (Los Angeles, CA) and University of South Florida (Tampa, Florida). He was research scholar-in-residence at the Brookings Institution, Washington DC during 1974–75, and then again in 1977. He was also distinguished Visiting Professor at the Indian Institute of Public Administration, New Delhi, in 1998. In addition to various academic assignments, Dwivedi was invited by the Government of Ontario to be a member of its Environmental Assessment Board,

Toronto, 1986–1989; and as its panel member, he conducted public hearings and delivered as many as seven decisions.

Among the positions Professor Dwivedi held with professional organizations are: President of the Canadian Political Science Association, Ottawa, 1986–87; President of the Canadian Asian Studies Association Montreal, 1998–2000, re-elected in 2005–06. From 1989 to 1999, he was elected three times, Vice President of the International Association of Schools and Institutes of Administration (IASIA), Brussels (Belgium). In 2001, he was elected President of the Canadian Council of Area Studies Learned Societies (a federation of the Asian, African, Latin American, and Middle Eastern scholarly associations in Canada), Montreal, Canada. Also, he established and was Chair of the Research Committee on Technology & Development, International Political Science Association from 1991 to 2003.

Besides his academic and professional activities, Professor Dwivedi has devoted ample time for community service both in Canada and India. He was spiritual counsellor to the Guelph Correctional Centre (the province of Ontario's largest prison at the time) in 1996–97, a voluntary work for which he was recognized by the Government of Ontario; established a junior high school in his home town in 1985; to serve the rural poor community around the town of Bithoor (near IIT Kanpur, India), he started a no-fee walk-in-clinic in 2002, which was extended in 2008 into a full-fledged Eye Hospital with 20 beds where patients receive free treatment including cataract operations and medicine; appreciating the need for minority religious groups to serve faculty and students at a university campus, he spearheaded the idea of multi-faith campus ministry where, besides three Christian ministers, a Hindu priest, a Muslim Imam, a Rabbi and others could interact together in a congenial manner and offer spiritual counselling to their faith members. Dwivedi has acted as a part-time Hindu priest at the Guelph University campus; and finally, he, along with his wife Sarla (both are trained yoga teachers), has been conducting yoga classes at the campus since January 2010.

Dwivedi passed away in Guelph, Ontario, Canada on January 29, 2013, from complications due to cancer. He was 76 years old.

Contributors

Christopher Key Chapple, Ph.D., is the Doshi Professor of Indic and Comparative Theology at Loyola Marymount University, Los Angeles, California, where he has been teaching since 1985. A specialist in the religions of India, he has published over one hundred articles and more than a dozen books. Winner of the Gandhi Prize for Excellence in Dharma Studies, he has also edited several books on religion and ecology. He serves as an advisor to the Forum on Religion and Ecology (Yale), the Green Yoga Association (Oakland), and the Ahimsa Center (Pomona).

Kathryn Dey earned her undergraduate degrees in International Development Studies and in Conflict Resolution Studies from the University of Winnipeg (Menno Simons College) in Winnipeg, Manitoba, Canada. During the completion of her degrees, she spent time as Research Intern studying local governance structures with an environmentally focused non-profit organization in Rajasthan, India. She is currently working as a Project Research Assistant with Dr Kirit Patel at the Canadian Mennonite University in Winnipeg.

Jane Dougan, Ed.D. (Instructional Technology and Distance Education), has had a lifelong interest in researching, writing and teaching adults about sustainability and equity-related concerns. Her M.S. (University of Bristol) was in Comparative Development and International Policy. Since 2001, she has been Coordinator of Distance Learning at the Oceanographic Center, Nova Southeastern University, Florida. Earlier, she was with the University of Guelph, where she first forged a teaching partnership and friendship with Professor Dwivedi, which has continued with their co-development of online courses for students all across the globe, specially Canada and the USA. Jane is a Fellow of LEAD International, and a member of such organizations as the IUCN Commission on Education and Communication (CEC), the North American Association for Environmental Education, and the Climate Change and Environmental Leadership Network. Her research interests lie with the development and presentation of cross-cultural online learning.

Shrinath Prasad Dwivedi, M.A. (English, Hindi Literature and Political Science), has taught undergraduate classes both in India and Canada. He has organized and participated in several national and international conferences on literature, interfaith, peace and religion. He has published five books of Hindi poetry and two anthologies, and has more than 100 essays and articles published in the English and Hindi journals and magazines. He is the President of Hindi Literary Society of Canada, Global Hindu Foundation and South Asian Literary Society of Canada. He has been the chief editor of the first published Hindi journal of North America *'Samvaad'*. He has been often featured in print and electronic outlets; and media occasionally seeks his views on ethnic, multi-cultural and multi-faith issues. He is honoured and awarded for his peace, literary and social works by the Canadian government and other organizations around the world. He is deeply involved, for more than 30 years, in the inter-faith movement in Canada. He is a social, peace, multi-faith activist and journalist.

Anil K. Gupta, Ph.D., is a Professor at the Indian Institute of Management, Ahmedabad (IIM-A) and executive vice-chairman of National Innovation Foundation, Ahmedabad. He received Padma Shri from President of India in 2004 for distinguished achievements in the field of management education; he has been adjudged as one of the fifty most influential people in the field of intellectual property rights around the world in 2003; other awards include Star of Asia Award (Business Week, 2001); Asian Innovation Award Gold from Far Eastern Economic Review (October 26, 2000) for coordinating SRISTI and Honey Bee Network; and Pew Conservation Scholar Award, 1993–96, University of Michigan, USA. He has published more than 250 articles and currently co-teaches a management course with Dr A.P.J. Kalam, former President of India, at IIM-A. He was appointed a fellow of National Academy of Agricultural Sciences, Pew Conservation Scholar, and the World Academy of Art and Science. He currently serves on the National Innovation Council, chaired by the Prime Minister of India.

R.B. Jain, Ph.D., is a former Dean of the Faculty of Social Sciences, and Professor and Head of the Department of Political Science,

University of Delhi, Delhi. He has also served as Professor and Head of the Department of Public Administration, Punjabi University, Patiala, Professor of Public Administration at the Indian Institute of Public Administration, New Delhi, and a National Fellow of the Indian Council of Social Science Research. He has also been a Visiting Professor at various universities in Canada (including the University of Guelph), USA, and Germany and has lectured as Guest Professor at various universities and institutions in all the continents. He has authored/edited over 35 books and published more than 200 articles in refereed journals and compendiums all over the world. He is currently the President Emeritus of the International Political Science Association's Research Committee on Public Bureaucracies in Developing Societies. He has recently been honoured by the Indian Institute of Public Administration as its distinguished member for his contribution to the institute as well as to the discipline of public administration.

A.D. Kaushik, Ph.D. (Ecology), has had more than 25 years' experience of teaching and research in ecology, environment and disaster management. Presently, he is a faculty member of National Institute of Disaster Management, Ministry of Home Affairs, Government of India, New Delhi.

Tim A. Mau, D.Phil (Oxford) is an Associate Professor in the Department of Political Science at the University of Guelph, where he teaches primarily in the area of public management and administration. His current research interests lie in the area of political and public sector leadership. He has published articles and book chapters on topics such as leadership competencies in the public sector, leadership in the Canadian military, Quebec and Scottish nationalism and French-English relations in business interest associations. He is a co-editor of the book (with O.P. Dwivedi and Byron Sheldrick) *The Evolving Physiology of Government: Canadian Public Administration in Transition* (2009).

R.K. Mishra, Ph.D., is ONGC Subir Raha Chair Professor on Corporate Governance and Senior Professor and Director, Institute of Public Enterprise, Hyderabad, India. He has been a visiting fellow at London Business School, and has also studied International Teachers Programme at SDA Bocconi, Milan. Dr Mishra taught at the University of Bradford, and was a Visiting Professor at Maison Des Sciences De L' Hommes, Paris and Faculty of Economics, University of Ljubljana. He is a member of the UN Task Force on International Standards of Excellence in Public Administration and Education. He is a special invite on OECD Working Group on

Privatization and Corporate Governance of SOEs and Asian Network of Corporate Governance. He is non-Executive Director on some public and private enterprise boards in India. He has considerable experience of teaching and guiding research for doctoral degree in management, economics, public administration and commerce. His areas of interest include Corporate Governance, International Management, International Finance, Public-Private Partnership, Restructuring and Environmental Administration, etc.

Bruce Mitchell received his B.A. and M.A. from the University of British Columbia, and Ph.D. from the University of Liverpool. He is Professor in the Department of Geography and Environmental Management, and also Associate Provost, Resources, at the University of Waterloo in Canada. His research over more than four decades has focused on water policy, governance and management, with particular attention to 'integrated water resource management'. He has conducted research in Australia, Canada, China, Indonesia and Nigeria. He is a Fellow of the Royal Society of Canada, and also of the International Water Resources Association, as well as an Honorary Professor at four Chinese universities (Dalian University of Technology, Nanjing University, Shenyang University, Xi'an Jiaotong University).

M.V. Naidu holds the degrees M.A., LL.B., LL.M. and Ph.D. In his teaching career spanning over five decades, he has written many books, contributed chapters, published scholarly and newspaper articles and headed numerous academic and civic organizations including as Manitoba Human Rights Commissioner and as Visiting Professor in Canada, USA, India and Fiji. His two recent books are *Quebec Separatism, Canadian Unity* and *Dimensions of Peace*. He has received many awards and grants including the Canadian government's national *Citation for Citizenship*. Currently, he serves as Professor Emeritus (Political Science) at Brandon University and continues to remain Editor Emeritus of *Peace Research: The Canadian Journal of Peace and Conflict Studies*.

Kirit Patel, Ph.D., is Assistant Professor of International Development Studies at Menno Simons College, affiliated with the University of Winnipeg and Canadian Mennonite University, Winnipeg, Canada. Prior to completing his Ph.D. at the University of Guelph, Canada in 2008, he worked as a development practitioner and policy analyst in India. His research interests include food security, biodiversity conservation, participatory development, farmers' indigenous knowledge and rights, rural migration, and environmental policy. Currently, he is the principal investigator in a large interdisciplinary research project, funded by the International Development Research Centre (IDRC), Canada, on food and nutrition security in South Asia.

Melchior D. Powell Ph.D., J.D., is Executive Director of the Southern Maryland Higher Education Center and Professor Emeritus of Public Policy and Administration at California State University, Long Beach (CSULB). Earlier, he was founding Dean of the Graduate Center for Public Policy and Administration at CSULB, and in Washington DC, Director of the Office of Research Management at the Appalachian Regional Commission, and Director of Contract Research at the National Association of Counties. He is currently Chair of the IASIA Working Group on Accountability, Culture and Ethics; and has been President of the Urban Affairs Association and President of the Western Governmental Research Association.

Praveen K. Saxena, Ph.D., has been Professor at the University of Guelph, Canada since 1989. The focus of research in his Plant Cell Technology Lab is on conservation, sustainable use, and replenishment of rare and endangered plant species. Of special interest are the plants which are traditionally used in medicinal, religious, spiritual and cultural practices. He has contributed more than 150 research papers in peer reviewed journals, edited four books, and has served as editor and reviewer for many journals. He has also supervised over 40 graduate students and postdoctoral fellows and teaches courses related to plant biotechnology and plant based natural health products. His other interests include environment, spirituality and Vedic philosophy of life.

Vinod K. Sharma did his Ph.D. in Forest Ecology. He got special training in Environment and Sustainable Development in UK and USA and taught Ecology and Environment in India, USA, Iraq and Libya. He joined Indian Institute of Public Administration, New Delhi in 1992 and was instrumental in setting up the National Centre for Disaster Management (now NIDM). He has published 10 books and more than 40 research papers in Disaster Management and Environment. He guided six Ph.D. and 35 M. Phil students in Ecology and Disaster Management. At present, he is Professor of Disaster Management and Environment at IIPA, New Delhi.

Deeptima Shukla, Ph.D. is Assistant Professor in the Department of Political Science at Kanoria PG College, Jaipur, India. Her area of specialization deals with social, economic and political issues related to South Asia. She has numerous research papers and articles published to her credit. At present, she is working on a project dealing with developmental issues in India.

Mukund R. Shukla, Ph.D., is a professional research associate in Plant Cell Technology Laboratory of the Department of Plant Agriculture, University of Guelph. His main research interests include plant conservation, micropropagation and plant biotechnology. He has authored several original research papers, book chapters and technical reports. He currently supervises research on medicinal and ornamental plants in undergraduate projects and participates in plant conservation programmes. He has keen interest in Ayurveda and holistic approach to human health.

Amita Singh, Ph.D., is Professor at the Centre for the Study of Law and Governance, Jawaharlal Nehru University, New Delhi. Her work focuses on administrative reforms especially on issues related to the implementation theory, innovations and e-governance and bioethical concerns in reforms. She has conducted evaluation of best practices in a DARPG-Government of India project in collaboration with the Global Innovators Network at the Ash Institute of Democratic Governance, KSG Harvard University, Monash Institute (Melbourne, Australia) and University of Southern Australia (Adelaide, Australia). She is a serving Board Member of the National Committee on Stem Cell Research and a Member of the Indian Council of Medical Research. Among her latest publications are: *Hinduism: Contemporary Expressions, (*2012), *Religion and Social Justice, Bureaucracy as Circus Ring*masters (2011), and *Good Governance*. She is the Secretary General of NAPSIPAG (Network of Asia-Pacific Schools and Institutes of Public Administration and Governance).

B.N. Tiwari, Ph.D., worked on various responsible posts in the Department of Education, Government of Uttar Pradesh where his final assignment was Additional Secretary, Board of High School and Intermediate Education. He has also been associated with various professional and social organizations, advisory committees and societies. Having accepted reading, thinking and writing as his favourite pursuits, he has been associated with various research projects in environmental and religious studies. He has published 23 books for children and neo-literates and about 50 articles on different subjects. His articles on conciliatory approach of Hindu poets and Hindu saints, Hindu religions and philosophy and concept of environment, Hindu theology of ecology and Hindu concept of unity have appeared in various Indian and international journals.

Reeta Chowdhari Tremblay, Ph.D., is Vice-President Academic and Provost at the University of Victoria. She had previously served as vice-president (academic) and pro vice-chancellor, pro tempore of

Memorial University of Newfoundland from July 2009 to October 2010. Before that she held the position of dean of the Faculty of Arts at Memorial University from August 2006 to June 2009. Prior to her move to St. John's, she was a political science professor at Concordia University in Montreal, where she chaired the Political Science Department from 1998 to 2005. She has an M.Phil from the Jawaharlal Nehru University (India) and an M.A. and Ph.D. in Political Science from the University of Chicago. In particular, her writings on Kashmir and India-Pakistan relations, a subject on which she is widely considered to be the leading North American expert, are widely acclaimed. In the community, she has held several distinguished professional positions such as the president of the Canadian Council of Area Studies of Learned Societies, president of the Canadian Association for Asian Studies and chair of the India Studies Committee of the Shastri Indo-Canadian Institute of Canada. She is currently president of the Canadian Political Science Association. Her areas of research include comparative politics and comparative federalism, South Asian political economy, nation-state and secessionist movements in India and Indian popular cinema.

Neelam Trivedi, Ph.D., is Associate Professor and Head of Department of Sanskrit at Dayanand Girls Post Graduate College, Kanpur (India). She has published three books and 38 research papers and articles in reputed international and national journals. She is the Associate Editor of the *International Journal of Religion and Spirituality in Society* and the *International Journal of Environmental, Cultural, Economic and Social Sustainability.* She is the co-editor of national research journal '*Sidhant*', editor of '*Siddhidatri*' and adviser of '*Gaveshna*', a research journal. She is the secretary of an NGO '*Vaitarni*' and is the life member of the World Association of Vedic Studies (WAVES) and Swadeshi Science Congress. She has guided nine Ph.Ds and five M.Phil dissertations. She has propagated Vedic culture and human values in various countries such as New Zealand, Japan, USA and Canada, through her research work. She has been conferred the title of Sanskrit Kovid and Kalidas award.

R.K. Trivedi, M.Tech. and Ph.D., is currently Director at Harcourt Butler Technological Institute, Kanpur. Before this he was Director STEP-HBTI as well as Ambedkar Institute, Kanpur and Teaching Faculty in the Department of Oil & Paint Technology at HBTI, Kanpur for 17 years. He has published more than 55 research papers in national and international journals, edited five books, contributed two chapters in books and six technical feasibility studies. He has held two visiting assignments at the University of Guelph, Canada and Purdue University, USA, and has also chaired several international seminars. Presently, he is President of Oil Technologist Association of India (OTAI, CZ). He was chief co-investigator of two SICI-CIDA partnership projects between HBTI and University of Guelph, Canada, and has been consultant to MI, WHO, CPCB, MARKFED, HAFED.

Dhirendra Vajpeyi, Ph.D., is Professor of Political Science at the University of Northern Iowa. He has authored, co-authored and edited 16 books and numerous articles. He has lectured at universities in Moscow, St. Petersburg, Russia; People's Republic of China; Nigeria; Chile; and Klagenfurt, Austria. He was Senior Research Fellow at Hoover Institute at Stanford University (California). He is Chair of the Research Committee on Technology & Development, International Political Science Association; and in addition, is a member of various IPSA research committee executive boards.

Index